Spatial Pattern of Population in Rohtas District of Bihar

Abhay Kumar Rakesh

RAJESH PUBLICATIONS
NEW DELHI - 110 002

Spatial Pattern of Population in Rohtas District of Bihar

Published by :
Sanjay Gupta
RAJESH PUBLICATIONS
1, Ansari Road, Darya Ganj, New Delhi - 110002
Ph.: 011-23274550, 43084725
Website : www.rajeshpublications.com
Email : rajeshpublications@gmail.com

First Published in India 2021

ISBN : 978-81-94867-87-6

Price : Rs. 800.00

Printed in India by :
Belwel Process
Delhi - 110002

Foreword

I feel great pleasure in writing a foreword to this book entitled "Spatial Pattern of Population in Rohtas District of Bihar" written by Dr. Abhay Kumar Rakesh, Assistant Professor & Head Department of Geography, B.P.S. College, Bhore, Jai Prakash University, Chapra. The present book is the modified form of the Doctoral Dissertation. The book contains critical analysis of the impact of geographical conditions on the spatial pattern of population characteristics.

Dr. Rakesh has analysed the facts using adequate primary and secondary data and has also applied suitable research technique to prove the hypothesis and to reveal findings.

I believe this work will motivate scholars of different disciplines to analyse various aspects of population characteristics.

I hope and trust that the book will be of immense helps for keen research scholars and others.

Dr. V.N.P. Sinha
Former Head & Emeritus Fellow
Department of Geography
Patna University, Patna

Preface

Geography is most succinctly described as the study of earth's surface as the space within which the human population lives. Thus population geography is the study of the spatial variations in human population and study of primary objectives related to present research. Such studies are inevitable for determining various aspects and burning problems associated with the cultural geography of any region or country without which we can not hope to understand and optimise social conditions for development and progress.

As the Rohtas district represents the extension of Vindhyan system it witnesses an undulating surface condition throughout its extent. The district is also noted for a relatively dry climate and moderate to low ground water table. The economic and cultural aspects are, therefore, underdeveloped and marked by a high degree of spatial variations. The density and distribution of population are large only in fertile land and favoured localities of the district. The literacy and sex ratio of population also exhibit conspicuous spatial variations. The growing pressure of population is leading to numerous problems like food shortages, non availability of drinking water, transport, irrigation, non availability of fertilizer, better seeds, sanitation and others. Yet neither the academicians nor the planners have so far taken up a study of these problems in a right perspective.

The present work is based upon information derived from various sources including personal observation. A number of books, journals, reports, statistical records and many valuable maps have been consulted. Data on population of six sample villages have been collected during the field survey during the year 2008. The second chapter examines the role of geographical setting in shaping the spatial pattern of population in Rohtas district. The third deals the spatial pattern of land use and its bearing on spatial pattern of population. The fourth, fifth and sixth chapters deal with the spatial pattern of variables associated with population. The seven chapter deals the sample villages based on field survey. Except the first chapter, the discussion in all other chapters is supported by personal observation and data collected in the field. The geographical pattern has also been derived on the basis of some statistical techniques. The last chapter sums up the study and tries to answer the questions posed in the beginning of the study.

In a work like this one has to seek help from a large number of teachers, friends and authorities. I wish to convey may deep sense of gratitude to all of them.

I am highly obliged to my Supervisor Prof. L.K.P. Singh, Department of Geography, P.U. and Principal of Patna College, P.U. for going through the manuscript and providing supervision.

I am also highly obliged to Prof. R.B.P. Singh, Head of the Department of Geography, P.U. for motivating me to complete the work in time.

I am also grateful to Prof. S. Adhikari, Dean, and Ex. Head of the Department of Geography P.U. for encouraging and suggesting me for completion of the work.

I am also grateful to all my teachers Prof. V.N.P. Sinha, Prof. (Mrs.) S.L. Prasad, Dr. S.N. Prasad, Prof. K.N. Paswan, Prof. U. Verma, Dr. M.M.P. Sinha, Dr. A. Sami, Dr. Kailash Mahto, Dr. R.B. Mahto, Dr. (Mrs.) Ravi Kiran Sharma, Dr. S.R. Maltiar, Dr. (Mrs.) A. Sahay, Dr. M. Nazim and Dr. M. Kumar Sinha for their valuable suggestions and help in the preparation if this research work.

I also extend my thanks to my friends Deepak Kumar, Avinash Kumar, Arya, Gautam Kumar and Rohit for their valuable inspiration and help from time to time.

I also thanks obligations towards all the officials of the Government of Bihar who have helped me in the collection of data and maps.

Special thanks should also go to Sri Sanjay Gupta, Rajesh Publications, New Delhi for the interest in printing the book.

Abhay Kumar Rakesh

Contents

List of Maps and Diagrams

1

Chapter

Introduction

Conceptual Frame :

Watson (1955) has stated that "Geography is truly a subject of discipline in distance"[1], while Cole and King[2] (1963) describe that "Geography is concerned with the distribution of elements that occur on the earth's surface and with variation of distribution through time and space." In fact the earth's surface provides space on which all human activities develop with the progress of time. According to Demko (1970), Population Geography is the branch of the discipline which treats the spatial variations in demographic and non-demographic qualities of human populations, and the economic and social consequences stemming from the interaction associated with a particular set of conditions existing in a given areal unit." The surface of the earth facilitates us with two types of space-lithosphere and hydrosphere. Population are largely associated with the space of lithosphere. The morphology of lithosphere is not uniform throughout its span. It contains mountains and plateaus in some parts and plains and coastal lands in others areas. On the basis of climate, the space of lithosphere may further be subdivided in three broad units- humid regions, arid regions and cold regions.

People have made there abode in all morphological and climatic areas of the lithosphere. They, however, vary sharply in their distribution and qualities in different spatial units. This variation is increasing with the progress of time. A shift is also witnessed from less prosperous areas to the areas of plenty. According to Mandal[3] (1980) the mean centre of population is bound to shift due to changing physical, economic, social and technical abilities of the region.

Normally, the fertile plain lands in humid areas are the most favourable lands for growing a number of crops in the fields. These areas, therefore, provide livelihood to a large number of people in a result. Such areas exhibit the highest concentration of population. Usually the economic condition of people is sound and most of the inhabitants are culturally advanced. Settlements in such areas have a large population size and are in compact and clustered forms. Interspacing between settlements is small. Settlements contain a large number of houses which are well built and knit together with excellent transport and other services.

The plain lands in arid and cold belts of the lithosphere are hardly suitable for economic activities. The population is generally thinly distributed. The inhabitants are also culturally underdeveloped. The settlements represent small group of houses. They are however, in form of hamlets or small clusters. The houses contain poor constructional materials and are ill-managed.

Mountains, plateaus and forested belts also contain a sparse concentration of population. The settlements are few and are of scattered in layout. The inter-spacing found between these settlements is large. The houses are built up with poor building materials. The people of these areas are culturally backward. In such areas settlements are generally found along the transport lines, at the sites of mineral exploitation, near lumbering industries and health resort centres and at some favourable points along river valleys. Mandal[4] (1980) has explained that terrain conditions such as fertile plains having congenial climatic conditions attract people, while the high rugged mountains and plateaus, forest cover and marshy land with unfavourable climatic conditions adversely affect the concentration of population.

Coastal lands possessing oceanic influence on climate are

generally fertile and suitable for cultivation. Some points of coastal areas are important as parts, fishing centres, health resort, etc. The concentration of population and types of settlements are, however, of varied types depending on local variation in physical, economic and cultural parameters.

The study area consists of both plain and mountainous lands. The nature of distribution of population and its qualities differs from one area to another. The fertile plain areas comprising highly dissected terrain have a low density of population. Local factors, however, modify this general pattern of population distribution in a few localities of the study area.

Climatically, the plain areas of Rohtas district are semi humid, but because of cultural advancement, the population concentration is higher in the district. In contrast to this the rugged mountainous areas though humid have attracted small size of population because these areas are forested and relatively undeveloped. In general the entire such areas suffer from poor economy which has resulted in under development and low standard of living.

Besides, the spaces of the lithosphere may also be obtained on the basis of economic and cultural characteristics. Some of the areas of earth are economically and culturally sound. While other areas comprise poor economic and cultural variables. Consequent upon which the concentration of population and settlements have got dense manifestation in areas of healthy development of economic and cultural features. Population and settlements are, however, found thinly represented in areas of poor presence of economic and cultural parameters. It is quite evident that industrial and agriculturally rich areas of Rohtas district exhibits dense population. On the other hand, the areas showing poor development of industrial establishments and agricultural activities have gravitated smaller number of people because these areas lack in providing facilities of livelihood. Most of such agricultural areas are climatically and irrigationaly poor.

If one will examine the pattern of service centres, it will necessarily be found that service centres are also influencing the spatial pattern of population in the study area. Usually service centres provides a large number of facilities to the people residing in neighbouring villages. As a result, population of these villages exhibit increasing tendency. A good number of people become interested to settle at service centres. This situation does not exist in areas without service centres.

Review of Literature :

Zelinsky has described that population geography can be defined accurately as the science that describes the ways in which the geographic character of place is formed by, and in turn reacts upon, a set of population phenomena that vary within it through both space and time as they follow their own behavioural lows, interacting one with another and with a number of non-demographic phenomena.[5] In brief, population geography deals with the spatial pattern of population phenomena in the context of aggregate nature of places.[6] In other words, it is concerned with demonstrating and composition of population are related to the spatial variations in the nature of place.[7] Spatial variations in a population, no doubt, are a function of a host of physical, economic and cultural factors. These factors operate through the dynamics of population change.[8] To a great extent, the spatial disparity of population in the result of spatial disparity in economic development. The spatial pattern of population indicates a system of social and economic change and can be regarded as a form of human adjustment to economic, environmental and social problems.[9]

The place of man in geography has long been a matter of academic dispute. Among the earlier geographers attention was largely devoted to the natural environment, although this was considered meaningful only in relation to man.[10] In recent decades there has been progressive reorientation of view point, with increasing emphasis upon man as the main inhabitant of the earth. This approach found its greatest advocates in France, where in the first part of the 20th century a flourishing school of human geography sought to explain the multiple relationships between man, his activities and the environment. However, the view of Vidal-de-la-Blache, Jean Brunhes and Maximilien Sorre varied in detail, giving varied weight to the study of man. Systematic population geography is thus one of the youngest branches of geography.[11] Though a number of population studies have been published before 1953, they are mostly related to the distribution, density and growth of population to the complete neglect of other characteristics.

The aspects of population geography have been most lucidly stated by Trewartha.[12] He has provided a detailed framework for geographical studies of population. His view is that "numbers, densities and qualities of the population provide the essential background for all geography. Population is the point of reference from which all other elements are observed and from which they all, singly and collectively, derive significance and meaning." Apart from this Frank Lorimer (1959) and G.T. Trewartha (1953) also state the population geography is still in a period of germination and lacks adequate data as well as methodology. Besides both the branches : demography within the field of social sciences and population geography within the field of geography suffer from certain conditions which have not been conducive to their optimal growth.

Howe (1961) has examined the geographical variation in disease mortality in England and Wales in mid-twentieth century.[13] Cox (1961) has attempted to study demography in relation to physical and economic conditions.[14] Veyret-Verner (1962) has studied the aspects like merchants, structures and repartition.[15] Zelinsky (1962) has studied changes in the geographic pattern of rural population in the United States from 1790-1960.[16] Murray (1962) has written on the geography of death in England and Wales.[17] Kariel (1963) has examined the population growth on account of migration.[18] Melezin

(1963) describes Soviet Geography of Population as the study of population distribution and productive relationship existing within various population groups, the settlement network and its fitness, usefulness and effectiveness for productive goals of a society.[19] Pokshishevski (1962) has also contributed a detailed work on the population of U.S.S.R.[20] In principle the population geography of U.S.S.R. has a practical role in planned organization and development.[21] Lowton (1963) has worked on recent trends in population and housing in England and Wales.[22] Howe (1964) has prepared a National Atlas of Disease Mortality in the United Kingdom.[23]

Wilbur Zelinsky (1966) has written a text book designated, in his own words, to provoke thought and stimulate research in population geography. However, most of the work done by him is tentative and preliminary to real research in the subject.[24] Coldwell and Okonjo (1969) have studies the spatial growth and distribution of population in the Upper Region of Ghana.[25] Kosinski (1970) has studied the population of Europe. He has found that spatial differences of population distribution have developed in response to variation of the natural environment, but especially they are the function of spatial disparities in economic and social life.[26] Lawless (1972) has attempted to describe the changing population pattern of Iraq with an emphasis on changes in communal structure in relation to the changes in ecological structure in the country.[27] Dewdney (1972) has studied the regional variation of population distribution in Syria. He has tried to related the population pattern with physiographic features and land use pattern.[28]

Clark (1972) has examined the changing population pattern of Iran.[29] He has deduced that the greatest impact on the geography of the country has been as a result of the increased government investment in health and welfare services, educational facilities, infrastructure, planning and industrial and agricultural development policies.

Sulton (1972) has worked on changes in population in Algeria.[30] He has found that the coastal areas have densely populated and the rest have a thin population concentration. Sukhatma (1972) has worked on population food supply and nutrition.[31] Kuroda (1972) has discussed the migration, distribution of population and development of Japan.[32] Glem T. Trewartha (1972) has studied the geography of population in the less developed Realm.[33] Harrison and Boyce (1975) have attempted to study Ecology and population structure in the Arctic.[34]

A number of studies have been published in foreign countries since 1950 on different aspects of population geography P.F. James (1954) has studied certain aspects of population in geographical control.[35] Clark and Evans (1954) have attempted to examine distance to nearest neighbour as a measure of spatial relationship in population, ecology.[36] Glass and Grebenik (1956) have examined the trend and pattern of fertility in Great Britain.[37] Belshaw (1956) has done work on population growth and levels of consumption.[38] Franklin (1956) has studied the pattern the sex-ratio in New Zealand.[39] Brookfield (1957) has tried to know about the demographic upsurge and prospect in Mauritius.[40] Scott (1957) has examined the changing population of Tasmania.[41] Duncon (1957) has worked on the measurement of population distribution.[42] Saville (1957) has done research on rural Depopulation in England and Wales from 1851 to 1951.[43] Newton (1957) has examined the Internal Migration in England and Wales.[44] Rose (1958) has done research on the geographical pattern of European immigration in Australia.[45] Kiser and Whelpton (1958) have studied the social and psychological factors affecting fertility.[46] Stewart and Warntz (1959) have worked on some parameters of the geographical distribution of population.[47] Bogue (1959) has attempted to examine Internal Migration. He has tried to relate his studies with physical conditions of the area.[48] Ackerman (1959) has examined the relationship between population and natural resources.[49] Howe (1960) has made studies on the geographical distribution of cancer mortality in Wales.[50] Glass

(1960) has worked on population growth, fertility and population policy.[51] Hooson (1960) has taken the progressive change in view point to its logical extreme and postulates that in essence geography is concerned with the problem of the uneven distribution of population over the earth. Distribution of population acts as a masterthread capable of weaving into a coherent pattern the otherwise disparate strands of the subject and expressing into philosophical unity particularly in the context of regional geography.[52]

It would be seen from the above studies that apart from the text books, there have been very few studies on the population of any small area where an attempt may have been made to correlate the growth and distribution of population or its various components with physical parameters. Even where such as attempt has been made, only generalised statements have been made which may or may not apply to the region under study. Besides the studies by foreign geographers are frequently carried out in developed countries where the conditions are entirely different from those obtaining in India, particularly a traditional agricultural area such as the Rohtas district.

Many papers have been published in India on population geography in the 20th century. The pattern of population density and distribution has, however, not changed much and George Kuriyan's map prepared in 1936 still has some value.[53] In a country of the size of India which stretches for 29 degrees both along the parallels and the meridians, regional contrasts in physical phenomena are inevitable, and this has made a profound influence on the distribution of population density and distribution.

Population studies on individual districts were somewhat popular with Madras University during the thirties. Krishnaswami (1930) traced the causes for the variation of population density and distribution within Coimbatore District and emphasised the special role played by the bigger towns of the district.[54]

Lokanathan (1931) has studied the migration of labour with special reference to South India.[55] Differentiated between the casual, the seasonal or periodic and the permanent forms of migration. He found that permanent migration was absent in South India, while other forms of migration were related to new agricultural developments.

Raghavan (1935, 1936 and 1937) has studied Anantapur district of Andhra Pradesh,[56] Salem[57] and Tanjore[58] district of Tamil Nadu respectively. His studies revealed that the population of Anantapur district has been steadily declining principally due to migration to more prosperous areas. The other two districts of his study showed increasing trend of population with much regional variation at the micro level.

Kuriyan (1933) has discussed the distribution of population in Kerala against the background of the physical, climatic, soil and agricultural conditions of three regions-lowlands, foothills and highlands.[59]

Rajagopal (1940, 1941) has studied the demography of Tirunelveli[60] and Chittor[61] districts of Tamil Nadu with particular reference to the growth of population, both rural and urban since 1921, occupation structures, education and sex ration.

Ahmad (1941) has analysed the distribution of population in India in relation to the elements of physical and cultural environments.[62] Yunus (1941) has examined the problem of growing population in Uttar Pradesh during the decade 1931-41 in relation to the production of foodgrains.[63] Geddes (1942, 1953) has dealt with the theme of variability in the rate of population growth in India from decade to decade.[64] Lateron he studies regional variations in variability in population change.[65]

Chatterjee and Ganguli (1943) have critically examined the growth of population in Nadia district of Bengal and Tirunelveli district of Tamil Nadu.[66] They have concluded that although soils and climate were more favourable for growth of population in Nadia, the decline of industry had resulted in a continuous decrease in population, whereas in Tirunelveli development of industries had helped in the growth of towns and consequent increase in population.

Chatterjee (1961) in his Presidential Address to the Geographical Society of India discussed the Salient features of the physical landscape of the different regions of West Bengal and traced their influence on the distribution of population, especially in giving rise to Calcutta conurbation, and three belts of varied population concentration to the east of conurbation and on the west a belt of relatively low density in the Rarh Region.[67] The most exhaustive account of distribution of population in India is available from the population sheets (41, 1959) published by the National Atlas Organization. On the basis of these sheets, Chatterjee (1962) has described in detail the distribution pattern of rural and urban population in the country's seven macro regions.[68] He has examined the role of physical factors the great age of India as a human habitat, and political events in introducing regional variations in population distribution.

Bose (1946, 1962) has examined the population of Damodar valley in West Bengal and Bihar respectively. He has found that the density of population in the Lower Damodar Valley (West Bengal) ranged from 200 persons per sq. km. in forested areas to over 1200 persons in industrial areas of Asansol and Kulti and the pattern of population are of varied character dependent on the mineral and agricultural resources.[69] In the upper Damodar Valley (Bihar) the pattern of population in rural as well as urban areas reflected even better the effects of topography, forests agriculture and accessibility.[70]

Singh (1947) has discussed in detail the trend of the growth of population in Uttar Pradesh with particular reference to the influence of geographical phenomena on the distribution and growth of population, total, rural, urban and communitywise.[71] Singh (1956) has also studied the population problem in Umland areas of Varanasi and has evaluated first the degree of concentration on the basis of administrative unit and has then explained how the difficulty of terrain, bad drainage, climate and soil factors have created contrasts in population concentration in the various micro regions.[72]

Raza (1950) has given facts and figures to prove that India is not overpopulated.[73] There will be no difficulty of feeding the increasing population if the country develops her industries.

Bidwai (1951) has studied the variation of population in Amravati district of Maharashtra.[74] He has established that, besides natural causes, migration due to drought and crop failure have remained responsible for the variation of population. Davis, K. (1951) has rendered a thorough analysis of the history of accelerating rate of population growth in the Indian Subcontinent.[75] His work, however, lacked strict geographical orientation.

Bhat (1953) has examined the relationship between the physical environment and the distribution of population in the Upper Panchaganga Basin, one of the important headwaters of the Krishna river.[76] He has found that the control of relief is more rigid in middle reaches than at either ends and the population has increased from the west to the east along the valleys. Bhat (1961) has also analysed the need for regional approach of population studies because of uneven distribution and variations in population concentration.[77] His study indicates that different area levels have different planning implications. In another paper (1961) he has developed his idea further and has emphasized sharp regional variations in density and growth of population in India during 1951-61.[78] He has got the same regional pattern but for every region, there was a critical density above which the growth rate of population tended to be slow.

Geddes and Learmonth (1953) have followed up the earlier studies of Geddes by examining the total change of population in India during 1921-40 along with an estimate of the variability.[79] Their study points out the impact of epidemics in 1918 and concludes that the turning point in demographic history was reached only after 1931.

Spate (1956) has concluded in his study on population that India is overpopulated.[80] His analysis of food trends indicated no possibility of increase of staple food grains in near future.

Verma (1956) in his study of the density and patterns of population in Punjab has observed that there is greater concentration of rural population in areas which are highly irrigated and intensively cultivated.[81] He has found that the urban density is governed by the commercial and industrial activities.

Prasad (1956) in his research on population distribution and dynamics of supply of labour in Bihar concluded that the flow of population between North and South Bihar was the direct result of economic differences between the two.[82]

Kayastha (1956) has studied the demography of the Himalayan Beas Basin of Uttar Pradesh.[83] He has established definite relationship between density and distribution of population and the physical setting.

Khan (1956) has studied the bearings of geographical conditions on the pattern of population in Allahabad District.[84] Gosal (1956) has studied all significant aspects of population in his doctoral thesis named as A Geographical Analysis of India's Population.[85]

Anantapadmanabhan (1957) has indicated a method of choosing the density grades and examined their relationship with relief, soils and availability of water in Madras.[86]

Trewartha and Gosal (1957) have provided geographic treatment to the spatial pattern of population change in India during 1891-1951.[87]

Mamoria (1957) has traced the growth of population

during each successive decade of India since 1981.[88]

Gosal (1958) has analysed the occupational structure in India.[89] His study has revealed that the rural population in India is not quite synonymous with agricultural workers. In another paper (1961) he has studied the internal migration of population in India and has found that the proportion of migrant population to the total population is rather small.[90] He concludes that the number of immigrants is related to the pressure of population on arable land.

Sinha (1958) has analysed the population distribution in Orissa (1871-1951) and has found that the rate of population growth has remained slow in earlier decades and has witnessed a much faster rate during later decades, outstripping the means of subsistence.[91] Sinha (1962) has further examined the influence of population growth on the economy of Orissa concluding that the carrying capacity of the land has far outstripped its limit.[92]

Dayal (1959) has attempted to correlate population growth and rural-urban migration in India.[93] His study has revealed that as a result of population growth and consequent decrease of per capita arable land, there has been an accelerated migration of the people to cities in search of employment.

Sharma (1960) has made a detailed study of the cultural trends in relation to physical variables in Etah district of Uttar Pradesh.[94] Lal (1961) has worked on in- migration problem in Indian Cities.[95] His study has revealed that the in- migration has remained pronounced in the cities where there is possibility of employment in railway transport and public administration. Arunachalam and Mathura (1961) have studied the settlement pattern and population distribution in the Ulhas basin which lies north of Bombay city and have emphasized the predominance of agriculture in the upper valley and the urban characteristics in the lower valley.[96]

Padhye (1961) has worked on population in Gwaligarh hills of the Satpura range.[97] He has established a relationship between population density and physical, climatic and other geographical factors. Ahmad (1961) has analysed the migration in two macro- region i.e. the Ganga Plain and Chotanagpur Plateau in Bihar in relation to geographical background.[98] He has concluded that immobile nature of population is a natural phenomenon in an area of intensive cultivation.

Gosal (1961) has brought to light wide regional contrasts in sex ratio in India and has examined the factors associated with these variations.[99] He has conducted another study (1962) for regional aspects of population growth during 1951-61.[100] Through a comparative study of maps, it brings out inverse correlation between density and growth of population.

Sen (1963) has studied the pattern of sex ratio in India's population, as in 1961.[101] Gosal (1964) has further made in interpretative study of literacy in India in which he has discussed the regional variation in literacy, mentioning a variety of factors with which these variations are associated.[102] In 1967 he analysed the regional aspects of rural literacy in the presidential address to the Indian Council of Geographers.[103] Gosal and Krishan (1965) have in another paper studied the occupational structure of rural population in Punjab.[104]

Mitra (1965) has reviewed the position of India with respect to its population and food supply.[105] Ramachandran (1965) has studied the trend of population in Malnad.[106]

Schwartzberg (1965) has explained the role of caste in Indian rural society and has analysed the distribution of some selected castes in North Indian Plain.[107] He has established that their distribution is not random but is related to specific facts of history and to the distinctive role played by caste in the total socio-economic system. Singh (1965) has studied the demographic features of Nagaland.[108] Tirath (1966) has studied areal patterns of literacy in India.[109] Nitya Nanda (1966) has published a study on "Distribution and Spatial Arrangement of Rural Population in East Rajasthan."[110] In addition to distribution, he has also discussed arithmetic physiological, agricultural and nutritional densities.

Visaria (1967) has made an elaborate discussion on regional variations in changes in sex ratio during 1901-61 in the population of India and Pakistan.[111] Desai (1967) has made a similar study on sex-ratio in India but of a highly generalised type.[112] Krishan (1968) has studied the distribution and density of population in Orissa.[113] In another paper (1968) he has worked on regionalism in growth of population in Punjab's border district of Amritsar and Gurdaspur.[114] The latter is based on maps prepared from data from individual villages and is quite a detailed study.

Mitra (1967) has studied the relationship between pattern of shift from agriculture to non-agriculture and the levels of development.[115] Chandana (1969) has also worked on female working force of rural Punjab, 1961.[116] Mehta (1969) has attempted to examined some aspects of population of the Himalayas which lies west of Nepal.[117] Mehta (1970) has also made a detailed study on some aspects of changes in the demographic character of Bist Doab.[118]

Gyanchand (1972) has written a text book on population in perspectives in which he has explained the spatial pattern of population growth, fertility and mortality in the World and in India.[119] Ambannavar (1975) has attempted to examine the fertility and mortality trend, long term prospects of population growth and long term prospects of urbanization and growth of labour force in India.[120]

Mahto (1976) has worked on frontiers of research in population mobility.[121] He has emphasized the importance of population mobility in his attempt. Roy (1977) has studied the growth of population in Bhojpur and Rohtas districts of Bihar.[122] He has concluded that the growth of population has a direct bearing on land use. The growing population numbers has resulted in the decrease of per capita net sown area and consequently the people suffer from poverty and unemployment. Bhattacharya (1978) has studied the spatial and temporal distribution of population in India.[123] Bhende and Kanitkar (1978) have written a text book on principles of population studies of the World and India.[124]

Mehta (1978) has studied the regional population growth of Rajasthan in relation to geo-physical and socio-economic setting.[125] Sinha, et. al. (1980) have examined the rural-urban migration as a factor for population growth and social chang.[126] L. Das (1981) has studied the spatial character of population pressure in North Bihar Plain, west of the Kosi river.[127] He has studied it in relation to geographical factors. Singh (1981) has gone through the distributional characteristics of tribal population in India.[128]

Kumar (1983) has examined the impact of environment on the distribution of population in Nagaland.[129] Bhatia (1983) has studied the density of population and social pathology in India.[130] Jha (1978) has worked on agricultural land use and population in the Kamala-Balan plain, North Bihar.[131] Prasad (1980) has studied the land use and population of Ranchi district.[132] Singh (1984) has studied the spatial pattern of population and settlement in Nawada Plain. He has concluded that the distribution of population in Nawada Plain is uneven. It is large in fertile agricultural areas and small in infertile hilly areas.[133]

Statement of Problem and Hypothesis :

In the present research, it is proposed to study the spatial pattern of population in Rohtas district of Bihar. The above review of literature reveals that these aspects have never been studied. This research is, therefore, likely to add to the state of knowledge in population geography.

It is proposed to study the spatial pattern of population distribution and density, occupational structure, sex and literacy and to correlate them to physiography, slope, watertable, rainfall, irrigation, soil, intensity of agriculture and cropping pattern. Relation between these parameters will be established either with the help of map or some statistical techniques.

The validity of correlation between different aspects of population with physical, economic and cultural variables would also be studied with the help of sample villages.

A major hypothesis of the proposed study is that slope controls the pattern of physical, economic and cultural aspects of the district. Thus slope is most closely associated with the pattern of several aspects of population in Rohtas district. Spatial pattern of irrigation also controls the economic and cultural aspects.

The above aspects of the present thesis may be hypothesized in the form of following questions :

1. Can Rohtas district be divided into physical regions based on physical parameters of relief, slope, watertable, climate, soil and vegetation ?

2. What is the relationship between physical regions and the regions based upon land use and population characteristics in Rohtas district ?

3. Do physical and land use attributes have deterministic influence upon population characteristics in Rohtas district and to what extent ?

4. Will it be feasible to identify geographical regions in Rohtas district based upon various parameters ?

5. Are the characteristics of micro region identified on the basis of cartographic and statistical analysis reflected in sample village studies made on Rohtas district ?

It is proposed to study in detail the geographical parameters of Rohtas district while attempting to answer the above questions.

Methodology :

The method of study adopted in the following pages is strictly analytical. Original data generated in course of fieldwork has been tested and analysed both cartographically and statistically. The study of sample villages is partly descriptive and pertly analytical. The conclusions drawn are the result of a combination of reliable published data (such as census data), data generated in the field (through questionnaires and sample village studies) and personal observations made during the course of frequent visits to the area.

Sources of Data :

The data for the present work has been collected from various sources including published and unpublished official records, published and unpublished maps, government publications and from field investigation.

A good deal of data were compiled from the Census Tabulation Office and Statistics Department of Rohtas District regarding the land use, crops, rainfall, industry, etc. The author has collected data from seven sample villages of the Rohtas district based on purposive random survey. The data for these sample villages include almost all physical, economic and cultural information.

Slope data has been extracted from topographical sheets published by the survey of India.

Original data was generated in the field for sample villages by administering questionnaires and personal observation.

Sources of Maps :

The following maps were available and have been used in the present study :-

(1) 1 cm. = 2 kms. District Maps of Bihar, published by the Government of Bihar.

(2) 1" = 1 mile and 1" = 4 miles topographical sheets of the Survey of India, Dehradun.

(3) 1" = 2 miles Blocks Maps of 19 Blocks of Rohtas District which have been published by the Census of India in the District Census Handbooks of Rohtas (1970).

(4) 16" = 1 mile Cadastral Maps of sample villages, published by Survey office, Government of Bihar, have been used for detailed study of these villages.

(5) Various Atlases such as National Atlas, Bihar in Maps, Monograph of Bihar, School Atlas and Census Atlas of Bihar have been used for preparing certain outline maps of the study region.

Methods of Analysis :

A systematic approach based on a firm statistical footing and with a critical eye have been adopted to get a balanced geographical account of population in the Rohtas district. The analysis of geographical conditions have been made keeping in view the intimate relationship with population. The study region has been broken into several micro-geographical units to highlight this relationship. The economic and cultural data have been analysed on block level. Most of the data have been mapped by choropleth techniques. Several scatter Diagrams, which also contain lines of linear regression have been drawn for exhibiting the relationship between many population parameters. It has been rightly remarked that any data that can not be subjected to cartographic analysis may not be treated to be geographical. As such all data have been depicted upon maps using suitable techniques.

The cadastral maps and data generated during field investigation of sample villages have been used for interepretating the details of physical region, land use region and population regions of the Rohtas district.

In this work an attempt has been made to find out the deterministic influences of environmental phenomena on various aspects of population. It is suggested that the geographical analysis presented for Rohtas district in the following pages makes some original contribution towards technique of study as well as throws light upon the geography of the study region.

References :

1. Watson, J.W. (1955) : "Geography : A Discipline in Distance," Scottish Geographical Magazine, Vol. 71, pp 1-13.
2. Cole, J.P. and King, C. A.N. (1963) : Quantitative Geography, Wiley, New York.
3. Mandal, R.B. (1980) : Spatial Dynamics of the Centres of Population, Recent Trends and Concept in Geography, Concept Publishing Company, New Delhi, Vol. 3, pp. 275-283.
4. Ibid.
5. Zelinsky, W. (1966) : What does the Population Geographer Study ? A Prologue to Population Geography, Prentice Hall, Inc., Englewood Cliffs, New Jersey, p. 5.
6. Ibid.
7. Clarke, John I. (1966) : What is Population Geography ? Population Geography, Pargamon Press, London, p. 2.
8. Mahto, K. (1980) : Population Mobility and Economic Development in Eastern India, Unpublished Ph.D. Thesis, Patna University.
9. Demko, G.J. et. al. (1970) : Spatial Pattern of Population Geography, A Reader, McGraw Hill Book Company, New York, p. 1.
10. Clarke, J.I. (1966) : Op. Cit., p. 1.
11. Gosal, G.S. (1972) : Population Geography, A Survey of Research in Geography, Indian Council of Social Science Research, New Delhi, p. 173.
12. Trewartha, G. T. (1953) : The Case for Population Geography, Annals of the Association of American Geographers, Vol. 43, p. 71.
13. Howe, G.M. (1961) : The Geographical Variation in

Disease Mortality in England and Wales in the Mid-Twentieth Century, Advancement of Science, p. 415.

14. Cox, P. R. (1961) : Demography.
15. Veyret-Verner, G. (1962) : Populations : Movements, Structures, Repartition.
16. Zelinsky, W. (1962) : Changes in the Geographic Pattern of Rural Population in the United States, 1790-1960, Geographical Review, Vol. 52, p. 492.
17. Murray, M. (1962) : The Geography of Death in England and Wales, Annals of the Association of American Geographers, Vol. 52, p. 130.
18. Kariel, H.G. (1963) : Selected Factors Areally Associated with Population Growth due to net Migration, Annals of the Association of American Geographers, Vol. 53, p. 210.
19. Melezin, A. (1963) : Trends and Issues in the Soviet Geography of Population, Annals of the Association of American Geographers, Vol. 53, p. 144.
20. Pokshishevski, V.V. (1962) : Geography of Population and its Tasks, Soviet Geographical Review and Translation, Vol. 3, p. 9.
21. Clark, J.I. (1966) : What is Population Geography, Population Geography, Pergamon Press, p. 4.
22. Lowton, R. (1963) : Recent Trends in Population and Housing in England and Wales, Sociological Review, Vol. 11, p. 303.
23. Howe, G.H. (1964) : A National Atlas of Disease Mortality in the United Kingdom Geographical Journal, Vol. 130, p. 15.
24. Zelinsky, W. (1966) : Introduction, A Prologue to Population Geography, Prentice-Hall, INC, Englewood Cliffs, N.J., p. 1.
25. Caldwell, J.C. and Okonjo, C. (1969) : Population Growth and Distribution in the Upper Region of Ghana in a book named as the Population of Tropical Africa by T.E. Hilton, Longmans, pp. 278-290.

26. Kosinski, L. (1970) : Distribution of Population, The Population of Europe, Longman, p. 21.

27. Lawless, R.I. (1972) : Iraq : Changing Population Patterns, Population of the Middle East and North Africa edited by Clarke, J.I. and Fisher, W.B., University of London Press Ltd.

28. Dewdney, B.D. (1972) : Syria : Pattern of Population Distribution, Population of the Middle East and North Africa, edited by Clarke, J.I. and Fisher, W.B. University of London Press Ltd.

29. Clarke, B.D. (1972) : Iran : Changing Population Pattern, Population of the Middle East and North Africa, edited by Clarke, J.I. and Fisher, W.B. University of London Press Ltd.

30. Sulton, K. (1972) : Algeria : Changes in Population Distribution, Population of the Middle East and North Africa, edited by Clarke, J.I. and Fisher, W.B. University of London Press Ltd.

31. Sukhatma, P.V. (1972) : Population, Food Supply and Nutrition, Asian Population Study, Series No. 28, Population Strategy in Asia, The Second Asian Population Conference, Tokyo.

32. Kuroda, T. (1972) : Migration, Distribution of Population and Development in Japan-Asian Population Study Series, No. 28, Population Strategy in India, The second Asian Population Conference, Tokyo.

33. Trewartha, G.T. (1972) : The Less Development Realm: A Geography of its Population.

34. Harrison, G.A. & Boyce, A.J. (1975) : Ecology and Population Structure in the Arctic in the Structure of Human Population, written by William S. Laughlin, Clarendon Press Oxford, pp. 379-392.

35. Lames, P.E. (1954) : The Geographic Study of Population in James, P.E. and Jones, C.F. (eds.) , American Geography : Inventory and Prospect, p. 134.

36. Clark, P.J. and Evans, F.C. (1954) : Distance to Nearest

Neighbour as a Measure of spatial Relationship in Population, Ecology, Vol. 35, p. 445.

37. Glass, D.V. and Grebenik, E. (1954) : The Trend and Pattern of Fertility in Great Britain : A Report of the Family Census of 1946.
38. Belshaw, H. (1956) : Population Growth and Levels of Consumption.
39. Franklin, S.H. (1956) : The Pattern of Sex Ratio in New Zealand, Economic Geography, Vol. 32, p. 162.
40. Brookfield, H.C. (1957) : Mauritius : Demographic upsurge and Prospect, Population Studies, Vol. 2, p. 102.
41. Scott, P. (1957) : The Changing Population of Tasmania, Geographical Studies, Vol. 4, p. 13.
42. Duncan, O.D. (1957) : The Measurement of Population Distribution, Population Studies, Vol. 11, p. 27.
43. Saville, J. (1957) : Rural Depopulation in England and Wales, 1851-1951.
44. Newton, M.P. (1957) : Internal Migration : Some Aspects of Population Movements Within England and Wales.
45. Rose, A.J. (1958) : The Geographical Pattern of European Immigration in Australia, Geographical Review, Vol. 48, p. 512.
46. Kiser, C.V. and Whelpton, P.K. (1958) : Social and Psychological Factors affecting fertility, Milbank Memorial Fund Quarterly, Vol. 36, p. 1323.
47. Stewart, J.G. and Warntz, W. (1950) : Some Parameters of the Distribution of Population, Geographical Review, Vol. 49, p. 270.
48. Bogue, D.J. (1950) : Internal Migration in the Study of Population, ed. By Hauser, P.M. and Dunean, O.D., Chicago.
49. Ackerman, E. A. (1954) : Population and Natural Resource, The Study of Population, ed. By Hauser, P.M. and Duncen, O.D., p. 717.

50. Howe, G.M. (1960) : The Geographical Distribution of Cancer Mortality in Wales, 1947-53, Transactions and Papers of the Institute of British Geographers, Vol. 23, p. 189.

51. Glass, D.V. (1960) : Population Growth, Fertility and Population Policy, Advancement of Science, Vol. 17, p. 353.

52. Hoosan, D.J.M. (1960) : The Distribution of Population as the Essential Geographical Expression, Canadian Geographer, Vol. 17, p. 10.

53. Kuriyan, G. (1936) : Population and its Distribution, Journal of Madras Geographical Association, Vol. 11, No. 1.

54. Krishnaswami, S.S. (1930) : Population of Coimbatore District, Journal of Madras Geographical Association, Vol. 5, No. 2 & 3.

55. Lokanathan, P.S. (1931) : Migration of Labour with Special Reference to South India, Journal of Madras Geographical Association, Vol. 6, No. 1.

56. Raghavan, K.S. (1935) : Population of Anantapur District, Journal of Madras Geographical Association, Vol. 9, No. 4.

57. Raghavan, K.S. (1936) : Population of Salem District, Journal of Madras Geographical Association, Vol. 11, No. 2.

58. Raghavan, K.S. (1937) : Population of Tanjore District, Journal of Madras Geographical Association, Vol. 12, No. 3.

59. Kuriyan, G. (1938) : Population and its Distribution, Journal of Madras Geographical Association, Vol. 13, No. 2.

60. Raghavan, M.P. (1940) : Population of Tirunelvelley District, Journal of Madras Geographical Association, Vol. 15, No. 3.

61. Rajagopal, M.P. (1941) : Population of Chittor District,

Indian Geographer, Vol. 16, No. 4.

62. Ahmad, K.S. (1941) : Environment and its Distribution of Population in India, Indian Geographical Journal, Vol. 16, No. 2.
63. Yunus, M. (1941) : Trends of Population and Crop Production in Uttar Pradesh, Indian Geographical Journal, Vol. 16, No. 2.
64. Geddes, A. (1942) : The Population of India : Variability of Change as a Regional Demographic Index, geographical Review, Vol. 32, pp. 562-573.
65. Geddes, A. and Learmonth, A.T.A. (1953) : Variability in Population Change in India and Regional Variations Therein, Indian Geographical Review, Vol. 28.
66. Chatterjee, S.P. and Ganguli, A.T. (1943) : Population Distribution in two District of India, Calcutta Geographical Review, Vol. 5, No. 3.
67. Chatterjee, S.P. (1961) : Presidential Address : Physical Features and Population Distribution in West Bengal, Calcutta Geographical Review, Vol. 23, No. 1.
68. Chatterjee, S.P. (1962) : Regional Pattern of Density and Distribution Population in India, Geographical Review of India, Vol. 24, No. 2.
69. Bose, S.C. (1946) : Density and Pattern of Population in the Lower Damodar Basin, Calcutta Geographical Review, Vol. 8, No. 1 & 2.
70. Bose, S.C. (1952) : A Demographic Study of the Upper Damodar Basin, Indian Geographical Journal, Vol. 27, No. 3 & 4.
71. Singh, R.L. (1947) : Trend in the Growth of Population in Uttar Pradesh, Bulletin of National Geographical Society of India (Varanasi), Vol. 3.
72. Singh, R.L. (1956) : Population and its Problem in the Umland of Banaras, proceedings of International Geography Seminar.
73. Raza, M. (1950) : Is India Overpopulated ? geographer,

Vol. 3, No. 1.

74. Bidwai, B.K. (1951) : The variation of Population in Amravati District, Geographical Review of India, Vol. 13, No. 1.

75. Davis, Kingsley (1951) : The Population of India and Pakistan, Princeton University Press.

76. Bhat, L.S. (1953) : A Population Map of the Upper Panchaganga Basin, Bombay Geographical Magazine, Vol. 1, No. 1.

77. Bhat, L.S. (1961) : Population Studies :The need for regional Approach, Bombay Geographical Magazine, Vol. 8 & 9, No. 1.

78. Bhat, L.S. (1961) : Population Density and Growth in India, 1951-61, Proceedings of the Indian Council of Geographers, Vol. 1.

79. Geddes, A. & Learmonth, A.T.A. (1953) : Variability in Population Change in India and Regional Variations There in, (1921-40), Indian Geographical Journal, Vol. 28, No. 3 and 4.

80. Spate, O.H.K. (1956) : Population and Food in India, Proceedings of International geography Seminar.

81. Varma, S.D. (1956) : Density and Patterns of Population in Punjab, National geographical Journal of India, Varanasi, Vol. 2, No. 4.

82. Prasad, A. (1956) : Population Distribution and the Dynamics of Supply of Labour in Bihar, Geographical Outlook, Vol. 1.

83. Kayastha, S.L. (1956) : Demographic Features of the Himalayan Beas Basin, National Geographical Journal of India, Varanasi, Vol. 2, No. 1.

84. Khan, M.N. (1956) ; Distribution of Population in Allahabad District, National Geographical Journal of India, Vol. 2, No. 4.

85. Gosal, G.S. (1956) : A Geographical Analysis of India's Population, Unpublished Ph.D. Thesis, Wisconsin

University.

86. Anantapadmanabhan, N. (1957) : Density of Rural Population and terrain Types in Madras State, Bombay Geographical Magazine, Vol. 5, No. 1.
87. Trewartha, G.T & Gosal, G.S. (1957) : The Regionalism of Population Change in India, Cold Spring Harbor Symposia in Quantitative Biology, Vol. 22, pp. 71-81.
88. Mamoria, C.B. (1957) : Growth of Population in India, Geographical Review of India, Calcutta, Vol. 19, No. 4.
89. Gosal, G.S. (1958) : Occupational Structure of India's Rural Population, National Geographical Journal of India, Vol. 4, No. 3.
90. Gosal, G.S. (1961) : Internal Migration in India- a Regional Analysis, Indian Geographical Journal, Vol. 36, No. 3.
91. Sinha, B.N. (1958) : Population Analysis of Orissa, National geographical Journal of India, Vol. 4, No. 4.
92. Sinha, B.N. (1962) : The Bearing of Population Growth on the Economy of Orissa, Deccan Geographer, Hyderabad, Vol. 1, No. 1.
93. Dayal, P. (1959) : Population Growth and Rural-Urban Migration in India, National Geographical Journal of India, Vol. 5, No. 4.
94. Sharma, T.R. (1960) : Historical and Cultural Geography of the Ganga Valley in Etah District, U.P., Agra University Research Journal, Vol. 8, No. 122.
95. Lal, A. (1961) : Pattern of in-migration in Indian Cities, geographical Review of India, Vol. 23, No. 3.
96. Arunachalam, B. & Mathura, R.R. (1961) : Distribution of Population in the Ulhas Basin, Bombay Geographical Magazine, Vol. 8 and 9, No. 1.
97. Padhye, S.S. (1961) : Melghat- a Study in Population, Bombay Geographical Magazine, Vol. 8 and 9, No. 1.
98. Ahmad, E. (1961) : Migrations in Bihar, Bombay Geographical Magazine, Vol. 8 and 9, No. 1.

99. Gosal, G.S. (1961) : Regionalism of Sex Composition of India's Population, Rural Sociology, pp. 122-137.

100. Gosal, G.S. (1962) : Regional Aspects of Population Growth in India, Pacific View Point, Vol. 3, pp. 87-99.

101. Sen, J.C. (1963) : The Sex Composition of the Population of India, The Deccan Geographer, pp. 43-62.

102. Gosal, G.S. (1964) : Literacy in India : An Interpretative Study, Rural Sociology, pp. 261-277.

103. Gosal, G.S. (1967) : Regional Aspects of Rural Literacy in India, Presidential Address, transactions of the Indian Council of Geographers, pp. 1-15.

104. Gosal, G.S. and Krishan, G. (1965) : Occupational Structure of Punjab Rural Population, Indian Geographical Journal, p. 40.

105. Mitra, D.K. (1965) : India's Population and Food Supply, Observer, p. 11.

106. Ramachandran, R. (1965) : Population Trend in Malnad, Deccan Geographer, p. 3.

107. Schwartzberg, J. (1965) : The Distribution of Selected Castes in North Indian Plain, Geographical Review, pp. 477-496.

108. Singh, L.R. (1965) : Demographic Features of Nagaland, National Geographical Journal of India, p. 11.

109. Tirath, Ranjit (1966) : Areal Patterns of Literacy in India, Manpower Journal, pp. 88-118.

110. Nanad, N. (1966) : Distribution and Spatial Arrangement of Rural Population in East Rajashtan, Annals of Association of American Geographers, p. 6.

111. Visaria, P.M. (1967) : The Sex Ratio of the Population of India and Pakistan and Regional Variations during 1901-61 in Ashish Allied Publishers.

112. Desai, P.B. (1967) : Variations in Population Sex Ratio in India, 1901-61, in Ashish Bose, ed., Patterns of Population Change in India, Bombay, Allied Publishers.

113. Krishan, G. (1968) : Distribution and Density of Population in Orissa, National Geographical Journal of India, Vol. 14, pp. 250-257.

114. Krishan, G. (1968) : Regionalism in Growth of Population in Punjab's Border Districts of Amritsar and Gurdaspur, Geographical Review of India, Vol. 30, pp. 1-17.

115. Mitra, A. (1967) : Relationship Between Patterns of Shift from Agriculture to Non-Agriculture, 1951-61 and the Levels of Development, in Ashish Bose, ed., Pattern of Population Change in India, Bombay, Allied Publishers.

116. Chandana, R.C. (1967) : Female Working Force of Rural Punjab, Manpower Journal, Vol. 2, pp. 47-62.

117. Mehta, S.K. (1969) : Aspects of Population of the Himalaya, west of Nepal, in Ram Rahul, ed. Social work in the Himalaya, Delhi School of Social work, University of Delhi.

118. Mehta, S. (1970) : Some Aspects of Changes in the Demographic Character of Bist Doab : 1951-61, Unpublished Ph.D. Thesis, Punjab University.

119. Gyanchand (1972) : Growth of Population, Fertility and Mortality, Population in Perspectives, Orient Longman, pp. 102-162.

120. Ambannavar, J.P. (1975) : Second Indian Studies, Population, The Macmillan Company of India Ltd. Delhi, Bombay, Madras, Calcutta.

121. Mahto, K. (1976) : Frontiers of Research in Population Mobility, Indian Geographical Studies, Patna, R.B. No. 6, pp. 61-66.

122. Roy, S.R. (1977) : Growth of Population in Bhojpur and Rohtas, Indian Geographical Studies, R.B. No. 8, pp. 38-44.

123. Bhattacharya, A. (1978) : Distribution of Population, Population Geography of India, Shree Publishing Company, New Delhi, pp. 1-28.

124. Bhende, Asha, A. and Kanitkar, T. (1978) : Principle of Population Studies, Himalaya Publishing House, Bombay.

125. Mehta, B.C. (1978) : Regional Population Growth - A Case Study of Rajasthan, Research Books, Sundar Marg, Tilak Nagar, Jaipur.

126. Sinha, V.N.P., Sinha, S. and Rashmi (1980) : Rural-urban Migration as a factor for Population Growth and Social Change, Indian Geographical Studies, R.B. No. 15, pp. 58-65.

127. Das, K.K.L. (1981) : Population Pressure in North Bihar Plain, west of Kosi : A Spatial Analysis, Indian Geographical Studies, R.B. No. 16, pp. 23-32.

128. Singh, J.P. (1981) : Distributional Characteristics of Tribal Population in India Geographical Studies, R.B. No. 17, pp. 1-10.

129. Kumar, G. (1983) : Nagaland : A Study in Environmental Determinism of Population Distribution, Indian Geographical Studies, R.B. No. 20, pp. 38-41.

130. Bhatia, J.C. (1983) : Density of Population and Social Pathology in India, Indian Geographical Studies, R.B. No. 20, pp. 6-17.

131. Jha, G.P. (1978) : Agricultural Land Use and Population in the Kamala Balan Plain, North Bihar, Unpublished Ph.D. Thesis, Patna University.

132. Prasad, S.N. (1980) : Land Use and Population in Ranchi District, Unpublished Ph.D. Thesis, Patna University.

133. Singh, L.K.P. (1984) : Spatial Pattern of Population and Settlement in Nawada Plain, Unpublished Ph.D. Thesis, Patna University.

2

Chapter

Geographical Setting

Geographical Location :

Rohtas district of Patna Division is situated in the central western part of Bihar. It lies between 24°30' north latitude to 25°39' north latitude and 83°14' east longitude to 84°20' east longitude. The district is bounded by Bhojpur and Buxar district on the north, Jehanabad and Aurangabad districts on the east, Palamau and Garhwa districts on the south and Kaimur district on the west. The river Son embraces the district from the south-west to east giving a natural boundary to it (fig. 2.1).

Size and Shape :

Geographical area of the districts 3839.26 km^2. It represents 2.20% of the total area of Bihar. According to 2001 census 2450748 persons (12,83,485 males and 11,67,263 females) have been enumerated in the district. 21,23,942 persons (86.64%) are found living in 1695 inhabited villages and 3,26,806 persons (13.33%) in 6 towns of the district. The district is predominantly rural in character. About 18.13% of total population belongs to scheduled castes and 1.05% belongs to scheduled tribes. The density of population is 638 persons/km^2 which is lower than the state average of 881 persons/km^2.

The district is elongated in a long narrow belt for about 170 kms from south-west to north-east. The width of the district is greatly wavering. It shrinks in south-west. The width expands towards the north.

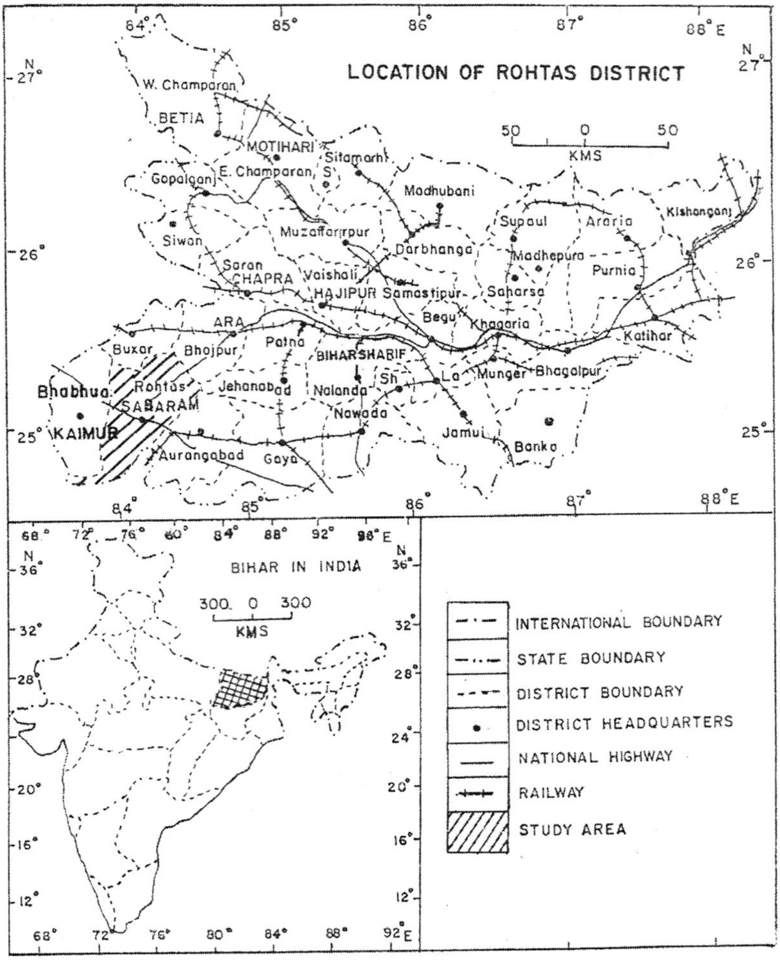
LOCATION OF ROHTAS DISTRICT
BIHAR IN INDIA
INTERNATIONAL BOUNDARY
STATE BOUNDARY
DISTRICT BOUNDARY
DISTRICT HEADQUARTERS
NATIONAL HIGHWAY
RAILWAY
STUDY AREA

Fig. 2.1

Nomenclature :

The district is named after Rohitashwa, the son of great Raghubanshi king Satya Harischandra. Rohtas is mot important name from very ancient times. Perhaps this part was the empire of the Rohitashwa. In the honour of that very honest king Satya Harischandra this tract of country is always referred after his son's name. The remains of Raja Rohit's fort are present even by now over Rohtas plateau and know as "Rohitas Fort".

Administrative Division :

The district has been divided into three sub-divisions and nineteen community development blocks. The administrative set up of the district is given below in fig. 2.2 and table no. 2.1.

Table - 2.1
Administrative Set-up of Rohtas District

Sl. No.	Name of Sub-division	Name of Community Development Blocks
1.	Sasaram	Sasaram, Chenari, Sheosagar, Nokha, Kargahar, Kochas.
2.	Bikramganj	Bikramganj, Dinara, Dawath, Suryapura, Karakat, Nasriganj, Sanjhauli.
3.	Dehri	Dehri, Rohtas, Nauhatta, Tilouthu, Rajpur, Akorhi Gola.

The History of the District as an Administrative Unit :

The existing district of Shahabad (except Chausa) formed, in 1685, part of the district of Sahabad and Rohtas. Sarkar Shahabad includes the northern Pargana of the present district with the addition of the three Parganas on the west Ratan, Kotha and Mangror. The southern Parganas of the

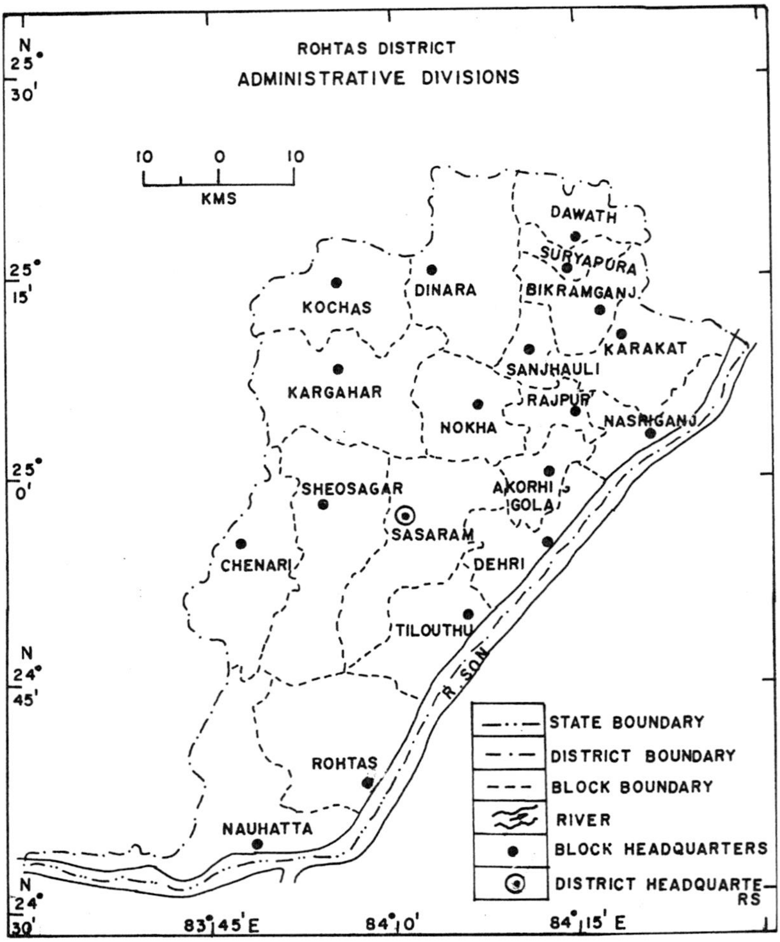
ROHTAS DISTRICT
ADMINISTRATIVE DIVISIONS
10 0 10
KMS
DAWATH
SURYAPURA
BIKRAMGANJ
DINARA
KOCHAS
KARAKAT
SANJHAULI
KARGAHAR
RAJPUR
NOKHA
NASRIGANJ
SHEOSAGAR
AKORHI GOLA
SASARAM
CHENARI
DEHRI
TILOUTHU
R. SON
ROHTAS
NAUHATTA
STATE BOUNDARY
DISTRICT BOUNDARY
BLOCK BOUNDARY
RIVER
BLOCK HEADQUARTERS
DISTRICT HEADQUARTERS
N 25° 30'
25° 15'
25° 0'
N 24° 45'
N 24° 30'
83°45' E
84°0'
84°15' E

Fig. 2.2

district Chainpur, Sasaram and Rohtas were in Sarkar Rohtas which then included also Siris-Kutumba, Japla and Belaunja on the eastern bank of the Son.

In 1784, Rohtas district was separated. The new district Rohtas includes Chainpur and Sasaram Parganas. Zila Rohtas was split up, its eastern portion forming part of the new district of Bihar while the western portion fell into Shahabad district with William Augustus Brooke as the first collector. Shahabad district was then constituted of the area now included in the Shahabad district, without Chausa and with the addition of the Doaba Pargana on the northern bank of the Ganga. The new arrangement came into effect in July, 1787. Chausa Pargana became a part of the Shahabad district in 1818. Further details of the history of the district as an administrative unit have been given elsewhere.

The district has always formed a unit of the Patna Division. For administrative purpose the district is divided into four sub-divisions, viz., Arrah Sadar, Sasaram, Buxar and Bhabua there are 11 revenue within the district.

Brief History of the District :

The present district of Rohtas consists of areas under Sasaram and Bhabua sub-divisions of the old Shahabad district. The district of Rohtas came in existence in the year 1972.

Geographically this district can be divided into two parts, viz., (i) hilly and (ii) plain areas. The hilly areas comprise the plateau of Kaimur while the plain area on the eastern side is formed by the mighty current of Son and on the western side by the rivers of Karmanasa and Durgawati. It is bounded on the north by the district of Bhojpur and part of Ghazipur in Uttar Pradesh, on the south by the district of Palamau, on the west by the districts of Mirzapur and Varanasi in Uttar Pradesh on the east by the district of Aurangabad and part of Gaya. The district has a close linkage with the history of the parent district of Shahabad which till 1685, formed part of old Sarkars of Rohtas and Sahabad.

Rohtas has an old and interesting history. In pre-historic days the plateau region of the district has been the abode of the aboriginals whose chief representatives now are the Bhars, the Cheros and the Savars. According to some legends, the Kharwars were the original settlers in the hilly tracts near Rohtas. The Oraons also claim that they ruled over the country between Rohtas and Patna. The local legend also connects King Sahasrarjun with Sasaram, the headquarters of Rohtas district. It is believed that Sahasrarjun had terrible fight with Saint Parsuram, the legendary Brahmin protector as a result of which Sahasrarjun was killed. The term Sasaram is supposed to have been abbreviated from Sahasrarjun and Parsuram. Another legend connects the Rohtas hills to Rohitashwa, son of Raja Harishchandra, a famous king who war known for his piety and truthfulness.

The district of Rohtas formed part of the Magadh Empire since 6th century B.C. to 5th century A.D. under the Pre-Mauryans. Mauryans and late Gupta rulers of Magadh. The minor rock edict of Emperor Ashoka at Chandan Sahid near Sasaram confirmed the Mauryans conquests of this district. In the 7th century A.D. this district came under the control of Harsha rulers of Kannauj. There is an inscription in the Mundeshwari temple near Bhabua which refers to kind Uday Sena as the ruling chief of the area. Another inscription at Deo Barunarak records the dedication of the temple there by Jivita Gupta, and one of the later Guptas. The next was King Sasanka, the king of Gauda in Bengal whose seal is inscribed at the Rohtasgarh. The famous Chinese pilgrim, Hieun-Tsang, who journeyed through the country in the seventh century A.D. passed through Arrah, the headquarters of old Shahabad district and new outside the region of newly created Rohtas district. The district successively came to the rulers of Shail dynasty of central India and Pal dynasty of Bengal. The first ruler of Pal dynasty controlled this district as observed by C. Mark later on the Ghadwals controlled Varanasi and also the Rohtas district in the twelfth century as confirmed by the Tarachandi rock inscription near Sasaram. After the fall of the Guptas, the district in all probabilities relapsed into the hands of the aboriginal tribes and came under the control of petty chieftains. The Rajputs who came afterwards from Ujjain in the province of Malwa has a series of conflicts with the aboriginals and it took them many hundred years to subdue the aboriginals completely. The following excerpt from the Census Report of 1961 gives a brief account of Medieval and British period history of Rohtas which at that time was a part of the old Shahabad district:

"When Bakhtiar Khilji attacked Bihar in 1193 A.D. he found Shahabad in the hands of petty Rajput chiefs who were often fighting among themselves. They were not united and strong enough to offer any powerful resistance to the Muslim invader. Consequently, Bakhtiar Khilji had an easy victory over them and the district soon became a part of his kingdom. The history of the district thereafter is linked with that of the Saba or the province of which it now forms part. In the year 1397 A.D. it was annexed, along with the rest of Bihar, to the kingdom of Jaunpur. A hundred years later, it passed into the direct hands of the Muslim emperor of Delhi."

"Sher Shah's father, Hassan Khan Sur, was an Afghan adventurer. He got the Jagir of Sasaram as a reward for his services to Jamal Khan, the Governor of Province, during the latter's engagement with the king of Jaunpur. But the Afghan Jagirdar was not able to exercise full control over his subjects. The allegiance of the people was very loose and the landlords were practically independent. In 1529, Babar invaded Bihar. He was apposed by Sher Shah who lost. Babar has left in his memoirs an interesting account of the place. He mentions about the superstitions of the Hindus in regard of river Karmanasa and also describes how be swam across the river Ganges at Buxar (now in Bhojpur district) in 1528. He has also recorded his visit to Maner (in Patna district) to see the tombs and offer his prayers there at noon."

"While encamping at Arrah in 1529 offer his victory over the Afghan rulers, Babar proclaimed his sovereignty over Bihar. In commemoration of this event, the place was called

Shahabad, which literally means "the city of the Emperor," This name was later applied to the Sarkar within which Arrah was included, and eventually to the entire district."

"When Babar died, Sher Shah became active again. In 1537 Humayun advanced against him and besieged his fortresses at Chunar and Rohtasgarh. Humayun proceeded to Bengal where he spent six months. While on his return journey to Delhi, he suffered a crushing defeat at the hands of Sher Shah at Chausa. This victory secured for Sher Shah the empirical throne of Delhi." The rule of Sur dynasty, which Sher Shah founded, was very shortlived. Soon the Mughals regained the empirical throne of Delhi. After his accession, Akbar tried to extend his empire and consolidated it. The district of Shahabad (which included the present Rohtas district also) was thus included in his empire.

British Period :

"In 1758 Shah Alam passed through Sasaram with a large army. He wanted to occupy Bihar in order to establish his claim over the throne of Delhi. He was, however, forced to retreat to Sasaram by Clive's army. The Mughal prince then proceeded to Durgawati where he was joined by a powerful Zamindar Pahalwan Singh, who helped him to cross the Karmanasa. Clive, who was then the Governor of the East India Company's settlements in Bengal, marched against Pahalwan Singh. The latter came to terms with the English after an interview with Clive."

"On becoming Nawab, Mir Kasim, tried to establish his control over this part of the country. He assembled a large force, marched to Sasaram and established his stronghold there. No resistance of any consequence was offered to him. He took measures to keep the district under his control, and returned to Munger thereafter. Mir Kasim was, however, defeated by the English at Udhwa Nala, near Rajmahal in the Santhal Pargana, on the 5th September 1763. He fled to Tilouthu near Sasaram, where he was joined by his women-folk. From here he fled to the kingdom of Oudh. In 1764, Mir

Kasim returned with Suja-ud-Daula. The English tried to stop his advance and there were fierce battles in Shahabad. But Mir Kasim's advance could not be checked until he reached Patna. Suja-ud-Daula fell back to Buxar and it was here that the English won a decisive battle over him in October 1764. This made then the absolute master of the area."

The next event of importance which turmoiled the district was the rebellion of Raja Chait Singh of Benares. His kingdom included large parts of Shahabad and his control extended up to Buxar. He raised the banner of revolt against the English people who had been passing through difficult, times. At Chunar and Ghazipur, the English troops suffered defeats and the very foundations of the English power in India were shaken. But, as is well known, Chait Singh lost eventually.

The district had a very uneventful history till 1857 when Kunwar Singh revolted against the British in line with the Mutineers of 1857. Most of the heroic details of Kunwar Singh is concerned with the present district of Bhojpur. The mutiny had however its impact and produced similar uprisings and incidents here and there. The hilly tracts of the district offered natural escape to the fugitives of the Mutiny. During independence movement the district had a substantial contribution to the freedom of India. After independence Rohtas remained a part of the Shahabad district but in 1972 Rohtas formed a separate district.

Rohtas District and Magadh :

The plain of Bihar consisting amazing fertility has naturally remained a nucleus of Indian civilization and culture.[1] Rohtas district, being a part of it, has also enjoyed the prevailing cultures of these ages. Scholars are of the opinion that even the Gangetic valley must have had numerous centres of urban civilization the like of which we find in the Indus valley.

The plains of Bihar constituted the Kingdoms of Magadha Anga, Videh and Vaishali during Pauranic period. The word

Magadha appeared in some of the pages of Atharva Ved before it took a definite shape during Mahabharat period. Magadh roughly spanned over the districts of Gaya and Patna and their adjoining lands.[2] General Cunningham holds that Magadha extended up to Karamanasa on the west and the source of Damodar river on the south.[3] According to B.C. Law, Magadha roughly corresponds to the old Patna and Gaya district.[4] P.C. Roy Chaudhury also holds the same view.[5] The limits of the Magadha Empire waxed and waned in its history. Jarasandh inscribed and expanded it, but his successors lost it to Sisung dynasty in seventh and eight century B.C. Ajatsatru annexed the country from Koshal to Bengal and enlarged its outline.

In the fourth century, Nanda's Magadha included the entire northern India and greater part of Deccan. Chandragupta Maurya united under the Magadha banner a territory larger than had come prior to him. Ashoka the Great stretched it from Afgainistan to Kamrup and from Himalaya to the Penner river. The outline thereafter shrinked with the decline of the empire.[6]

The Magadha proper has been associated with the names of Lord Buddha and Lord Mahavira who met in Rajagriha Bodh Gaya where Buddha attained enlightenment and Pawapuri where Mahavira attained Nirvana. The ancient international seat of learning, Nalanda University, which not attracted to its seminaries scholars from foreign lands, but also sent out to the for of regions its alumni proficient in varied branches of human lore, as representative of India culture and thought is also 220 kms. from Rohtas.

Relationship of Rohtas District with Patna, Gaya and Sasaram :

These cities play a vital role in transforming the socio-economic and cultural conditions of Rohtas district. Patna lies about 160 kms. and Gaya 104 kms. away from the Rohtas district and can be reached within four hours either by railways or by road. A broad gauge railway line and a national highway pass across this district and the same also link Rohtas with other metropolitan cities.

(1) **Administrative :** Sasaram is a District Headquarter handed by District Magistrate and has a Block Development Officer and a Circle Officers at block headquarter. Other higher administrative needs of the district are directly governed by Patna. Patna is, in fact, the pivot of administration for whole of Bihar State. Gaya-Patna is the Divisional Headquarter and has the offices of the Divisional Commissioner.

(2) **Education :** The Rohtas district has paucity of educational institutions. Only Sasaram town a few block headquarters have Government Colleges. Even affiliated colleges and Government High Schools are absent in most of the block headquarters. In hilly areas even middle schools are found at relatively long distance. Thus for higher education the people of this district are compelled to depend on the educational institutions of Patna, Gaya or Ara. The universities at these places provide facilities of learning in all faculties.

(3) **Religious :** Gaya town has conspicuously been known as one of the holiest spots for the Hindus from times immemorial and hardly a day passes when there is no Hindu Pilgrim to offer pandas in Gaya Kshetra or dham as it is called.[7] According to the religion of the Puranas, which is the modern religion of the Hindu of India, it is incumbent on every Hindu to visit Gaya and make offerings for souls of his ancestors.[8] Situated seven miles away, south of Gaya town, is Bodh Gaya, the holy place for Buddhists. Buddhists not only from India but also from different countries visit the spot in large numbers. It is at Bodh Gaya that Lord Buddha achieved enlightenment. The important sites of religious importance of Gaya are Vishnu temple, Manglagauri temple, Pretshila Pahar, Brahamyoni, etc. In addition to these this city observes a permanent Pitripaksh Mela which gravitates people in lakhs from different corners

of India.

(4) **Hospital and Health Centres :** The Rohtas district has medium facilities. Most of the health centres are located at block headquarters and a district level hospital is found at Sasaram town. The available health centres are, however, ill managed. Hence the people of the plain are forced to go to Gaya or preferably Patna for medical aids.

Besides the people of Rohtas district rush to Patna or Gaya town for recreation, trade and commerce etc.

Thus the Rohtas District is well connected with Sasaram, Patna and Gaya townships. These cities invariably support and encourage the socio-economic and cultural set up of the district of Rohtas.

Geology :

A general stratigraphical sequence of the geological formations is given below in table no. 2.2.

Table - 2.2
Stratigraphical Sequences

Systems	Series	Stages	Sub-stages	Thickness
Recent to Sub-recent		Alluvium	Sandstone	180 metres
Upper Vindhyan	Kaimur	Upper Kaimur	Bijaigarh	60 metres
		Lower Kaimur	Sand Stone	48 metres
Lower Vindhyan	Semri	Rohtas	Limestone and shales	152 metres
		Kheinjua	Glauconite beds	
			Fawn limestone	
			Olive shales	281 metres
			Forcallanites	
		Basal	Kagarhat Limestone and shales	
			Basal	

		Conglomerate etc.	610 metres
Pre Vindhyan	Bijawar and Gneissic Granite		

The plateau Rohtas is eastern most extension of one of the most famous geographical and geological feature of the Vindhyan table land. Of the numerous stratigraphical subdivisions related with the great Vindhyan system, only three are conspicuous in this portion of Peninsular India facing the vast Gangetic plain in the north. Those are by order of superposition :-

(i) The Kaimur Sandstone, (ii) The Bijaigrah Shales and (iii) The Rohtas limestones. Throughout the greater part of the region the rocks are hidden by the alluvium deposits of the Ganga River except for some small hillocks about 16 kms. north of Sasaram. There are no other exposed rocks in the area of study (Fig. 2.3).

The Vindhyan table land has come out of the Vindhyan geosynclines. In per-cambrian time after the formation of the cuddapah rocks in south India, it remained a sea in which the calcareous and argillaceous sedimentation took place. This sea might have extended around the granite massif of Bundelkhand in the heart of northern India extending in the great semi circle from near Agra in the north-west towards Chittorgarh, Hoshangabad in the south and Sasaram in the west. The plateau has remained as a stable mass since it has come in to existence. The epeirogenic upheaval which uplifted the sediments from the floor of the sea to form a continental land area were the last significant earth movement recorded in the history of this plateau. No other disturbance of similar magnitude has ever affected its stability during the long series of geological ages. After remaining an impassive solid block of the lithosphere the plateau was traversed by the cycle of erosion and new chapter of landscape evolution began in this area. But this cycle of landscape evolution was interrupted during the Gondwana

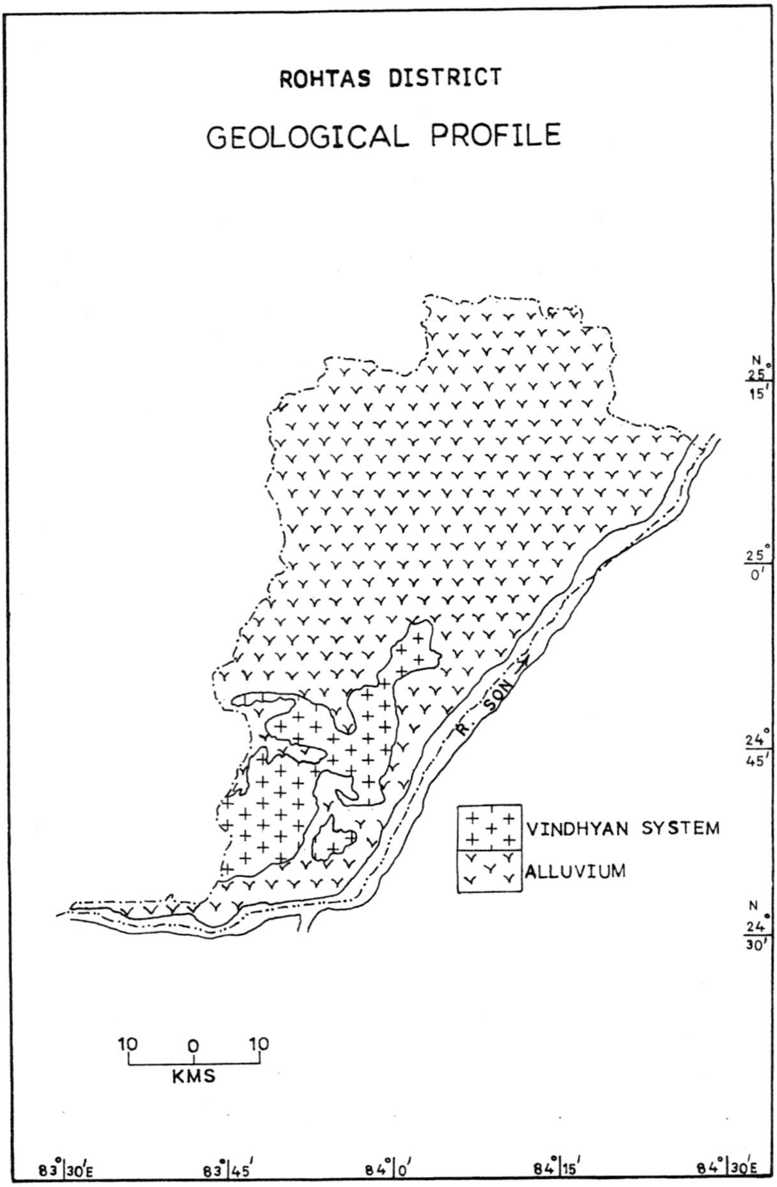
ROHTAS DISTRICT
GEOLOGICAL PROFILE
VINDHYAN SYSTEM
ALLUVIUM
R. SON
10 0 10
KMS
N 25° 15'
25° 0'
24° 45'
N 24° 30'
83°30'E
83°45'
84°0'
84°15'
84°30'E

Fig. 2.3

glaciation time. After deglaciation, the cycle again started to unroll the chapter of geomorphic features uninterruptedly till the tertiary upliftment.

The rocks of the Vindhyan formations comprise mainly sandstone, quartzites, limestone, dolomite and shales. The maximum thickness of sediments is over 2400 metres. The rocks usually exhibit horizontal alignment except some tilting affecting limestone area. Such area contains precipitious scarps around the edge of the plateau. The Rohtas sandstone constitutes an excellent building material and has largely been quarried at Karwandia near Sasaram. The Rohtas limestone and the Bijaigarh shales from the undercliff facing the Son river along the southern and south-eastern edges of the plateau outcrop, and are also present in the north in the deep river gorges of the Durgawati, where they cut through the anticlinal axis of the shallow corrugations. The Rohtas limestone is largely burnt for lime. The sacred limestone Gupteshwar cave of the Durgawati valley is a notable feature.

The Bijaigarh shales are intensely brittle, splintery and black in colour. It can be easily mistaken for coal. They are often impregnated with iron pyrites and have been used to a small extent to manufacture sulphate of iron. In the south-west of Rohtasgarh between the fort of the scarp and the Son river scarp of Vindhyan subdivisions underlying the Rohtas limestone are for a short distance. Some are remarkable for their porcellanic texture. The isolated hills north of Sasaram consist of a coarse quartzes and telepathic sandstone.

Below the foot of the plateau in the north, the whole district is covered with alluvial deposits of the Ganga.

Physiography :

The district is characterized with physiographical diversities which have developed with due to denudational processes and varied geological structure. The area of maximum relief is on the south-west skirts of the plateau (between 339 to 461 metres), where the plain directly meets the free face at its bottom. Four pediments are seen here.

The hills and streams are absent. The rock formation of the plateau mass represents massive limestone at the feet and hard sandstone at the top. The fringes of the plateau in the south, east and north attain the height of 260 to 339 metres. Rock free face scarps are common features in this meeting place of plateau and plain. Northern outskirt which has a gentle slope towards the Ganga plain has vegetative cover in lower reaches. Eastern and south portions are noted for limestone quarries. The 96 metre Shital Kund on the Durgawati river and 38 metre Dhuan Kund on the Kudra-Kao river are the beautiful waterfall spots in northern plateau fringes. In extreme north-east and in north-west of the plateau some residual hills are present to break the monotony of the area. These hills are named after their adjacent villages e.g. Bhitariban hill near Bhitariban village, Salempur hill near Salempur village, Lohra hill near Lohra village and Babhani hill near Babhani village. Some springs are seen on the plateau are locally known as "CHUANS". Settlement is found near chuans as water have been providing only source of drinking water throughout the year over the plateau mass (Fig. 2.4).

The district may be divided into two major physiographic units :

(i) Plateau Rohtas

(ii) Plain Rohtas

(i) Plateau Rohtas :

This is a tableland and is the continuation of the Kaimur plateau in Rohtas district. It extends along the southern boundary of the region. At Rohtasgarh it attains the height of 461 metres above mean sea level. This tract is covered with mixed tropical forest. The boundary of the plateau is very irregular having some isolated hills in north and north-western corner. The north westerly continuation of the great Vindhyan range has bold escarpments facing the plain country. The western highlands of Rohtas plateau have an elevation varying from 304 to 425 metres. The sloppy sides of

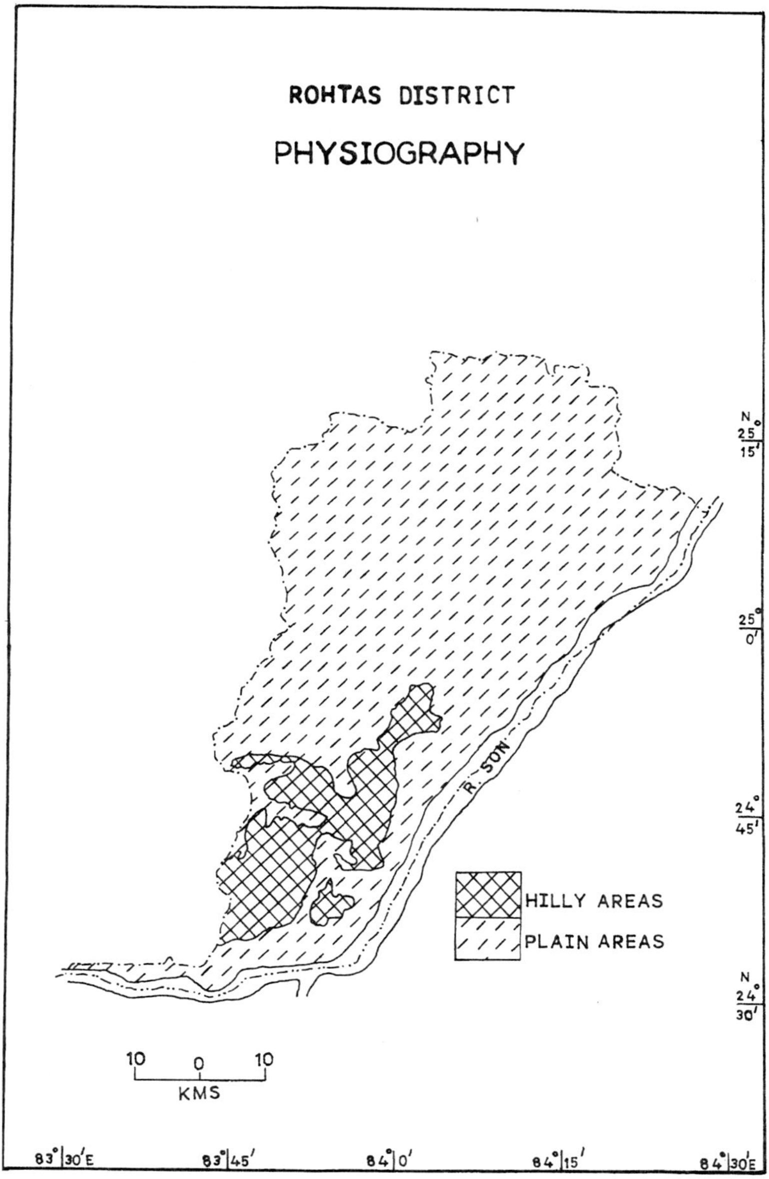
ROHTAS DISTRICT
PHYSIOGRAPHY
R. SON
HILLY AREAS
PLAIN AREAS
10 0 10
KMS
N 25° 15'
25° 0'
24° 45'
N 24° 30'
83° 30' E
83° 45'
84° 0'
84° 15'
84° 30' E

Fig. 2.4

the tableland are used for pasturage (Fig. 2.5).

(ii) Plain Rohtas :

Plain Rohtas may be divided in to two parts for its physiographic study :

(a) The Plain lying in the north of plateau

(b) The Plain lying in the south and east of the plateau.

(a) The plain lying in the north of plateau : This tract extends from the foot of the plateau to the northern fringe of the district. It is a flat country of alluvial formations having a very faint slope towards north. This densely populated and highly fertile area contains tenacious clay mixed with coarse sand. On the east the soil is comparatively light. The plain has a height of 80 to 93 metres from sea level and the thickness of alluvial deposits is 50 metres.

(b) The plain lying in the south and east of the plateau : The plain lying in the south and east of the plateau is a small area between south and east of the fringe of the Rohtas plateau and the river Son. Its slope is southward on the southern side and towards east on the eastern side of the plateau. It is crossed by the left affluent streams of the Son. In the north-east locality between Sasaram and the Son river the height of the plain is 12 metres from sea level. It merges into Bhojpur plain in the north quite imperceptibly.

Drainage :

The general slope of the region is from south to north. This is why almost all rivers drain towards north, north-east or north-west direction. In south and east of Rohtas, the most important river of the region is the Son. It flows to river Ganga, 16 km. north of Maner in Patna district. The details of the rivers (fig. 2.6) of the district are given below :

(i) The Son :

The Son river originates on the elevated plateau of Amarkantak near the source of Narmada and the Mahanadi

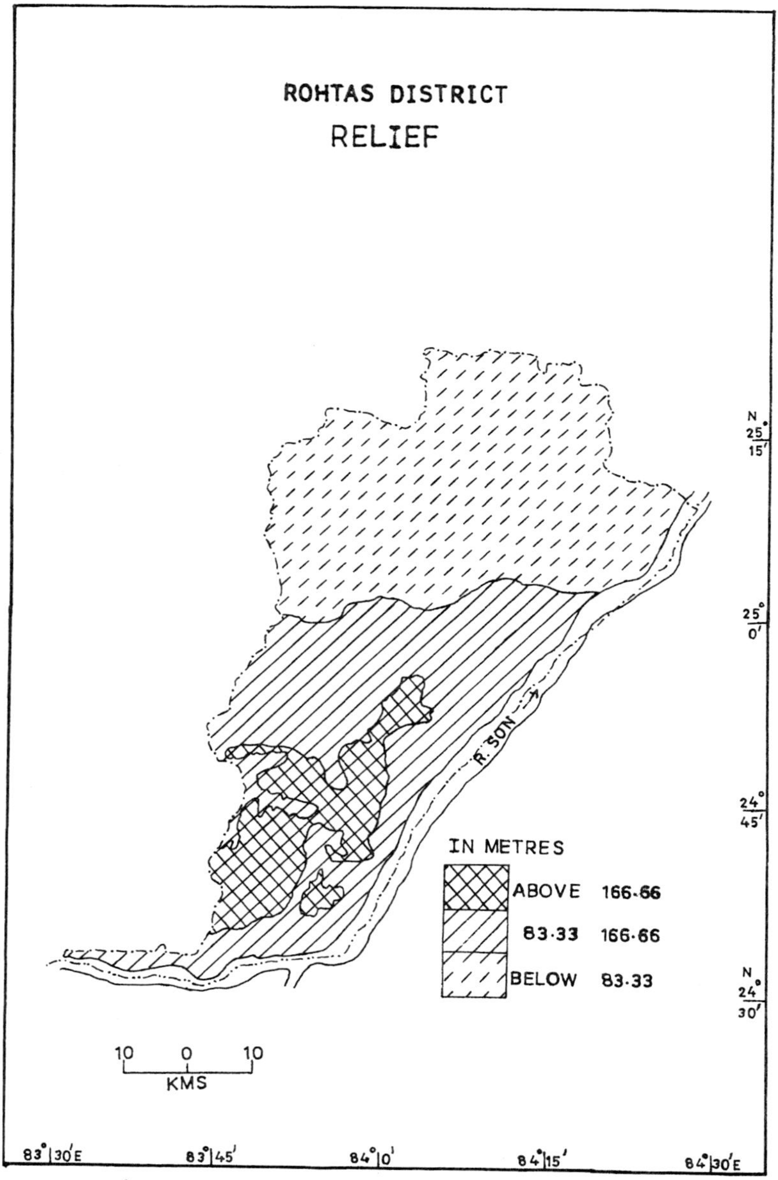
ROHTAS DISTRICT
RELIEF
R. SON
IN METRES
ABOVE 166.66
83.33 166.66
BELOW 83.33
10 0 10
KMS
N 25° 15'
25° 0'
24° 45'
N 24° 30'
83° 30'E
83° 45'
84° 0'
84° 15'
84° 30'E

Fig. 2.5

in Madhya Pradesh. It touches the Rohtas district at the tri junction of the district of Garhwa, Mirzapur of U.P. and Rohtas at Kosdera village near Jadanathpur. After a course of 507 km. flowing close to the steep slope it precipitates from Rohtas plateau in the south and east. Finally it merges into the Ganga between Arrah and Danapur, 16 km. north of Maner. During its course it attains great width generally exceeds 3.5 kms and amounts to 4.6 kms. The river in spanned by massive masonry dam forming a reservoir at Indrapuri for canals and by old long railway bridge and Jawahar Bridge for N.H. 2 between Son Nagar and Dehri-on-Sone.

The most noticeable feature of its courses is its meagre stream of water at ordinary times as compared with enormous width of the river bed, its vast size and paroxysmal violence at periods of floods. In dry season of summer days, the bed deposits exhibit wide stretch of drifting sand with an unimportant stream of water barely hundred metres wide meandering from bank to bank and fordable at most places. But in rainy season the river presents a wonderful contrast. During this period the entire rainfall of its enormous catchments area has to find an outlet by this channel clearly becomes incapable in carrying near about 8,30,000 cubic feet per second. Consequently, the flood water rushes down so violently as to spill over its broad bed and cause disastrous inundations in the low lying plains of the Rohtas and Bhojpur districts.

The Son does not entertain any important tributary up to Dehri from the point where it enters the region. At Indrapuri Son water is distributed east to Gaya and Patna districts and west to Rohtas and Bhojpur districts through a large irrigation system of the Son canals. The bed of the Sone is entirely made of sand, but in a few parts clay is found and cultivated.

The Son bed at Dehri has a large turn-over of business of timber and bamboos.

The Son possesses historical interest as being identical

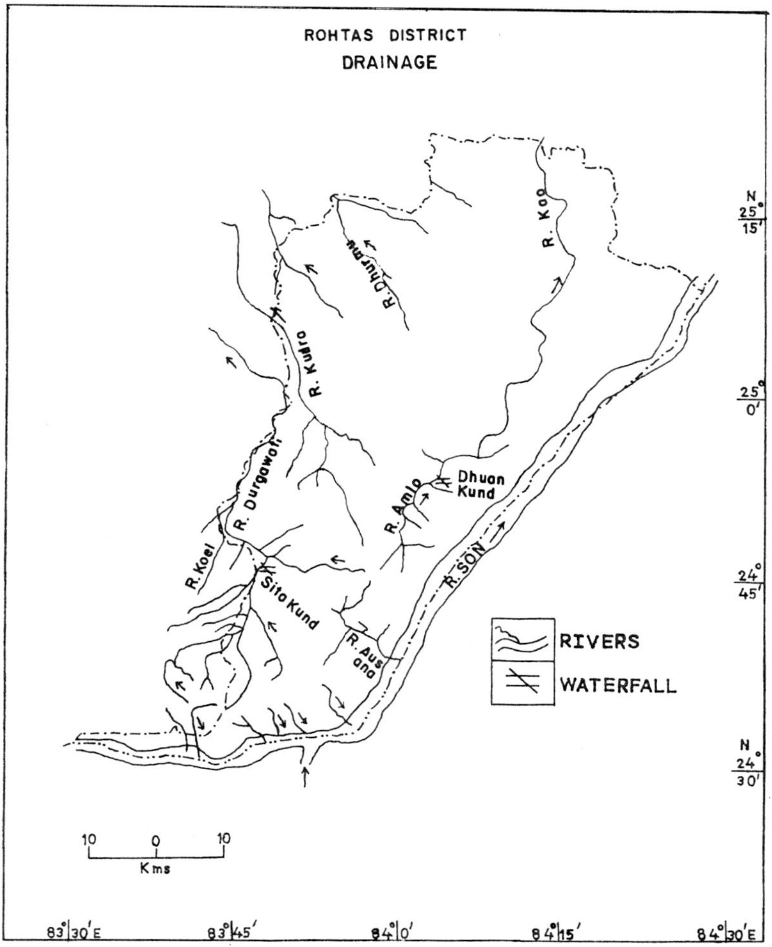
ROHTAS DISTRICT
DRAINAGE
R. Kao
R. Dhurma
R. Kudra
R. Durgawati
R. Koel
Sita Kund
R. Amla
Dhuan Kund
R. SON
R. Ausana
RIVERS
WATERFALL
10 0 10
Kms
N 25° 15'
25° 0'
24° 45'
N 24° 30'
83°30'E
83°45'
84°0'
84°15'
84°30'E

Fig. 2.6

with Eranrohoas, which is mentioned by Magasthenes as the third in all India and inferior to none but the Indus and the Ganges. The ancient town at Pataliputra (modern Patna) was situated at its confluence with the Ganges. It has gradually receded further westward and made fresh channels for itself. In the Ain-i-Akbari it is said to have jointed the Ganga at Maner and in Rennall's Bengal Atlas of 1772 the junction is market at the same place.[9]

(ii) The Durgawati :

The Durgawati rises in the village of Bhakma, on the southern ridge of the Kaimur plateau, a few miles north of the source of the Karmanasa. It rises at an elevation of 615 metres. After flowing for about 14 kms in northerly direction it rushes over a precipice 93 metres high into the deep glan of Khedar Khoh, where other hill torrents help to swell its volume. There is a waterfall of 96 metres on its way near the limestone cave of Gupteshwar. The Durgawati enters into the plain country at Karmchat (Kaimur district) where a large scheme of irrigation project is under construction. Running towards north for about 19 km. it embraces Kudra (kaimur district) a urban settlement on N.H. 2. The Kudra river joins it as a tributary in the way. The total length of the river is 169 kms from source to month having a catchments area of 409.4 km2. Near the source its width is two metres with nine metres depth. Over the plateau its maximum width is 9 metres, but as it advances in plain it become wider and wider. It is perennial in nature. In upper part it has a roack channel. The Karmchat project, a big scheme of irrigation, is under construction near the village 'Bhitari Bandh' on this river.

(iii)The Kao :

The Kao or Dhoba rises on the plateau six miles south-west of Tilothu and after flowing through a glen in a northerly direction, forms a fine waterfall (38.7 metres) known as Dhuan kund about 8 kilometres south of Sasaram. It enters the plains at the Tarachandi pass, two miles south-east of Sasaram. At this place it bifurcates; one branch, the Kudra, turns to the west and ultimately joins the Karamnasa, while the other, which preserves the name Kao, flows to the north, and finally falls into the Ganges, near Gaighat. There is very little water in its bed during the cold and hot seasons but in the rainy days it is subjected to floods of the most violent character. In the hilly portion of its course the bed is rocky and full of enormous boulders wasted down during heavy rains. The bank are generally high and firm, but in the plains are less elevated. The river, which is nowhere navigable, except at flood time as far as the railway line, is the principal drainage channel of the southern and central parts of the district. With the completion of the Kao project it provides water for canal irrigation.

(iv) The Kudra :

The Kudra is a branch of the Kao, and carry off the overflow of that river when it rises in flood. After leaving the Tarachandi pass near Sasaram, it is swollen by a number of small streams, and flowing in a north-easterly direction crosses the Grand Trunk Road at Khurmabad, and falls into the Durgauti at Tendwa after a course of fifty miles. In the dry season it contains very little water : but during the rains, it becomes a large streams. The bed is rocky and full of enormous boulders until the river has fairly debouched into the plains, after which it varies according to the character of the soil through which it passes. According to local tradition, the origin of the Kudra is as follows :- A powerful Brahman Zamindar, who owned large estates near Kargahar, came down with a large following to the Tarachandi pass, and after defeating the local levies, proceeded to excavate a new channel from the Kao river to his own domains. This channel was called the Kudra because it was excavated with Kudaris and it is noticeable that an old bed of the kudra is still to be seen passing northwards towards kargahar.[10]

(v) The Ausana :

It is the only important river flowing south-east of the plateau. Its source is 4 kms north-west of the source of the

Kao river in the west of the village Kachhubar at an elevation of 465 metres. Its length is only 29 kilometres. After flowing for about 7 kms. it has curved out the deep-gorge on the southern flank land flows of through a precipice before entering the plain. It passes near Rohtas railway station (old centre gague) and joins the Son.

Springs :

In Rohtas plateau region springs are known as "CHUSNS." The chuans are the only regular source of water throughout the year for the neighbouring settlements over the plateau. The percolation and sinkage of water during rains through the upperlying sandstone has helped in storage over the underlying impervious shale bed. Where the sand stone has been eroded or reduced to the shale bed, springs appear. These springs are neither hot not very cool but in the summer season water is cool and refreshing.

Underground Water :

The plateau region the presence of underground water is insignificant. It is seen in narrow glen which are known as 'KHOH'. These Khoh are the deep cut narrow valleys of streams. A scene of underground water is viewed in Gupteshwar cave in which sub stream water flows through the PATALGANGA. These Patalgangas have their continuation with Sita Kund which is pool of cool water in Durgawati valley. As Khoh or glens are the lower land of the beds of rivers the percolation of water from the over lying beds remains in ation. The Suggi Khoh, The Gupta Khoh, The Khadar Khoh, The Tankari Khoh, The Katari Khoh, The Dharu Khoh etc. are the significant deep glens into which underground drainage can be seen in action even during summer days. These Khohs are the sources of drinking water for the wild animals in summer season when there is complete scarcity of water on the plateau surface.

Other Water Bodies :

There are no natural lakes in this district. As the terrain

has a well defined slope there is no question of water logging on the surface for a long duration.

The deep ditches, which are carved out by the down cutting of water action are found on the source of river valleys, are known as 'KUND'. These are the Dhuan Kund on the Kao River, the Sita Kund on the Durgawati river.

Physical Regions :

Rohtas district shows great diversity of physical land forms. These land form have widely influenced economic & cultural variables such as the land use pattern, means of transportation, irrigation and population distribution. Features of landscapes exhibit regional diversity due to which it has been divided into 5 physical regions. The demarcation of these regions has been done on the basis of various physical parameters like relief, slope, soil, vegetation, drainage pattern, etc. These physical regions are the following :-

(1) The Northern Low Plain :

This region covers 27.36% area of Rohtas district which is very fertile. This area comprises the blocks of Dinara, Dawath, etc. Its relief is less than 83.33 m. and show great population density due to various favourable conditions like-fertile plain, developed irrigational system high underground water table means of transportation, etc. per hectare production is high due to developed canal irrigation system. Prominent cereals grown here are rice, wheat, pulses, etc. The slope of this region is from south to north which is followed by two rivers 'Kao and Dharamu'. Loamy soil is mostly found in this region which is well known for its fertility. It has high water holding capacity and long cracks are usually which in dry state. Mango, Neem, Shisham, Jack-fruit, etc. are chief vegetation. This region has lack of dense forest because most of the areas have been under cultivation (fig. 2.7).

(2) The Central High Plain :

This region spread over an extensive part of Rohtas

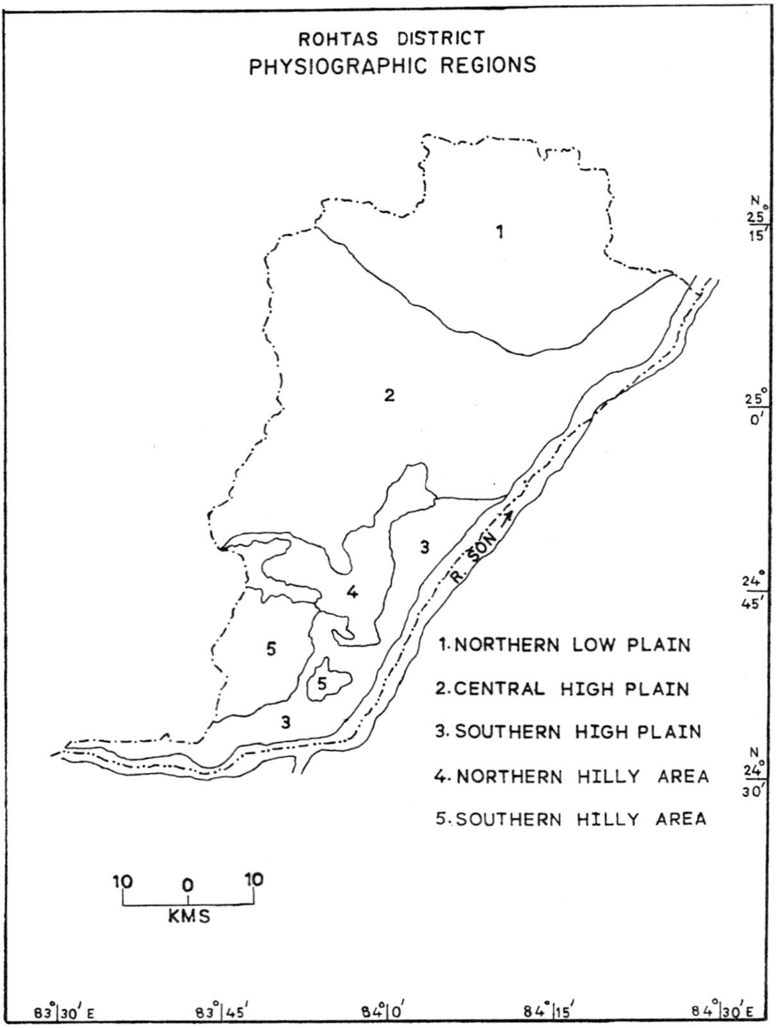
ROHTAS DISTRICT
PHYSIOGRAPHIC REGIONS
1
2
3
4
5
5
3
R. SON
1. NORTHERN LOW PLAIN
2. CENTRAL HIGH PLAIN
3. SOUTHERN HIGH PLAIN
4. NORTHERN HILLY AREA
5. SOUTHERN HILLY AREA
10 0 10
KMS
N 25° 15'
25° 0'
24° 45'
N 24° 30'
83°30' E
83°45'
84°0'
84°15'
84°30' E

Fig. 2.7

district, which is about 46.33% of the total area. It is a fertile plain having hilly structure on its southern part. Its slope is from north-south to east-west. Prominent rivers of this region are Son, Kao, Kudra and Durgawati. All these rivers represent Trellis pattern. Karail, Loamy Sigta soils are mostly found in this region. There is a network of canals in this region due to which crop production is very high. Prominent crops are rice, wheat, sugarcane, pulses, etc. In the Central High Plain population density is higher in its eastern part and it decreases westerward. In the eastern part population density is 800-1000 person per sq. km. which is the highest in Dehri (1442 persons per sq. km.). Sasaram contributes maximum of population i.e. 12.08%. Sasaram, Sheosagar and Chenari blocks comprise dense forest which is economically very useful in the region. In these forests Sal, Salai, Tendu, Gamhar, Mahua, Acacia and Bamboo are important plants which provide Honey, Mahua, Tendu Leaf, Gum, Catechu, etc. These products are widely used by local people as their main source of economy. These forests also facilitate the natural homes of wild animals like Tiger, Leapord, Fox, Bear, Dear, Hyena, Python etc. Some animals are going to be extinct in near future if process of exploitation persists in the region concerned.

(3) The Southern High Plain :

This region extents over the central and southern parts of Rohtas district along river Son. In some lower river valley regions of central west mountain small plains are found. This region is drained by Son river in the east and south while in the western and northern part of it is demarked by Kaimur hill. Its average elevation is 166m and its slope is towards east and south from west. Prominent rivers of this region are Son, Amlo and Ausana. Besides there are also some small seasonal rivers which meet to river Son in the rainy season by their small courses. Soil of this region is mainly of loamy type. Red soil is also found in the foot hills of Kaimur hills. In the eastern part of this region mainly rice, wheat are grown while in the western part pulses and millets are prominent.

Means of irrigation found in this region are monsoon rain, tubewell and wells. Canals have not been developed in this region. Average population density in this region is 400 persons per sq. km. which is maximum in the northern part (600 persons per sq. km.) and minimum in southern part (200 persons per sq. km.). Natural vegetation are found in western parts of Tilouthu and Rohtas blocks. Underground water table is moderate in this plain area.

(4) The Northern Hilly Area :

It covers 5.64% of total area of Rohtas district which is the northern most extension of plateau of Kaimur. Its average elevation is 166 m. and its slope towards north and east-west from south. River Amlo emerges from the northern part of this region and meets with river Kao. In the outer part of this region loamy soil is found while in the inner part red soil is found. Population density is about 200-400 persons per sq. km. In the eastern part of this hilly region dense natural vegetation is found. Which is very important for the economic activities of people in this region. Prominent crops are mountain rice, pulses, millets etc.

(5) The Southern Hilly Area :

Its covers 5.85% of total area of Rohtas district and is the highest region (more than 166.66 m.) of the district. Its slope is towards north-west from south-east and towards south-east from north-west. Many small rivers emerge as a small streams during the rainy season and meets with Son in the south and Durgawati in the west. It has mainly Red Soil. Due to uneven land forms population density is very low which is less than 200 persons per sq. km. Prominent crops are mountain rice, jowar, maize, pulses, etc. Products gathered from trees are also included in the livelihood of the people. Dense forests are found in the northern part. The average depth of level water table is extremely deep.

Climate :

As such this district lies far off the Himalayan region and

is in extreme western part of the south Ganga plain, the climate of this district is generally dry for the greater part of the year. The cold season starts early in November and extends to late March. The hot season is from April to about the middle of June. The monsoon season commences during late days of hot season. The monsoon contains till the end of September. October is a transition month of the monsoon season.

Climate is the indicator of average conditions of the different meteorological elements such as, precipitation, temperature, wind, relative humidity, etc. So in any region, climate is the most prominent constituent of physical environment. Human activities in any region are related to climate. Agricultural activities are exclusively influenced by climatic conditions.

Rohtas district is characterised by the Caw or Humid subtropical climate with dry winter according to Triwartha's classification of climate. Normally the district enjoys the monsoon type of climate which is characterised by a seasonal rhythm of water. The monsoon rains, at a place is either earlier or delay than the normal. The variability of rainfall has adverse impact on agricultural activities including the production of crops.

Seasons :

The seasonal characteristics of the monsoon climate are direct result of seasonal alternation between the two prevailing winds known as south-west monsoon and north-east monsoon. Traditionally Indian year on the basis of climatic characteristics has been divided in to (i) Summer season (ii) Rainy season and (iii) Cold season.

Indian meteorological department has divided a year in to two parts. Viz. (i) Summer season (from March to 15th October) and (ii) Cold season (from 15th October to February). Further sub-division of the summer season (a) dry summer (from March to mid June) and (b) wet simmer (from mid June to mid October).

Summer Season :

(a) Dry Summer :

Temperature rises gradually from last February up to mid June; being May the hottest month. The mean maximum temperature in °c recoded is 26.40, 31.40, 34.65 and 33.40 in March, April, May and June respectively. The season is characterised by hot scorching and stormy wind know as 'Loo'. Loo is common in May and June.

(b) Wet Summer :

It starts with the advent of the monsoon, usually by the 10th June. The temperature decreases and the whole environment is drenched in wet and earthen fragrance. The mean daily maximum temperature is 38.6°c and 32.7°c in June and July the mean daily minimum temperature is 28.2°c and 26.4°c in June and July respectively. The region receives 150.4 mm. rainfall at Rohtas and 133.9 mm. at Sasaram in the month of June and 322.1 mm. at Rohtas and 317.0 mm. at Sasaram in July. August is the month of the heaviest rainfall (fig. 2.8) when Sasaram receives 387.1 mm. of general rainfall.

Cold Season :

In the mid of October winter starts gradually with uncloudy dustless day and cool pleasant night with mean daily range or 9.6°c of temperature. The daily range of temperature is 13.1°c and 13.5°c in November and December respectively. The mean daily maximum temperature is 28.3°c and 25.1°c in November and December. Mean daily minimum temperature is 15.2°c and 11.6°c in the same months. January is the coldest month when mean daily maximum temperature comes below 23.0°c and mean daily minimum 11.0°c late December and early January are almost similar in cold experience. 19.6 mm. to 29.0 mm. rainfall is also recorded in January and February due to the winter depressions. This rain provides a facility for the growth of Rabi crops, especially to wheat in the plain of Rohtas.

Temperature :

Meteorological data are available for Dehri. Dehri is the only one observatory new existing in the district. From the middle of March temperature begins to rise and hot dry westerly winds blow. May is the hottest month. Towards the peek of summer preceding the onset of the monsoon maximum temperatures can reach which values as high as 47°c (117°F) on individual days. With the setting on of the monsoon day temperature drop by about 8° to 9°c without appreciable drop in might temperatures. After the withdrawal of the monsoon by the beginning of October temperatures begin to decrease reaching the lowest value in January which is the coldest month with minimum temperature sometimes going down to 4° or 5°c.

Humidity :

The summer months are very dry and relative humidities can be as low as 20 per cent to 25 per cent in the afternoon. In the monsoon season air is very humid; during the rest of the year humidity averages about 50 per cent in the afternoon.

Cloudiness :

During the winter and summer months skies are generally clear or lightly clouded but towards late summer cloudiness is more in the afternoon. In the monsoon months skies are heavily clouded or over cast.

Winds :

Light south-westerly or westerly winds prevail in the winter and early summer months. Towards the end of summer easterlies set in and continue throughout the monsoon season. During extreme hot months storms are also witnessed in different parts of the study area.

Special Weather Phenomena :

Locally heavy rain and strong winds are experienced in the district in association with some of the storms or

Table - 2.3

Temperature, Relative Humidity and Wind Speed Rohtas

Months	Mean Daily Maximum Temperature in c	Mean Daily Minimum Temperature in c	Relative Humidity (Hours I.S.T.)		Mean Wind Speed (km/hr)
			830 (in %)	1730 (in %)	
January	23.9	11.4	74	50	4.2
February	27.6	14.2	63	39	5.6
March	33.7	19.1	45	26	6.9
April	38.9	23.9	38	23	7.4
May	41.6	27.7	47	26	7.4
June	38.6	28.2	64	50	7.6
July	32.7	26.4	84	77	6.4
August	32.1	26.2	85	80	5.3
September	32	25.5	84	80	5.0
October	31.5	21.9	74	66	3.5
November	28.3	15.2	68	52	3.2
December	25.1	11.6	72	49	3.4
Annual	32.2	21.23	67	51	5.5

Source : Bihar District Gazetteers, Shahabad, 1966, pp. 42-43.

depressions which move inland from the Bay of Bengal during the monsoon and post monsoon months. Thunder storms and occasional dust storms accompanied with squalls occur in the summer months. Even during the monsoon months rain is sometimes associated with thunder. Morning fogs are possible during the winter months.

Table - 2.4

Special Weather Phenomena of Rohtas District : Mean Number of Days with

Months	Thunder	Dust storm	Squall	Fog
January	0.4	-	-	1.6
February	0.3	-	-	-
March	0.8	-	-	-
April	0.4		-	-
May	0.5	0.3	0.1	-
June	0.4	0.3	-	-
July	0.4	1.3	-	-
August	-	-	-	-
September	0.3	-	-	-
October	-	-	-	0.6
November	-	-	-	0.5
December	-	-	-	2.1
Annual	3.5	1.9	0.1	4.8

Source : Bihar District Gazetteers, Shahabad-1966, p. 43.

Table - 2.5

Meteorological Station	Annual Rainfall in mm.
Dehri	1122.6
Sasaram	1226.6
Koath	1079.8
Akbarpur	1169
Chenari	1337.8
Kochas	1110.3
Kargahar	1280.4

Source : Bihar District Gazetteers, Shahabad -1966, pp. 40-41.

Table no. 2.3 give the temperature, relative humidity and mean wind speed and table no. 2.4 give the frequency of special weather phenomena respectively for Dehri meteorological station and table no. 2.5 give the details of the rainfall at the 7 rain-gauge stations with records extending in most cases to 70 or 80 years.

Rainfall :

Rohtas district has a network of 7 rain gauge stations with records extending in most cases to 70 or 80 years. Table no. 2.5 provides the details of the rainfall at 7 stations and for the district as a whole. The average annual rainfall recorded in the district is 1189.5 mm Western and Central parts of the district around Chenari, Sasaram and Kargahar receive a little more rainfall than the rest parts of the district. The district gets 88 per cent of the annual Rainfall during the monsoon months. The maximum rainfall occurs in August. The variation in the annual rainfall from year to year is not large. In the fifty years, i.e., 1901 to 1950, the highest rainfall amounting to 143 per cent of the normal fell in 1936; the year 1908 had the lowest annual rainfall amounting to 61 per cent of the normal. During these fifty years there were only 6 years when the district rainfall was less than 80 per cent of the normal. None of these were consecutive years. At individual stations two or three consecutive years of low rainfall have occurred once or twice. The average number of rainy days per year for the district in 52.

The highest rainfall in 24 hours recorded at any station in the district was 389.4 mm. (15.33") at Chenari on 11th September, 1936.

Rohtas district represents three periods of rainfall as detailed below :

(a) Monsoon rainfall (June to October)

(b) Winter rainfall (November to February)

(c) Summer rainfall (March to May)

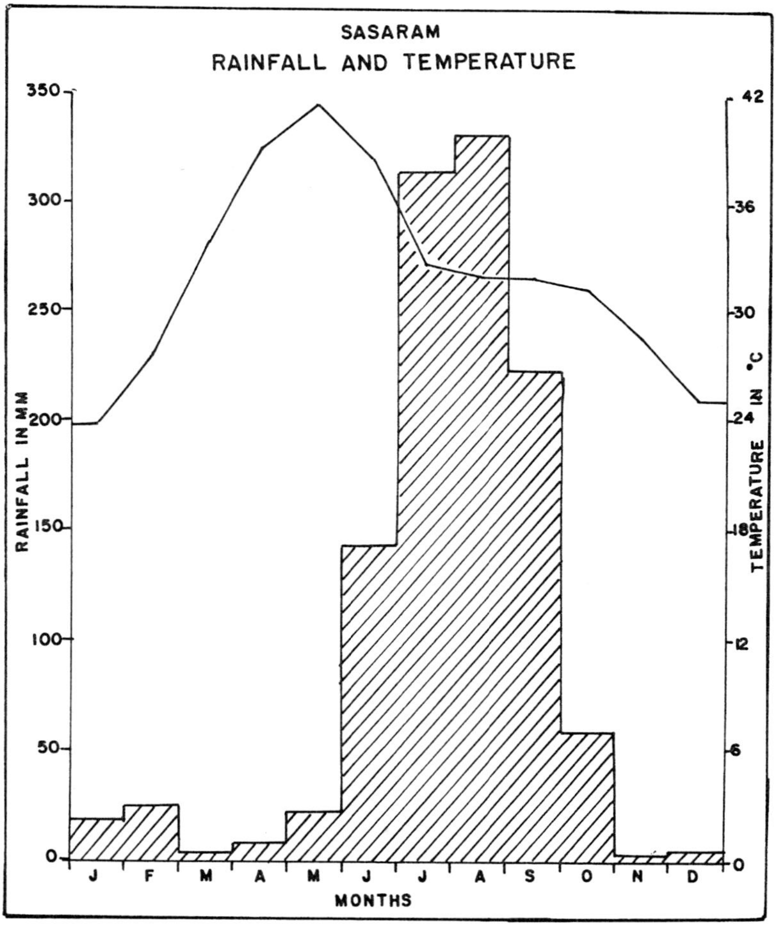
SASARAM
RAINFALL AND TEMPERATURE
RAINFALL IN MM
TEMPERATURE IN °C
350
300
250
200
150
100
50
0
42
36
30
24
18
12
6
0
J
F
M
A
M
J
J
A
S
O
N
D
MONTHS

Fig. 2.8

Monsoon Rainfall :

The hot and dry weather season from March to May paves the path for the advent of S.W. monsoon which starts from the Bay of Bengal and enters into the region in mid of June and remains up to mid September, the period of high percentage of total rainfall. In this period "The monsoon bursts, storms, flows clouds March from east to west and rains fall." July and August are the months of heaviest rain. Sasaram receives 317 mm. in July and 387.1 mm. in August.

Winter Rainfall :

The winter rain is associated with western cyclonic depressions. It brings much clouds and light rain. It is beneficial for the Rabi crops. January and February are the months of winter rainfall. Akabarpur gets 21.3 mm. and 29.0 mm. in January and February respectively while Sasaram receives 21.3 mm., 25.4 mm. in the same month.

Summer Rainfall :

From March to May is the most hot and dry period of region. Rainfall in April is meagre. The variation of rainfall is 1 to 5 mm. from March to May. Sasaram receives 12.2 mm. in March 6.6 mm. in April and 14.7 mm. in May.

Soils :

The weathering process disintegrates rocks into pieces that form a thin surface layer of fragmented material. In the beginning the fragmented mass of this layer has the characteristics of parent rocks. With the passage of time, this mass becomes finer and supports plant life if temperature and rainfall conditions permit. This thin surface layer of broken rocks which can support plant life is known as soil. Under the soil layer are gravels of parent rock and concretion formed by the accumulation of leached materials collectively known as sub-soil.

Soil is the main stay of agriculture and forestry and the detailed soil map is the base of land use planning. The soil map of Rohtas district is based on intensive field study. Hence the alluvial soil is dominant no doubt, but soil in situ, residual type covers a vast tract of the plateau and foot hill regions contributing a lot in alluvial deposition. The soils of the plain are sandy, sand clay mixed and heavy clay in nature.

The variety of soils has been distinguished on the constituent materials and their physical, chemical and morphological characteristics. The spatial distribution of soil depicted in fig. 2.9 is classified on their native nomenclature and further grouped on the basis of geographical location and merit of landforms. The following are the types of soils based on constituent materials and native nomenclature :

(i) Sigata Mati (Sandy loam)

(ii) Doras Mati (Loamy clay)

(iii) Karail Mati (Clay)

(iv) Lal Mati (Red soil)

Sigata Mati (Sandy Loam) :

It is a light coloured sandy soil with mixture of clay. Its nomenclature has been based on the Sanskrit word 'Sikata' which indicates high proportion (75%) of sand contents. It is well aerated, friable and inceptive of irrigation. It is spread in the vicinity of lower reaches of rivers. Its constituents are iron, phosphate, lime and nitrogen in small chemical quantity. Being more sandy it is highly triable and suitable for Bhadai and Rabi crops. Where it has been underlained by hard pan contains more silt than sand. It is also suitable for rice cultivation. This soil is largely used in pot, tile and brick manufacturing. The district contains less than 4% of the total area of sandy soil in Rohtas district.

Doras Mati (Loamy Clay) :

It covers 36.65% of the total area of the region. This soil is also called as 'Bhat Mati' by local people. It is fairly fertile and contents 25% to 30% of lime. Hence it is suitable for

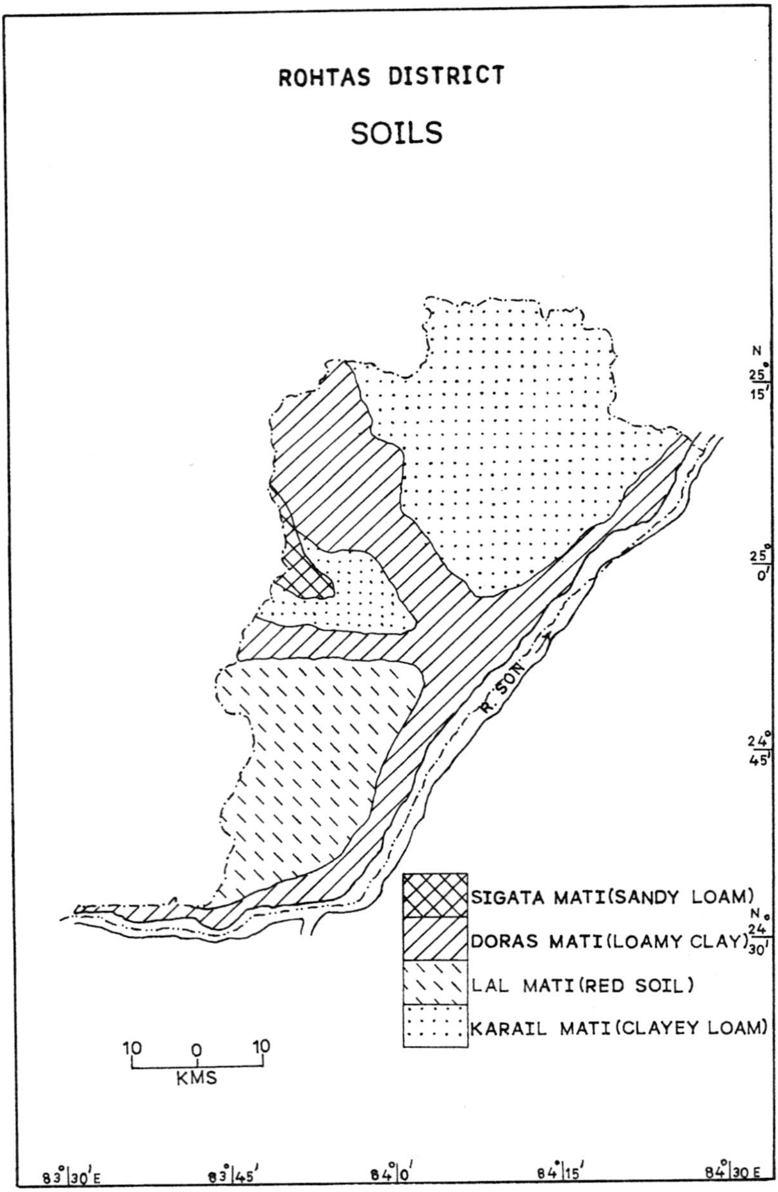
ROHTAS DISTRICT
SOILS
N
25°
15'
25°
0'
24°
45'
R. SON
SIGATA MATI(SANDY LOAM)
DORAS MATI(LOAMY CLAY)
N
24°
30'
LAL MATI(RED SOIL)
KARAIL MATI(CLAYEY LOAM)
10 0 10
KMS
83°30'E
83°45'
84°0'
84°15'
84°30 E

Fig. 2.9

raising sugarcane. Cultivation of rice, gram, pea is also common in the tract of this soil. Agronomical evidences show that the organic matter, the nitrogenous contents of these soils decrease rapidly with depth. It is a soil being favourable for two crops in a year.

Karail Mati (Clay Loam) :

It contains higher clay percentage. It swells up after containing large quantity of water in the rainy season. In dry season intricate pattern of deep cracks are formed. This soil is highly productive under careful management. But even a slight diversion from the agricultural time schedule renders them almost inploughable, because soils get either too dry or too wet for tillage. Rice, wheat, gram and linseed crops are raised in this soil. Thus, is a multi-cropped soil. It is spread over 28.85% area of the district. This soil is found mainly Dinara, Dawath, Kochas, Suryapura, Nokha, Bikramgamj and Sanjhauli blocks.

Lal Mati (Red Soil) :

This type of soil is found over the plateau surface. Its texture, colour and fertility vary from north to south. There is a symmetrical distribution of this soil from the uplands (Tanrs) to the valley troughs (Dons). The low valley tracts contain black soils and the gently rising slopes change the colour of the soils from grey to red on the crest of the upland.12 It is a poor soil for agricultural purposes. Only coarse grains are grown in areas of such soils Nauhatta, Rohtas, Chenari, Sasaram blocks are contain this soil.

The following groups of soils are based on geographical setting in the plain tract of the region :

(i) Khadar (land facing flood effects)

(ii) Bhangar (land beyond flood approach)

Khadar :

The soil of the flood affected parts is called 'Khadar'. The term khaddar denoted 'khal' the low tract where surface cover is washed away every year by flood water. Sometimes this tract is covered by a thin silt deposit as is discernable in the lower riches of Durgawati rivers. A vast area of Sigata soil corresponds with this group of soils.

Bhangar :

As the expansion of floods depends upon quantity of rain, it is difficult to delimit the Bhangar area with a boundry line. But in spite of this fluctuating tendency of river flood 62.32% of total land of plain tract has never gone under flood. The non-flood affected area is designated as Bhangar land. The soil is usually heavy clay and loam.

Based an terrestrial features the following types of soils are quite apparent :

(1) Pather (Plateau soil over hills)

(2) Uthar (Upland soil over pediplane)

(3) Hethar (Low lands)

Pather :

Pather is the plateau part of the region. It is the eastern most part of the great vindhyan range. Its 5.44 per cent area is under Rohtas district.

Uthar :

Uthar means comparatively high portion of land. Therefore, this type of feature has been keenly observed in plain part of the region. Uthar or Uchas is a local term for the upland in Bhojpuri language.

Hethar :

Though a particular part of the middle Ganga plain under Bhojpur district is called hethar, yet the teem is used for comparatively low land by the river side. 32.28 per cent land of the total Rohtas district comes under this land. This terrestrial feature is a blessing for Rohtas plain for paddy cultivation production.

Vegetation :

The plateau Rohtas is covered with forest reserves of dry deciduous type. The largest compact forest area occurs towards the south and south-west bordered by the river Son. Rohtas block records maximum area under forest (60.91%) followed by Nawhatta (51.77%).

Formerly forest were owned by Zamindars. In 1952 all privately owned estates were declared as protected forest. A forest division was created in 1954 with headquarters at Sasaram. Prior to it unsystematic and indiscriminate felling of trees were the order of the day. The forest are completely ruined and Sal is confined to Rehal plateau and in patches at other places. Salai, Kendu, Siddha, etc. are seen scattered about. Bamboos are spread over an area of 82 km2 but the clumps had been pitiably damaged by the graziers who lop the tops of the clumps to feed their cattle.

Importance of Forest in the Economy of Region :

The forest of Rohtas region are meeting raw material requirements of many large and small scale industries besides meeting the requirements of the local people. It provides many of them their livelihood. Bamboo shrubs of the area are thick and are previously supplied to M/S Rohtas industries at Dalmianagar (now it is closed) for the manufacture of paper pulp. Local people also use bamboo for construction of house roofs. A good quantity of bamboo and palas leaves are used as raw materials for small scale industries of basket and leaf plate (Pattal) making, carried on by scheduled castes of this locality. Timber of Gamhar, Mahua, Kendu, Babool are profusely used for agricultural implements like 'Hal', 'Juath', 'Parihath', 'Henga' and 'Harish'. Toy making woods are supplied to Varanasi and Gaya.

The bulk supply of wood for aforesaid purposes gives a good return to forest department. The area of forest is situated over Rohtas plateau and wants of plateau people are few and simple. Their main requirements are grasses and leafs for cattle, fodder, fuel, small timber, bamboo and thatch for house construction and some small timber for agricultural implements. The demand by big size timber is gradually increasing in the vicinity of the plateau for the construction of pucca building and this has become a thickly populated plain of north and west. Apart from meeting the need of local market a large quantity of timber moves to Varanasi market of Uttar Pradesh.

Collection of Kendu leafs for preparation of bid is an important source of livelihood of plateau people. The collection of Honey, Mahua, Chiraunjee and Katha also play valuable role in the economy of plateau Rohtas. Poor people have privileges of collecting and selling dry fire-wood and pattal (leaf plate) free of cost. Charcoal is also prepared in sufficient quantity and is sold in Varanasi market after meeting local requirements. Sabai grass is widely used for making ropes and strings. Salai wood is used in manufacturing of wooden utensils.

Over the plateau fruits of Mahua, Kendu and Piar, constitute a considerable proportion for food especially for the poor people. The forest area affords grazing of thousand of cattle of the plain in addition to the cattle belonging to the inhabitants of the Rohtas plateau. When all the fields of the plains are cultivated and there is no grazing ground left, herds of cattle are driven to the plateau every year and are allowed grazing in the forest area on the normal charge.

The production of these forests is gradually increasing year after year. Bamboo, Kendu leafs, Fodder grass, Sabai grass, Bharuhi grass, Hides and Skins. Myrabolalnce, Koryadana, Gum, Thatch grass, Kattha are important forest produce of Rohtas district.

Fauna :

Rohtas forest is noted for Royal Bengal Tigers. Royal Bengal Tigers, Leopards, Hyena, Wolf and Bears are also found in large number. Deers and Nilgai sometimes move on the bank of Son and in south-east of the plateau. After the extension of irrigation system and advancement of cultivators the existence of forest, the wild animals are restricted only in the move remote parts. Their number is dwindling. The unrestricted shooting before the creation of forest divisions has heavily declined the population of wild life. But out of recent post decades rising prices of weapons and bullets and the policy of preservation and protection of forest and wild animals have affected the organised hunting and owing to this wild life is again prospering. The entire plateau has been notified as a game sanctuary from 1960 where all shootings are strictly prohibited for preservation of wild life.

Resource Base :

Resource is the manifestation of man and environment relationship. According to Prof. Zimmerman, "resource do not refer to a thing or a substance but to a function which is performed by the thing or substance. Each and every thing becomes a resource if it is operated by a skilled and literate person and vice-versa."

Zimmerman has classified resources into following types:-

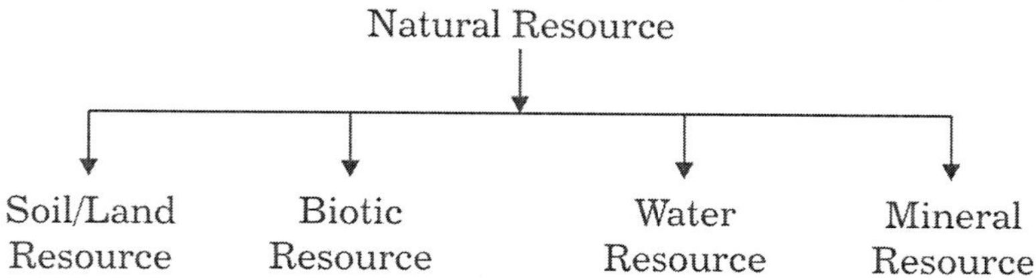

Soil resource and Biotic resource are described in previous pages.

Water Resources :

Water is an important as well as an essential resource. Existence of life depends upon it. Being a limited resource, water assumes critical importance for those areas where economy is primarily based on agriculture. Cultivation is the main occupation of Rohtas district. 66.15% of the total geographical area and 80.11% of main workers are engaged in agricultural activities. So, it is obvious that water it huge quantity is required in the district for agricultural and domestic purposes.

The main source of water, both surface and ground water, is precipitation in the form of rainfall available mostly during S.W. monsoon period. The run off from precipitation drains through streams and rivers or collected in surface depressions in form of tank. Apart from this, rainfall is stored as ground water through percolation and infiltration.

Thus the district has both the sources of water i.e.

(i) Surface water and

(ii) Underground water

(i) Surface Water :

When the rainfall that has not been intercepted by vegetation reaches the ground surface, part of it fills small surface depressions, partly percolates into the soil and remainder if any, flows over the surface as overland flow and it is the surface water. The surface water is seen in the form of rivers, tanks, etc.

(a) Rivers :

River Son along with its tributaries is the main source of surface water in the district. It drains an area of 5 lakh hectares. The catchments area of Son in the district is 2513 km^2. The river Kao has 602 km^2 catchments area in the district.

(b) Tank Water :

In Rohtas district tanks are found in almost every village, irrespective of their size. Here tank water is used for domestic, fishing and agricultural purposes. In revenue records of Rohtas district there were 3221, 2995, 2821 tanks in 1971, 1981 and 1991 respectively.

Highest number of tanks is observed in Sasaram (345) and lowest in Nauhatta development block (126).

(ii) Underground Water :

Underground water is the water which occurs beneath the surface of the earth within saturated zone. The largest source of fresh water is the ground water. Agricultural economy is largely dependent on assured water i.e. ground water.

Rainfall is the major source of underground water recharge. Infiltration and storage of underground water are governed by the geological formation. So the occurrence of underground water varies from area to area.

In Rohtas district rainfall varies from south to north. As regards geological formation Archaean's granite and Gneiss occur in the most of the area of plateau Rohtas. Sandstone, limestone, shale and conglomerate of Vindhyan system mostly occur in south-western parts of the district. Below the foot of the plateau in the north, the whole region is covered with alluvial deposits of the Ganga. The water holding capacity of these structure are affected by rift, joints and porousness of the rocks. Normally Rohtas district holds a good amount of underground water.

Mineral Resources :

Though a detailed geological survey of the district is awaited, considerable mineral resources occur in the district. The western fringe of the Son valley of Rohtas has some important mineral deposits such as limestone, sandstone, pyrite and glass sand.

(i) Limestone :

The quarrying of limestone is being carried on since the early 19th century or even earlier. This contains both ordinary quality and good quality of limestone. The composition of the limestone is as follow:

$CaCO_3$ - 25.0 percent

$MgCO_3$ - 2.0 to 3.5 percent

SiO_2 - 3.0 to 12.0 percent

Limestone of the area is used by the cement factories at Dalmianagar and at Banjari. The limestone quarries of Banjari are operated by three concerns viz. M/S Kalyakpur lime and cement works Ltd., Dehri lime company and Kuchhuer lime and stone company. These quarries high grade limestone with about 78 to 86 per cent $CaCO_3$. The limestone is well developed in this part and some of the bands cover a thickness of ten metres. Another important areas of limestone are (i) The Murli Hill, about one kilometre south of old Banjari railway station and (ii) Baulia, south - west of Murli Hill. The latter is worked by the Son valley Portland cement Co. Ltd. Japla.

The region has the distinction of being the largest limestone producing area in Bihar and it ranks second in India after Sandargarh district of Orissa.

(ii) Pyrite :

A large quantity of pyrite deposits was discovered in 1960. These deposits are two in number viz. Amjhor deposits and Ghogha deposits. These deposits have created a good hope of mineral (pyrite) based industrial development in Rohtas. Amjhor deposits are situated nearby 2 kms west of old Tumba railway station at the fact of the upper Kaimur Sandstone. The Sulphar content in the pyrite of Rohtas (Amjhor) varies between 40 to 46 per cent. Ghogha deposit occurs at the base of the upper Kaimur scarp about two kilometres north-west of the former. It contains 39 per cent Sulphar of the pyrite deposit so far known in India, Amjhor is by far the best quality and have the largest known reserves.

(iii)Sandstone :

Several exposures of fine grained sand stone are visible which are extensively utilized for civil engineering purposes.

Quarries are scattered in Karwandia -Trachandi -Sasaram area.

(iv) Glass-sand :

The lower Kaimur sandstone is considered a potential glass-sand rock. It is white in colour and friable, so that it can be easily crushed as powder. The rock is fine grained and occurs just below the Rohtas limestone.

(v) Bauxite :

Bauxite deposits also occur near some of the foot hills. A prospecting pit was put down to a depth of 2.35 metres without reaching the bottom of the deposit. The Bauxite is mostly red or reddish in colour and apparently contains a fairly high percentage of iron. This deposit requires detailed investigation for its economic exploitation.

References :

1. Singh, R.P. & Kumar, A. (1970) : Unrolling the Map of Bihar, Monograph of Bihar, Bharati Bhawan, Patna, p. 1.
2. Singh, R.P. : Op. Cit., p.1.
3. Cunningham, (1929) : Ancient Geography of India, edited by S.N. Mazumdar, London, p. 281.
4. Law, B.C. (1954) : Historical Geography of Ancient India, Paris, p.44.
5. Chaudhary, P.C. (1953) : Political History of Ancient India, Calcutta, p. 110.
6. Singh, R.P. and Kumar, A. : Op. Cit, pp. 1-2.
7. Chaudhary, H.C. : Op. Cit., p. 2.
8. Shastri, H.P. (1928) : Journal of the Bihar and Orissa Research Society, p. 330.
9. Singh, H.P. (1979) : Resource Appraisal and Planning in India, Rajesh Publications, New Delhi, p. 31.
10. Roy Chaudhary, S.P. (1966) : Land & Soil, National Book Trust, New Delhi, p. 5.

11. Singh, R.L., India : A Regional Geography, N.G.S.I., Varanasi, p. 192.
12. Singh, R.P. & Kumar, A. (1970) : Monograph of Bihar, Bharti Bhawan, Patna, p. 28.
13. District Gazetteer of Shahabad (1966), p. 14.

3

Chapter

Land Use

The utilization of land to meet various needs of man is known as land use. Land being the fundamental asset of mankind is one of the greatest resources.[1] Land is the most important means of agricultural production and at the same time the field of activity of Production.[2] The need for an appraisal of land resource is thus imperative. Of all human wants food has been of prime importance and making it available particularly in the developing world has engaged huge population and covered large land surface.[3] Consequently its proper use brings prosperity and misuse untold misery to the people.[4] The concept of land use is after considered a relatively stable subject of study. But its effect is the result of continuous field of tension created between available resources and human needs and acted upon by human efforts.[5]

A large part of Rohtas district exhibits undulating topography. There is a general lack of rainfall even during the monsoon days. Forests and hills occupy a vast territory. The soil is generally of poor quality. Even the cultivable land has to be left fallow to region fertility. It is, therefore, an area of food scarcity and low standard of living for the ever increasing population. In view of the above facts, a proper utilization of land with the application of advanced techniques and better field management becomes necessary.[6]

Land Use Categories :

The main source of information on land use in the region is provided by the Directorate of Statistics and Evaluation,

Government of Bihar. Every year land use statistics (Bhumi Udyog Vivarni) for each block of Bihar are compiled. These are the aggregates of village figures collected through field to filed survey by the Karmacharis under the direction of revenue officers. Land is classified into nine major categories, viz, (1) Forest land, (2) Barren and unculturable land, (3) Land put to non- agricultural uses, (4) Permanent pasture and other grazing land, (5) Miscellaneous trees, crops and groves, (6) Culturable waste land, (7) Other fallow land, (8) Current fallow land and (9) Net sown area.

In comparison, the British land use classification groups land under : (1) Forest and woodland, (2) Meadow land and permanent grasses, (3) Arable and tilled land, (4) Health land, more land, commons and rough hill pastures etc., (5) Garden, orchards, nurseries, etc. and (6) Unproductive land e.g. buildings, yards, mines, wasteland etc. But in the international land use classification nine major land use classes are recognised : (1) settlement, (2) Horticulture, (3) Trees and permanent crops, (4) Crop land, (5) Improved permanent pasture, (6) Unimproved grazing land, (7) Woodland, (8) Swamps and marsh and (9) Unproductive lands. These two schemes are on the whole comparable to the Indian Scheme of land use given above but are less suited to Indian conditions.

Table no. 3.1 gives the acreage under various land use categories in Rohtas district during 2004-2005. Here only six significant land use classes have been determined out of the nine reported categories.

It is clear from the above table no. 3.1 that the net area sown exceeds all other land use categories. It accounts for 63.94 per cent of the total area of the region and occupies mainly the plain pockets. The highlands have very little sown area, but where plains appear, they permit this category to exist. The net area sown denotes the actual land sown with crops during a particular year.

The net sown area is followed by forest and barren lands

which account for 20.60 per cent of the total area of the district and extend over the southern and western parts of the district. Forests in different parts of Bihar are mere relics of their vast extent in either lowland or highland Bhiar.[7] These forest are paradise for hunters, gatherers and lumberers.[8] Forest includes all forest land or administered as forest under any legal enactment dealing with forests whether state-owned or private.[9] Barren lands represent bare rocks, usar lands, etc.

Table - 3.1
Land Use (2004-05)

Sl. No.	Land use categories	Area in acres	Rohtas district area in per cent
1.	Net Sown Area	616445.31	63.94
2.	Fallow Land	31221.29	3.23
3.	Cultivable Waste	4675.95	0.48
4.	Land Put to Non-agricultural Uses	115365.99	11.96
5.	Forest and Barren Land	192777.95	20.00
6.	Land Under Pasture and Plantation	3780.58	0.39
	Total	964267.07	100.00

Source : Department of Statistics, Rohtas District & Self Computation.

The thirds important category is land put to non-agricultural uses which accounts for 11.96 per cent of the total area of the region. The lands used for settlement, communication, water bodies and pasture coupled with other lands given to use other than farming are grouped under this head.

The fourth category is fallow land which shares 3.23 per cent of the total area of the region. It describes these lands which are generally cultivated but remain uncultivated during the year under review.[10] The proportion of fallow land is usually higher over infertile soil which can not bear the

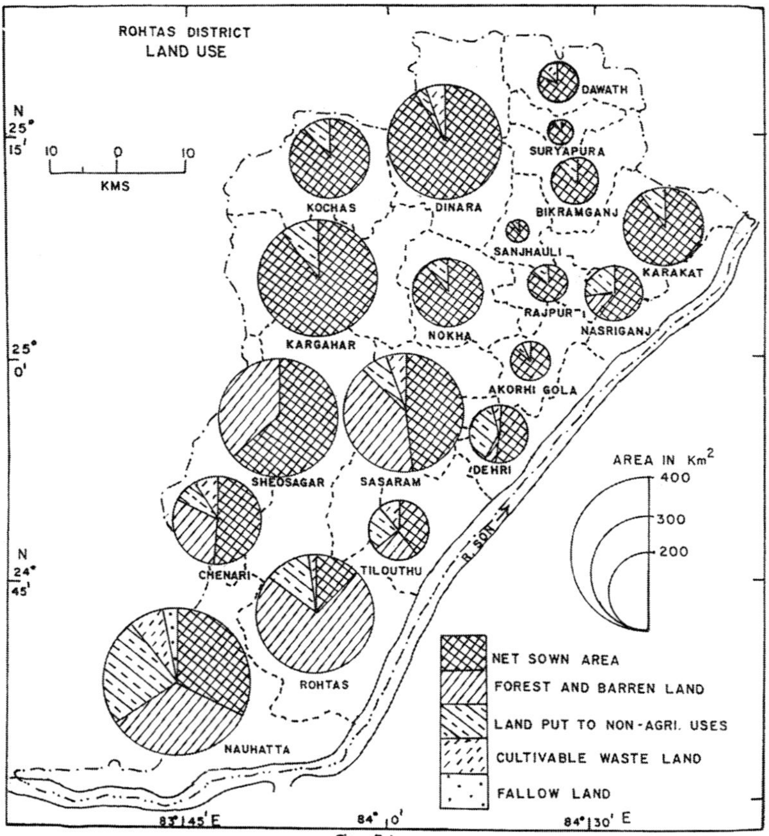
ROHTAS DISTRICT
LAND USE
N
25°
15'
10
0
10
KMS
25°
0'
N
24°
45'
DAWATH
SURYAPURA
BIKRAMGANJ
KARAKAT
KOCHAS
DINARA
SANJHAULI
KARGAHAR
NOKHA
RAJPUR
NASRIGANJ
AKORHI GOLA
SHEOSAGAR
SASARAM
DEHRI
CHENARI
TILOUTHU
ROHTAS
NAUHATTA
R. SON
AREA IN Km²
400
300
200
NET SOWN AREA
FOREST AND BARREN LAND
LAND PUT TO NON-AGRI. USES
CULTIVABLE WASTE LAND
FALLOW LAND
83°45' E
84° 10'
84° 30' E

Fig. 3.1

strain of annual cropping.[11]

Cultivable waste lands cover 0.48 per cent land of the region. It includes all land available for cultivation, whether not taken up for cultivation or abandoned after a few years for one reason or the other.[12]

The last category is land under pasture and plantation which cover 0.39 per cent of the total area of the region. The land used for grazing for cattle, plantation along banks of rivers and canals by government are put under this class of land use. Some farmers do plantation in his own farms.

DISTRIBUTION PATTERN OF LAND USE :

Like any other region of India the Rohtas district has an established sedentary subsistence agriculture from the very beginning of its occupance and despite some regional variation there is a general emphasis on the utilization of land as crop land.[13] The land use pattern is absolutely different from that of British or American rural landscape. Of course the principles of land use that have evolved from mid-latitude experience can not be applied directly to tropics.[14] Owing to different environmental and socio-economic settings.

Table no. 3.2 and fig.-3.1 provides a detailed account of the geographical distribution pattern of land use classes in Rohtas district.

(A) Net Sown Area :

The percentage of net sown area varies greatly in different parts of the study area. In the highly undulating and forested blocks of Rohtas, Nauhatta, Tilouthu, the percentage is less than 40, rising to between 40 and 65 in Sheosagar, Sasaram, Chenari, Nasriganj and Dehri. These blocks, thus, have less than the district overage of 63.96% land under varied crops. Among these blocks Rohtas, Nauhatta and Tilouthu have exceptionally high percentage of land under forests, hills and exceptionally low percentage of land under crops. Besides

Table - 3.2
Block wise Land Use (in %) Rohtas District (2004-05)

Sl. No.	Name of Blocks	Net sown area	Fallow land	Cultivable waste land	Land Put to non-agricultural uses	Forest and barren lands	Land under pasture and plantation
1	Sheosagar	63.48	0.08	-	0.29	36.15	-
2	Kargahar	90.25	0.32	-	8.1	0.77	0.56
3	Sasaram	48.23	4.26	0.21	6.98	40.32	-
4	Chenari	52.82	9.66	0.22	8.94	28.29	0.07
5	Nokha	89.96	-	-	10.02	0.02	-
6	Kochas	86.83	0.36	0.02	10.93	1.04	0.76
7	Karakat	87.92	0.26	-	11.25	0.06	0.51
8	Bikramganj	86.89	-	0.09	12.89	-	0.13
9	Nasriganj	62.96	-	-	27.8	9.24	-
10	Dinara	92.55	2.32	0.18	3.97	0.66	0.32
11	Dawath	80.98	11.11	0.27	2.19	4.95	0.5

12	Sanjhauli	87.06	-	-	12.94	-	-
13	Suryapura	86.6	2.02	-	0.17	10.86	0.35
14	Rajpur	85.75	0.87	-	0.33	12.96	0.09
15	Rohtas	12.85	2.12	0.06	12.27	72.57	0.13
16	Dehri	52.69	3.02	-	37.21	5.21	1.87
17	Nauhatta	33.89	7.99	3.38	23.25	30.6	0.89
18	Tilouthu	39.16	10.96	0.77	25.19	23.48	0.44
19	Akorhi Gola	87.57	0.56	0.02	6.97	4.58	0.3

Source : Land Use of Rohtas District, 2004-05, Department of Statistics.

being forested and undulating these blocks are inhabited by relatively illiterate people. The soil is rocky and unfertile and the water table is low. In the south, these blocks are spotted with the presence of Son river and outliers of the Chotanagpur plateau.

The blocks of Kargahar, Nokha, Bikramganj, Dinara, Sanjhauli, Suryapura and Akorhi Gola have exceptionally high percentage of land under N.S.A. which exceeds 86%. On the other hand these blocks exhibit a low percentage of land under forests and barren land which is less than 5 per cent of total area. Thus, there is negative relationship between the ratio of cropland and the forest and barren land. The high ratio of land under plough is due to the fertile nature of soil high water table, relatively developed irrigation by canals and heavy pressure of population inevitably requiring more land to grow more food.

The remaining blocks of Dawath and Rajpur also have more than the regional average of land under the plough. In all these blocks except Rajpur the percentage of net area sown is above 85%. Rajpur block is comparatively forested and contain barren land (12.96%), but others enjoy the facilities of fertile soil, canal irrigation and high water- table.

(B) Fallow Land :

Unlike the net sown area, the percentage of land under fallow land is largely uneven in different parts of the study area. The blocks of Dawath and Tilouthu have more than 10 per cent of their land under this category. Among these blocks of the region Dawath has the highest area (11.11%) of land under fallow land. This block has low water-table, poor soil and inadequate means of irrigation. The block of Tilouthu are hilly and have a low water table and poor soil coupled with poor means of irrigation. Other blocks account for less than 10 per cent of land under this category. Most of these blocks are generally fertile and have better means of irrigation. The blocks of Sheosagar, Sasaram, Chenari, Rohtas and Nauhatta are partly infertile and hilly but the plain land where ever is available is fertile and can not be allowed to remain fallow because of the paucity of agricultural land.

(C) Cultivable Waste Land :

The above table indicates that the percentage of waste land is high in the hilly and forested blocks of Sasaram, Chenari, Nauhatta and Tilouthu where it is around 0.20 to 3.4 per cent of total land. The other blocks exhibit below 0.20 per cent of land under this category. The majority of these blocks except Dinara and Dawath are plain and put to crops. This category of land becomes important as one can hope to increase the cultivated area only be utilising this land. Such land is definitely culturable although it is not under the plough at present. Reclamation measures like deep ploughing or levelling and copious use of water and fertilizers may bring such land under cultivation.

(D) Land Put to Non- Agricultural Uses :

The distribution of land under land put to non-agricultural uses of erratic. Dehri lies in the extreme east part of the region and has an exceptionally high percentage (37.21) of its land under this category. The conspicuous reasons are the inclusion of other fallows and pasture lands in this category, whose percentage is higher in Dehri block. Other important blocks in this regard are Kochas, Karakat, Bikramganj, Nasriganj, Sanjhauli, Rohtas, Nauhatta and Tilouthu, which account for 11 to 28 per cent land in this category. These blocks lie far apart from each other in different parts of the district. The remaining blocks except Nokha (10.02%) have below 10 per cent of their land in this class. Most of these blocks are hilly and forested which do not permit the origin and growth of settlements, communication, pasture, water bodies etc. The plain blocks of Kargahar, Nokha, Dinara, Suryapura and Akorhi Gola devote most of their land to crops. This type of land is bound to increase in extent in view of the growth of population in villages and towns and gradual expansion of the cultural landscape. Thus one can see indiscriminate encroachment on cultivated land in sub-urban areas.

(E) Forested and Barren Lands :

Forested and barren lands are also unevenly distributed in the district. Most of the forested and barren lands lie in the blocks of Sheosagar, Sasaram, Chenari, Rohtas, Nauhatta and Tilouthu which occupy the southern parts of the district. The percentages range from 72.59 in Rohtas to 12.96 in Rajpur. The percentage of this class of land is highest in Rohtas, Sasaram and Nauhatta blocks. These blocks are hilly and receive a good amount of rainfall. The rest of the blocks except Chenari (28.29) have below 12 per cent of total land under this category of land use, others blocks are flat and fertile.

MAN-LAND RATIO :

Table no. 3.3 consists of the average per capita cultivated land in 2005 and population pressure per acre on such land in 2005.

Table 3.3 shows that the per capita cultivated area is surprisingly low in all blocks of the Rohtas district. It is more alarming in hilly and infertile blocks of Sasaram, Rohtas and Tilouthu. The hilly and infertile character of these blocks have restricted the expansion of cultivated land. The blocks of Bikranganj and Dehri also show low per capita cultivated land. These blocks are densely populated and large area has been covered by non- agricultural uses.

In other blocks of Rohtas district the per capita cultivated land is higher. It is the highest in Kargaher, Kochas, Dinara and Nauhatta blocks which utilise most of their land under different harvests on account of relatively better means of irrigation. The population size of these blocks is also not large.

Table - 3.3
Block wise Average Per Capita Cultivated Area in Rohtas District (2004-2005)

Sl. No.	Name of Blocks	Per capita cultivated land in acre
1	Sheosagar	0.35
2	Kargahar	0.41
3	Sasaram	0.13
4	Chenari	0.29
5	Nokha	0.25
6	Kochas	0.40
7	Karakat	0.25
8	Bikramganj	0.21
9	Nasriganj	0.17
10	Dinara	0.37
11	Dawath	0.22
12	Sanjhauli	0.28
13	Suryapura	0.25
14	Rajpur	0.24
15	Rohtas	0.13
16	Dehri	0.08
17	Nauhatta	0.49
18	Tilouthu	0.16
19	Akorhi Gola	0.21

Source : Land Use Report of 2004-05, Department of Statistics, Rohtas.

IRRIGATION :

Nearly 89 per cent of land in the study area is cultivated. The average irrigated land to total cultivated land is nearly 83 per cent. Main means of irrigation in the region are canal and tube-wells.

Irrigation plays an important role in uplift of the economic conditions because it increases agricultural production. Development of irrigation is essential in the region due to variability and uncertainly in the amount of rainfall.

Distribution of rainfall (chapter II) varies from south to north in the district. Southern plateau receives higher rainfall where as northern plains receive lesser amount of rainfall.

Table - 3.4
Proposed Irrigation Projects

Sl. No.	River basins	Name of projects	Location	Estimated area of irrigation (in laks hect.)
1.	Durgawati	Durgawati reservoir	Karamchat	0.27
2.	Kao	Kao reservoir	Near Dhualund	0.90
3.	Son	Son reservoir	Near border of Bihar & U.P.	5.00

The Son river project is the first irrigation project in Bihar. It is constructed by British Government in 1874 to feed the eastern and western canals, built up at Dehri-on-Sone. After independence a barrage is completed near Indrapuri in 1968. It is the biggest reservoir of the region. Its irrigation capacity is 4 lakh hectares.

Kao weir in Kao river is another project in the district.

The 93.27% geographical area of the region lies in Son command area. It provides permanent irrigation to 2.02 lakh hectares of agricultural land. The irrigated lands are mainly in 16 development blocks. Canal is the main source of irrigation and it stands for 93.27 per cent of total irrigation (table no. 3.5) in the Rohtas district. The spatial pattern of irrigated land by various mean of irrigation is given in table no. 3.6 and 3.7.

Table - 3.5
Percentage of Average Irrigated Land in 2006 by Different Means of Irrigation in Rohtas District

Sl. No.	Means of irrigation	Percentage of area under irrigation
1	Canal	93.27
2	Government Tubewell	0.13
3	Private Tubewell	6.60
	Total	100.00

Source : Agriculture Department, Rohtas.

The table no. 3.5 further on explains that private tube-well irrigation is another means of irrigation. It, however, does not play important who as means of irrigation in the study area (fig. 3.2).

Table - 3.6
Spatial Pattern of Irrigated Land in Percentage by Different Means of Irrigation (2006)

Sl. No.	Name of Blocks	Canal	Government Tubewell	Private Tubewell
1	Sheosagar	92.59	-	7.41
2	Kargahar	98.14	-	1.86
3	Sasaram	93.16	0.19	6.65
4	Chenari	93.75	-	6.25
5	Nokha	99.00	-	1.00
6	Kochas	97.77	-	2.23
7	Karakat	98.24	-	1.76
8	Bikramganj	97.93	-	2.07
9	Nasriganj	98.50	-	1.50
10	Dinara	99.10	-	0.90
11	Dawath	98.76	-	1.24
12	Sanjhauli	96.59	-	3.41
13	Suryapura	96.91	-	3.09
14	Rajpur	97.59	-	2.44

15	Rohtas	-	-	100.00
16	Dehri	89.68	1.34	8.98
17	Nauhatta	-	-	100.00
18	Tilouthu	-	2.44	97.56
19	Akorhi Gola	89.56	0.49	9.95

Source : Agriculture Department, Rohtas.

The table no. 3.6 describes that canal irrigation exhibits dominating role as means of irrigation in most of the blocks of the district of Rohtas. In majority of blocks canal irrigated land is more than 90%. Other blocks also represent high percentage of canal irrigated land. It has happed because of the presence of Son river in the region across which a big dam has been made at Indrapuri near Dehri. From here many canals has been constructed in different direction for irrigation purposes.

The table no. 3.7 portrays that the irrigated land is highly represented in the northern parts of the study area followed by the central part. The southern part contains small percentage of irrigated land of the district. It has so happed because the southern part is hilly where canal is difficult to construct and secondly low percentage of cultivable available. On the other hand the northern part of the study area comprises fertile soil where construction of canal is easily. Here large area is cultivable.

Table - 3.7

Block wise Percentage of Irrigated Land Out of Total Irrigated Land in Rohtas District (2006)

Sl. No.	Name of Blocks	Irrigated land in percentage
1	Sheosagar	3.81
2	Kargahar	15.17
3	Sasaram	5.3
4	Chenari	3.39
5	Nokha	7.13
6	Kochas	6.35

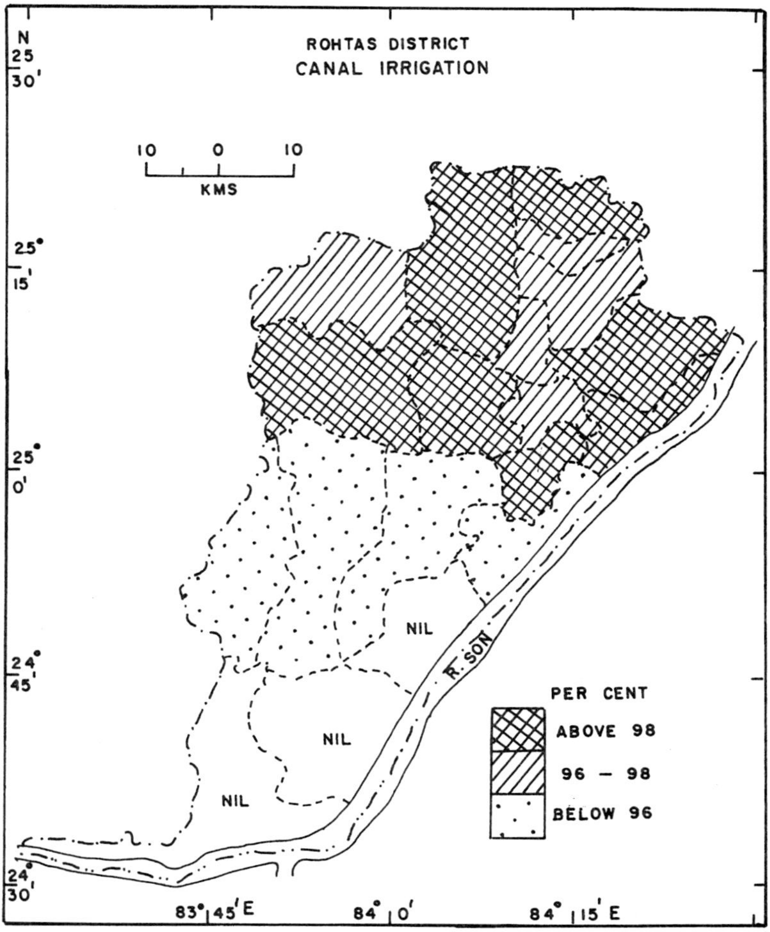
ROHTAS DISTRICT
CANAL IRRIGATION
10 0 10
KMS
NIL
NIL
NIL
R. SON
PER CENT
ABOVE 98
96 – 98
BELOW 96
N 25° 30'
25° 15'
25° 0'
24° 45'
24° 30'
83° 45' E
84° 0'
84° 15' E

Fig. 3.2

7	Karakat	10.1
8	Bikramganj	6.85
9	Nasriganj	4.73
10	Dinara	11.92
11	Dawath	5.72
12	Sanjhauli	3.1
13	Suryapura	2.28
14	Rajpur	2.89
15	Rohtas	1.05
16	Dehri	3.93
17	Nauhatta	0.56
18	Tilouthu	2.17
19	Akorhi Gola	3.55
	Total	100.00

Source : Agriculture Department, Rohtas.

LAND CAPABILITY :

This study is based on the fieldwork in six sample villages conducted during 2008. These villages lie both in the hilly and plain areas of Rohtas district. The categories of the cultivable lands are alike in both type of villages but they exhibit different capabilities in different areas. The capabilities of land classes are basically measured on the basis of fertility of soil, productivity and the resultant market price of a chunk of land. Table 3.8 provides a number of other variable including the above variables for the analysis and classification of land capability. The cultivable lands of the region may be put into the following generalised classes :

(i) Dihland (triple cropped land)

(ii) Intermediate land (paddy land in plain areas and Rabi-Bhadai land in hilly and forested areas)

(iii) Low land (Rabi land in plain and Dhankhet paddy land on hilly areas).

(i) Dihland : It consists of the best quality of agricultural land. The majority of the settlements are located on this type

Table - 3.8
Land Capability Classes

Land classes	Situation	Soil	Drainage	Fertility	Irrigation	Manuring	Chief crops	Maximum intensity of cropping	Yield	Market price	Grade
Dihland	Around village	Loamy	Good	High	Tubewells & wells	By Human & Animal refuses, chemical fertilizer	Maize, Wheat, Potato, Mustard, Oil, Chilli, Onion, Vegetables etc.	Triple cropped	Very high	Very high	I
Inter-mediate	Slightly away from village	Differen-tial	Excellent	Very high	Canal, tubewells, Wells	Compost and Chemical fertilizer	Paddy, Wheat, Masur, Gram, Oilseeds, Maize etc.	Double cropped	High	High to medium	II
Low-land	Away from village	Clayey & Sandy	Medium	Medium	Canal, tubewells, Wells	Chemical fertilizer	Wheat, Gram, Masur, Khesari etc.	Single cropped	Moderate	Medium	III

of land. Such land has a small ratio to total cultivated areas. It is the most potential land for the expansion of the village becomes it in found close to the settlement. It is well drained and remains beyond flood reach throughout the year. It does not however, retain water or obstruct the natural drainage.15 It is well irrigated by surface well and hence it is cropped all the year round. Thus it is a multi cropped area raising a variety of valuable crops such as vegetables, onion, chilli, maize, oilseeds, etc. Texturally the soil is sandy loam and fertile. In addition it gets household refuses. The yield of crops is therefore very high. Because of the above characteristics it fetches the highest price in the market.

(ii) Intermediate Land : These lands occupy an intermediate position between the Dihland and Lowland. These lands share a large proportion of land in the village. it has a medium quality and texturally ranges from loam to sandy loam in hilly areas and loam to clayey loam in plain areas. This land is well irrigated by canal and surface wells in plain areas. Here Aghani and Rabi crops are sown. In hilly areas this land is not provided with irrigation and only Rabi crops are grown. During dry years, a part of this land is left fallow. The yield of the crops is high. In areas of maximum use of manures and application of irrigation there is very high production per unit of land. On the other hand the production is moderate where the facilities of irrigation are not good.

(iii)Lowland : This types of land shares nearly 28 per cent of total land in the study area. It is largely 'Ahar Land' in plain areas and is waterlogged during rainy days. The soil is invariably clayey (kewal). Its fertility is medium and the land has a high moisture retaining capacity. It is single cropped area. The main crops raised are masur, wheat, gram and khesari, etc. The yields are quite variable.

In hilly tracts the soil is also clayey but is wet even during the summer months. Such land is situated near the bed of the streams which are usually fed by perennial springs from which moisture oozes even in the hottest months of the year. The land is double cropped. The main crops harvested are paddy, mustard, wheat and maize etc. The yield is moderate.

LAND USE PATTERN IN PHYSICAL REGIONS :

The physical regions do not conform with the political boundaries of different blocks. However, the land use data of blocks are taken into account for analysis and discussion in different physical regions. Discussion has been made on the basis of keeping the maps of both physical region and blockwise land use.

(i) Northern Low Plain :- This physical region contains higher percentage of net sown area in areas of plain surface conditions. Dinara block which lies in this part has the highest percentage of N.S.A. (92.55%) and is followed by Nokha block (89.96%). Other blocks also contain more than 80 per cent land under this category.

The fallow lands, over the entire northern low plain except Dawath (11.11) and Suryapura (2.02) represent low percentage i.e. below 5 per cent.

The cultivable waste land is below 1 per cent in most parts of this region. Land put to non- agricultural uses is low i.e. between 2 to 13 per cent in majority of the blocks Bikramganj contains larger percentage of such land. The forest and barren land is exceptionally high in northern blocks and exceptionally low in southern blocks. Rajpur and Bikramganj exhibit 12.96 and 0 per cent of land under this category respectively.

(ii) Central High Plain :- It exhibits the dominance of net sown area all over the plain. The most important block is Kargahar which has 90.25 per cent of land under this class. All other blocks falling in this plain also have more than 50 per cent of their land under this class except Sasaram contains only 48.23 per cent. This is because the entire net sown area is evenly plain and has less than 166 metre relief. The plain does not get sufficient rainfall. The irrigational needs of the fields are provided by canals, tube-wells. The soil is usually fertile.

The percentage of fallow land is low except in Chenari (9.66). A large part of this block is infertile. The percentage of cultivable waste land in this plain is exceptionally low. The percentage of forest and barren land categories is high in Sasaram block (40.32) and Chenari (28.29) block. In this area land put to non- agricultural uses are between 1 to 9 per cent. Dehri block has some land under industrial use and has also a good percentage of land under trees and water bodies.

(iii)Southern High Plain : Here net sown area exceeds other land use classes. Even if it is much below the regional average (63.96%). The proportion of fallow land under non-agricultural uses, and forest and barren land is comparatively higher in this region. The proportion of fallow land, however, dominates the forested and barren lands category in Tilouthu block. The percentage of cultivable waste is also high (3.38%) in Nauhatta block and it is low (0.06%) in Rohtas block.

The entire southern high plain undulates frequently and exhibits low water table. These factors have most probably helped in establishing an important share of land under non-agricultural uses. The average relief of the area varies between 83.33-166.66 metres. The region receives low amount of rainfall.

(iv) Northern Hilly Area : It comprises the northern hills of Kaimur plateau which mainly lie in Sasaram and Tilouthu blocks. The relief of the hills is not the same in its entire area. The remaining northern parts of Sasaram and eastern parts of Rohtas block are completely plain and fertile. The rainfall in the area is moderate and there are sufficient irrigational facilities.

As such the area gets moderates amount of rainfall and contains a fertile plain, the net sown area covers 48.23 per cent of land and dominates the other categories of land use. The second important land use class in non- agricultural use which accounts for 6.98 per cent of total land of Sasaram block. The main uses of land under this category are towards communication, water bodies and settlements. Forest and barren lands share 40.32 per cent of land. Barren lands are more conspicuous in the form of sandy bed and banks of Amlo river and rocky foothills of Kaimur plateau. Only 0.21 per cent land under culturable waste land is in Sasaram block.

(v) **Southern Hilly Area**: Like the northern hilly area, it is hilly and gets good amount of rainfall. The slope of the area is steep. It, therefore, has a large percentage of land under forest and barren categories. Rohtas and Nauhatta blocks of the area comprise 72.57 and 30.60 per cent of land under this category of land. Nauhatta block has 33.89 per cent of land under net sown area, but this is only 12.85 per cent in Rohtas block. The percentage of land under other categories of land in Rohtas block is low. In Nauhatta block the percentage of other categories of land except the fallow land is moderate. Rohtas block also has the highest percentage of land under forest and barren land (72.57) in the whole of Rohtas district.

CROPPING PATTERN :

The total cultivated land in Rohtas district is 859976.64 acres i.e. 89.23 per cent of the total area of the region. Like other regions of India, the study area is also characterised by seasonal agricultural practices. Most of the crops grown in the region fall into four agricultural harvest namely Bhadai (Autumn), Aghani (Winter), Rabi (spring) and Garma (Summer). These harvests are shown in each block by table no. 3.9. The choropleth drawn in each block represents total cropped area. Table 3.9 exhibits the acreage and percentage of different harvests in Rohtas district as a whole.

Table - 3.9
Cropping Pattern Expressed in Percentage of the Total Cultivated Land (2004-05)

Sl. No.	Name of Blocks	Bhadai	Aghani	Rabi	Garma
1	Sheosagar	-	50.79	49.20	0.01
2	Kargahar	-	63.93	36.30	0.04
3	Sasaram	0.14	54.20	45.62	0.04

4	Chenari	0.28	57.76	41.96	-
5	Nokha	0.02	57.45	42.36	0.17
6	Kochas	-	47.02	52.98	-
7	Karakat	0.33	59.48	39.93	0.26
8	Bikramganj	0.01	55.25	44.74	-
9	Nasriganj	0.44	53.43	45.52	0.61
10	Dinara	-	57.94	42.06	-
11	Dawath	0.26	55.59	43.95	0.20
12	Sanjhauli	0.01	60.82	39.17	-
13	Suryapura	0.44	53.82	45.53	0.18
14	Rajpur	0.52	63.42	35.00	1.06
15	Rohtas	5.39	44.45	47.12	3.04
16	Dehri	1.36	51.89	45.22	1.53
17	Nauhatta	13.90	42.12	43.98	-
18	Tilouthu	3.36	48.10	45.04	3.50
19	Akorhi Gola	0.42	50.14	48.38	1.06

Source : Agriculture Department, Rohtas District.

Table - 3.10

Average Acreage and Percentage of Cultivated Land in Rohtas District in Different Harvests (2004-05)

Harvests	Area in acres	Area in %
Bhadai	4820.85	0.56
Aghani	476161.72	55.37
Rabi	376165.93	43.75
Garma	2828.14	0.32
Total	859976.64	100.00

Source : Agricultural Department, Rohtas District.

(1) Bhadai Crops :

Bhadai crops are sown with the onset of the rains (in May and June) and harvested in the month of Bhado or August-September. They consist of mainly quick maturing crops.16 The main crops are maize, marua, rice, vegetables, etc. They are grown over an area of 4820.85 acres i.e. 0.56% of the total cultivated area. Table no. 3.10 clearly indicates that Bhadai crops rank third in each blocks in terms of percentage of cultivated land. In majority of the blocks the percentage of such land hardly varies between 2 to 13. Nauhatta block exhibits the highest percentage (13.90) of such land followed by Rohtas (5.39) and Tilouthu (3.36). The remaining 16 blocks account for less than 2 per cent land in this category. Thus, the hilly areas exhibit higher percentage of land under this category than the plain areas. This indicates that Bhadai crops need comparatively less fertile land.

(2) Aghani Crops :

The Aghani harvest is dominant over the entire region. It is cultivated on an area of 476161.72 acres of land i.e. 55.37 per cent of the total cultivated area. The Aghani crops are sown in Mid-June, transplanted between July and Mid-August and harvested usually in the month of Aghan or November end and December. Paddy is the unrivalled crop of this season. Other crops are pulses and oilseeds which are generally grown on uplands (fig. 3.3).

On the basis of percentage of land in different blocks under Aghani crops, four categories may be established - (i) Blocks having more than 60 per cent of land under Aghani crops, (ii) Blocks having 55 to 60 per cent, (iii) Blocks having 50 to 55 per cent and (iv) Blocks having less than 50 per cent of land. The first categories covers the blocks of Kargahar (63.93%), Sanjhauli (60.81%), Rajpur (63.40%). These blocks have good canal irrigation system. The second category comprises the blocks of Chenari (57.76%), Nokha (57.45%), Karakat (59.48%), Bikranganj (55.25%), Dinara (57.94%), Dawath (55.58%). All these blocks have plain and fertile areas and are irrigated by canals. The third category consists of the blocks of Sheosagar (50.79%), Sasaram (54.20%), Nasriganj (53.42%), Suryapura (53.83%), Dehri (51.88%), Akorhi Gola (50.12%). These blocks have plain and moderate fertile area. A small per cent of land in Sasaram block is hilly. The fourth category encompasses the blocks of Kochas (47.02%), Rohtas (44.44%), Nauhatta (42.10%) and Tilouthu (48.07%). Nauhatta block is namely hilly and here irrigation

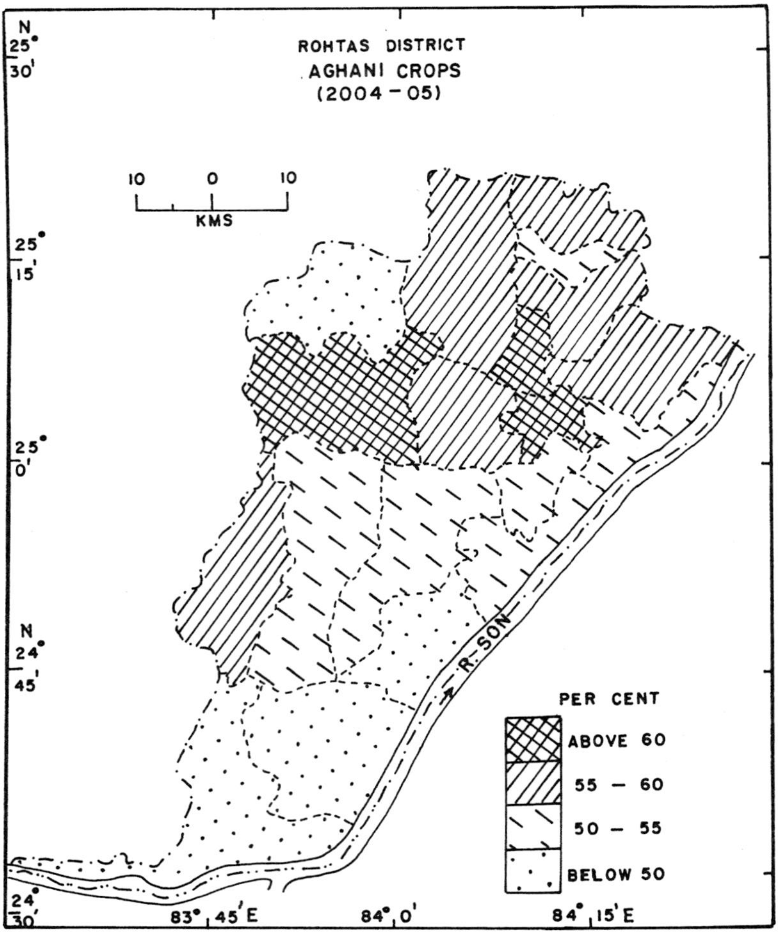
ROHTAS DISTRICT
AGHANI CROPS
(2004 - 05)
10 0 10
KMS
N
25°
30'
25°
15'
25°
0'
N
24°
45'
24°
30'
83° 45' E
84° 0'
84° 15' E
R. SON
PER CENT
ABOVE 60
55 - 60
50 - 55
BELOW 50

Fig. 3.3

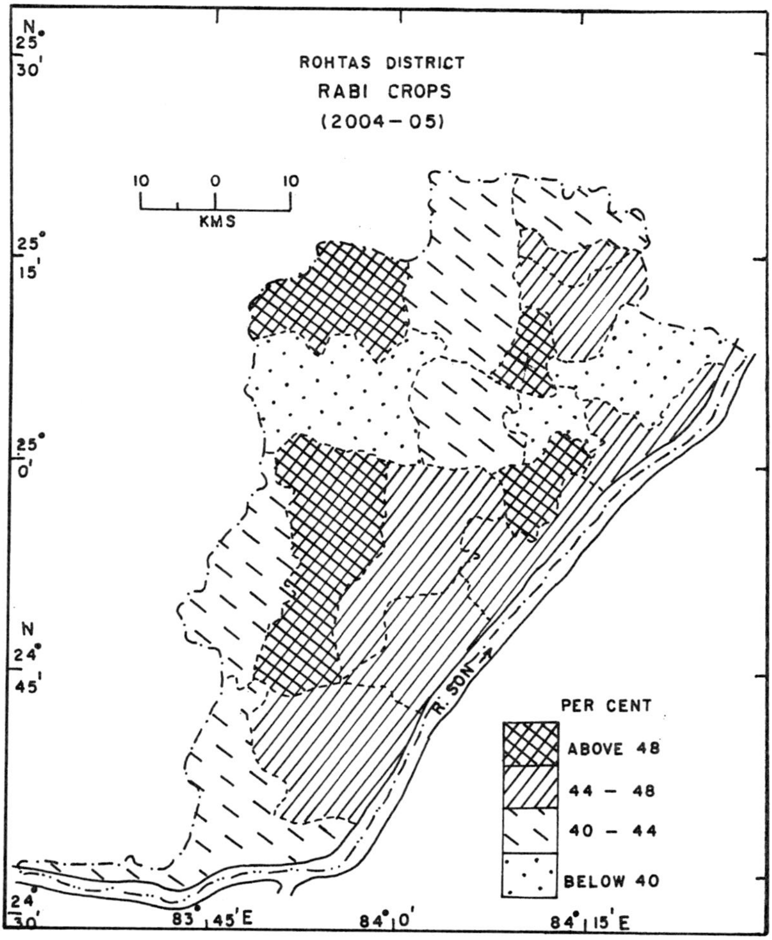
ROHTAS DISTRICT
RABI CROPS
(2004–05)
10 0 10
KMS
N
25°
30'
25°
15'
25°
0'
N
24°
45'
24°
30'
83° 45'E
84° 0'
84° 15'E
R. SON
PER CENT
ABOVE 48
44 – 48
40 – 44
BELOW 40

Fig. 3.4

source is mainly tube-well.

(3) Rabi Crops :

Rabi harvest is also known as winter harvest. Crops of this harvest are sown in October-November and harvested in March-April. Rabi occupies second position in the cropping pattern of the district. It is grown over an area of 376165.93 acres i.e. 43.75 per cent of the total cropped area. Stands for a long list of crops such as wheat, gram, khesari, arhar, linseed, masur, matar, mustard and others. The percentage of these crops is higher in North and Middle-eastern blocks like Kochas (52.97%), Sheosagar (49.20%), Sasaram, Nasriganj, Suryapura, Akorhi Gola and Tilouthu (45 to 55 per cent each). The favourable reasons are comparatively fertile soil, high watertable and canal irrigational facilities. Other blocks have less than 45 per cent of land under this harvest (fig. 3.4).

(4) Garma Crops :

The crops of this harvest are sown in March and harvested in May. It is grown over an area of only 2828.14 acres i.e., 0.32 per cent of the total cropped land. The Garma crops are grown where irrigation and regular manuring facilities are available. They include mostly summer vegetables and the new variety of paddies. Table 3.9 indicates that the percentage of land under this harvest is negligible and variable over the entire region.

Major Crops :

The dominant crops are paddy, wheat, pulses and others cereals. Table no. 3.11 shows that these four crops account for 375528 hectares of cultivated land of the region. Table no. 3.12 explains that five crops cover average total area of crops under important crops. Kargahar block has 27625 hectare of cultivated land under paddy crops followed by Dinara (23400 hectare) and Karkat (16870 hectare). Area under paddy crops is low in Rohtas block (2487 hectare).

Table - 3.11
Cultivated Land Under Principal Crops (2005-06) in Hectares

Principal Crops	Area in Hectare
Paddy	199128
Wheat	160000
Pulses	4800
Oilseed	11600
Total	375528

Source : Agriculture Department of Rohtas (2005-06).

Table - 3.12
Average Total Area of Important Crops (2005-06) in Hectares

Sl. No.	Name of Blocks	Paddy	Pulses	Oilseed	Maize	Wheat
1	Sasaram	11538	689	84	294	9700
2	Nokha	12375	34	-	-	11700
3	Sheosagar	13987	425	44	145	11200
4	Chenari	9452	890	74	149	6500
5	Kargahar	27625	48	-	-	25300
6	Kochas	13668	60	-	19	9200
7	Dehri	7423	328	63	111	8000
8	Akorhi Gola	6823	261	66	147	6700
9	Rohtas	2487	669	91	294	2500
10	Tilouthu	5940	280	79	55	3000
11	Nauhatta	3020	866	123	183	1500
12	Bikramganj	11745	110	-	35	8200
13	Sanjhauli	5700	-	-	38	4200
14	Dawath	8700	-	-	-	7200
15	Suryapura	4500	-	-	-	3200
16	Dinara	23400	-	-	-	20500
17	Karakat	16870	-	0.01	-	12200
18	Nasriganj	7645	105	-	-	5200
19	Rajpur	6230	35	0.02	-	4000

Source : Agriculture Department of Rohtas (2005-06).

(i) Paddy :- Paddy crop occupies the first position amongst all crops in the district. Table- 3.12 shows that paddy attains first position in all blocks. In Kargahar, Dinara and Karakat this crop is grown over an area of above 15,000 hectares of cultivated land. It is grown in plain and fertile parts of the blocks. These blocks are comparatively better irrigated by canal. The amount of rainfall is also high in these blocks. Other important blocks in paddy cultivation are Sasaram, Nokha, Sheosagar, Kochas, Bikramganj, Nasriganj and Rajpur blocks. Paddy is grown over an area of 10,000 to 15,000 hectares of cropped land in plain and fertile pockets. All these blocks have better irrigation facilities by canals and also receive a higher rainfall. The net sown area is exceedingly higher in Nokha and Kochas (89.96 and 86.83 per cent respectively) than Sasaram (48.23%). On the other Sasaram accounts for only 48.23% of N.S.A. due to the presence of forest and barren land area over large parts of its extent. The cropped land under paddy in other blocks ranges between 5,000 to 10,000 hectares. Chanari, Dehri, Akorhi Gola, Sanjhauli and Dawath receive irrigation from canals and tube-wells. The blocks of Chenari and Dehri exhibit a low percentage of land under net sown area an account of the presence of forest and barren land and land put to non-agricultural uses. Rohtas and Nauhatta blocks have low cropped land under paddy because of the prevalence of forest, hills and undulating land surfaces.

(ii) Wheat : Wheat cultivation is primarily controlled by winter rains.[17] Canal irrigation has helped in its production in the district. Wheat ripens in March when the weather turns warm. Heavy loan which retains moisture is an ideal soil for its production. This soil is available in good amount in the district. Still wheat is the second important cereal in the district. It is grown over 395360 acres of the total cropped land. The majority of the blocks of the district have more than 5,000 hectares of their cropped land under this crop. The crop is more important in these blocks which exhibit plain topography, moderate fertility of land, high water table and availability of different means of irrigation during the growing months. Such blocks are Kargahar and Dinara where 20,000 hectares of cropped land lie under this crop. Other block, which are comparatively hilly, forested, barren and land put to non- agricultural uses, have a low water table without irrigation facilities in winter and so account for less than 4,000 hectares land cropped under wheat. Rohtas, Tilouthu, Nauhatta and Suryapura blocks come under this group.

(iii)Maize : - It is the most important Bhadai crop in the district and is sown in July and harvested in September. It is grown over an area of 1470 hectares of total cultivated area. Maize grows luxuriantly on bhith or upland which is completely immune from early floods. It requires light and sandy loam soils. Its greatest enemy is standing water or water logged land.

Its distribution is not uniform in the district. Hilly blocks dominate the acreage under this crop such blocks are Sasaram, Sheosagar, Chenari, Akorhi Gola, Rohtas and Nauhatta.

(iv) Pulses :- These include Mung, Urad, Kurthi, Masur, Gram, Arhar, etc. They share 11860.74 acres of total cultivated area. The acreage is unevenly distributed. Pulses are, however, significant in the blocks of Sasaram, Chenari, Rohtas and Nauhatta followed by Sheosagar, Dehri and Tilouthu.

(v) Oilseeds :- It is the fifth important crops in this area. These include Mustard, Tisi and Sunflower. It is grown over an area of 28663.60 acres of total cultivated area. Its distribution is not uniform. Hilly blocks dominate the acreage under this crop, such blocks are Nauhatta, Rohtas, Sasaram, Chenari and Tilouthu.

CROP YIELD :

Yield and production of an agricultural unit is based on a number of factors. Chief among these are environmental, technological and institutional.[18] Slope, fertility, irrigation and rainfall are among the important deciding factors of agricultural output development. A major part of the cultivated area in Rohtas plain depends on rainfall. Soil fertility and productivity also depend on the water availability water is a therefore a very crucial variable in the development of agriculture in the study area. Frequent failures and widespread economic losses have been recorded due to the high variability of rainfall. However, weather is a key variable in agricultural production and land is the residual claimant of agricultural earnings.[19] No doubt some advances in irrigation have been made but it has touched only the fringe of the problem and on the whole monsoon is still a powerful factor to be reckoned with in agricultural planning, production and yield.

Table - 3.13
Spatial Pattern of Yield 2008 (in Mons per Bigha)

Sl. No.	Name of Blocks	Paddy	Wheat	Maize	Mustard oil
1	Sheosagar	28	11	5	5
2	Kargahar	31	12	7	6
3	Sasaram	27	11	6	6
4	Chenari	30	10	4	6
5	Nokha	35	15	10	5
6	Kochas	34	21	16	5
7	Karakat	38	24	17	9
8	Bikramganj	40	25	22	8
9	Nasriganj	39	26	18	9
10	Dinara	43	22	17	5
11	Dawath	40	21	15	4
12	Sanjhauli	38	24	12	5
13	Suryapura	39	23	14	6
14	Rajpur	34	16	9	5
15	Rohtas	19	14	7	9
16	Dehri	28	10	6	5
17	Nauhatta	8	4	5	3
18	Tilouthu	20	15	8	10
19	Akorhi Gola	37	24	10	5

Source : Field Survey.

Though environmental technological and institutional factors are all important for production, yield and even planning the implementation of technological and institutional measures is conditioned by the environmental determinism.[20] The physical factors affecting agricultural production and yield in Rohtas district are physiography, climatic variation, slope, soil and hydrological variables.

The technological and institutional variables include high yielding varieties of seeds, fertilizers, irrigation, pesticides farm machinery, size of holding, tenure systems, management factors, sociological factors, existence of infra-structure like electricity and transport.[21]

AGRICULTURAL REGIONS :

The Rohtas district exhibits a varied morphological, conditions, slope, water table, soils, rainfall and irrigation conditions in its different parts. Hence the spatial pattern of land use also differs from area to area. Net sown area, however, exceeds other categories of land use in large parts of the district. The percentage of land cropped more than once not uniform. Since agriculture is the mainstay of livelihood in the region, the percentage of land under net sown area and that sown more than once have been selected for determining the boundaries of agricultural regions. Regional boundaries of agriculture are drown where the above mentioned two variables are sharply different from the neighbouring areas. The agricultural regions thus obtained are the following :

1. Intensive Agriculture Region
2. Moderate Agriculture Region
3. Poor Agriculture Region.

1. Intensive Agriculture Region : It comprises the whole of Kargahar, Nokha, Kochas, Karakat, Bikramganj, Nasriganj, Dinara, Dawath, Sanjhauli, Suryapura and Akorhi Gola and northern areas of Dehri block. Thus it covers 50.17 per cent of total area of the study area. This region is fully

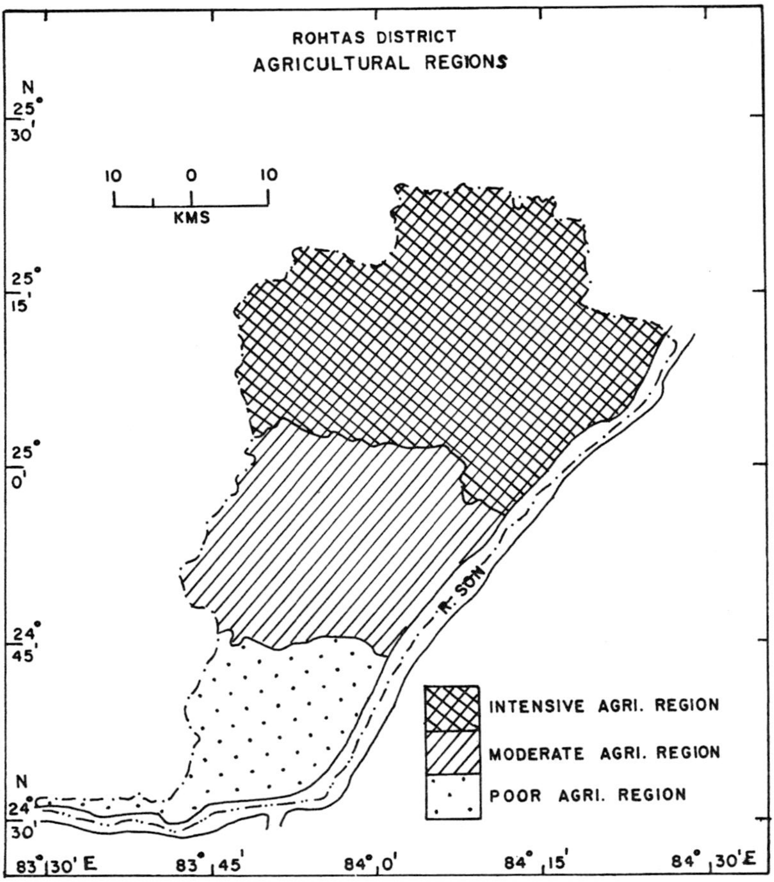
ROHTAS DISTRICT
AGRICULTURAL REGIONS
10 0 10
KMS
N
25° 30'
25° 15'
25° 0'
24° 45'
N
24° 30'
83° 30' E
83° 45'
84° 0'
84° 15'
84° 30' E
R. SON
INTENSIVE AGRI. REGION
MODERATE AGRI. REGION
POOR AGRI. REGION

Fig. 3.5

plain. The amount of rainfall is not adequate here. The water to irrigation has to be supplemented by canals and tube-wells. The soil is relatively fertile. The water table is high in this region. Thus the net sown area is very high (over 80%) in this agricultural region (table 3.14) except in Nasriganj (62.96%). Table 3.14 shows that the percentage of more than once cropped land is also higher in a majority of the blocks of this region (fig. 3.5).

The percentage of land sown more than once cropped to net sown area in these blocks ranges between 27 to above 75 per cent. The same out of total land of the blocks ranges between 23 to above 66 per cent. Other important categories of land use in this agricultural region are fallow land and land put to non- agricultural uses. They vary above 11 and 0.33 to 27 per cent in different blocks. The percentage of barren land and culturable waste lands is insignificant over the entire area (fig. 3.6, 3.7 & 3.8).

Table - 3.14
Percentage of Land Under Net Sown Area and More Than Once Cropped Land Out of Total Land and Net Sown Area of the Blocks (2004-05)

Sl. No.	Name of Blocks	Net sown area	More than once cropped land to NSA	More than once cropped land to total area
1	Sheosagar	63.48	44.6	28.32
2	Kargahar	90.25	37.44	33.99
3	Sasaram	48.23	38.93	1.88
4	Chenari	52.82	17.8	9.4
5	Nokha	89.96	63.9	57.48
6	Kochas	86.83	50.92	44.23
7	Karakat	87.9	42.96	37.76
8	Bikramganj	86.89	52.7	45.79
9	Nasriganj	62.96	75.57	47.56
10	Dinara	92.55	49.22	45.54
11	Dawath	80.98	46.03	37.27

12	Sanjhauli	87.06	47.34	41.21
13	Suryapura	86.6	46.17	39.98
14	Rajpur	85.75	27.51	23.58
15	Rohtas	12.85	23.57	3.02
16	Dehri	52.69	51.83	27.3
17	Nauhatta	33.89	60.84	20.61
18	Tilouthu	39.16	31.57	12.35
19	Akorhi Gola	87.57	75.48	66.08

Source : Land Use Report of 2004-05, Department of Statistics Rohtas District.

2. **Moderate Agriculture Region** : It extends over the whole of Sheosagar, Sasaram, Chenari and Tilouthu and southern parts of Dehri blocks. It thus covers 30.05 per cent of the total area of the Rohtas district. Physiographically a big part of the total area of this agricultural region is hilly and forested. The fertility of land and the underground water table is variable. The amount of rainfall is normally higher than in other agricultural regions but most of rain occurs in hilly and forested areas. Therefore, there is a gap between the percentage of net sown area in different parts of this region which varies from nearly 33 per cent in Nauhatta to 63 per cent in Sheosagar. The percentage of net sown area is higher in relatively fertile plain and irrigationally better managed blocks. Its percentage is low in hilly and forested blocks of Sasaram and Nauhatta. The table 3.14 shows that the percentage of more than once cropped land is higher in blocks which have a higher percentage a net area sown. This percentage ranges between 1.88 in Sasaram to 9.40 in Chenari. Amongst other categories of land use forest and barren lands account for a large percentage of total land in almost all blocks of moderate agricultural region. It is low in Tilouthu block (23.48%). In other blocks such lands lie between 28 per cent in Chenari and 40.32 per cent in Sasaram. Fallow land is significant in all blocks of this region and land put to non- agricultural uses is also conspicuous in all blocks. Cultivable waste land is not significant in this region.

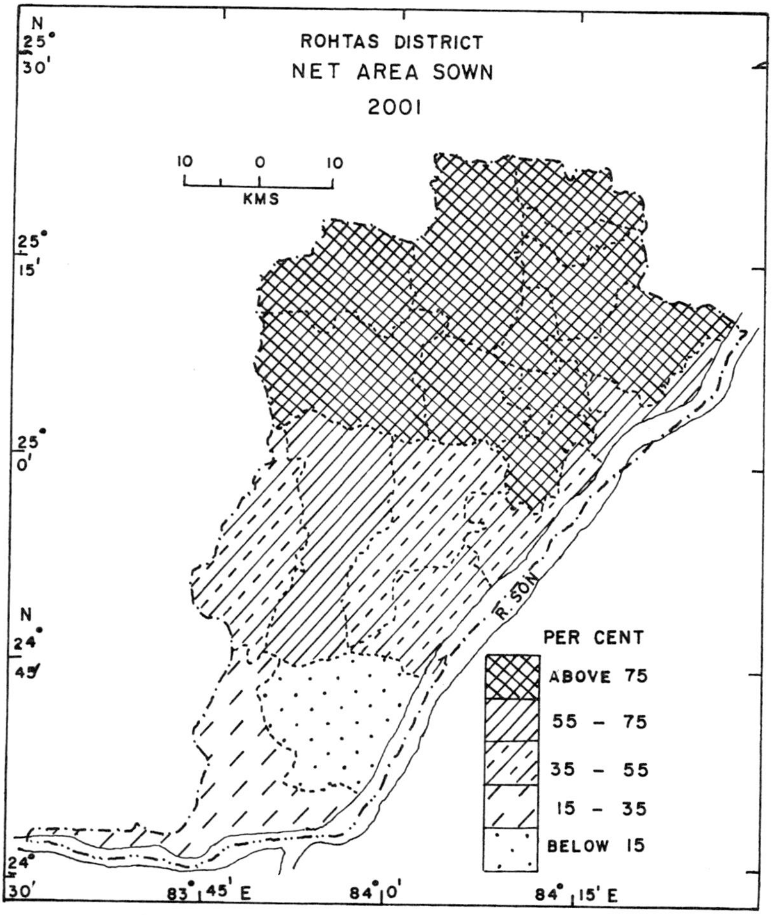
ROHTAS DISTRICT
NET AREA SOWN
2001
10 0 10
KMS
N
25°
30'
25°
15'
25°
0'
N
24°
45'
24°
30'
83° 45' E
84° 0'
84° 15' E
R. SON
PER CENT
ABOVE 75
55 - 75
35 - 55
15 - 35
BELOW 15

Fig. 3.6

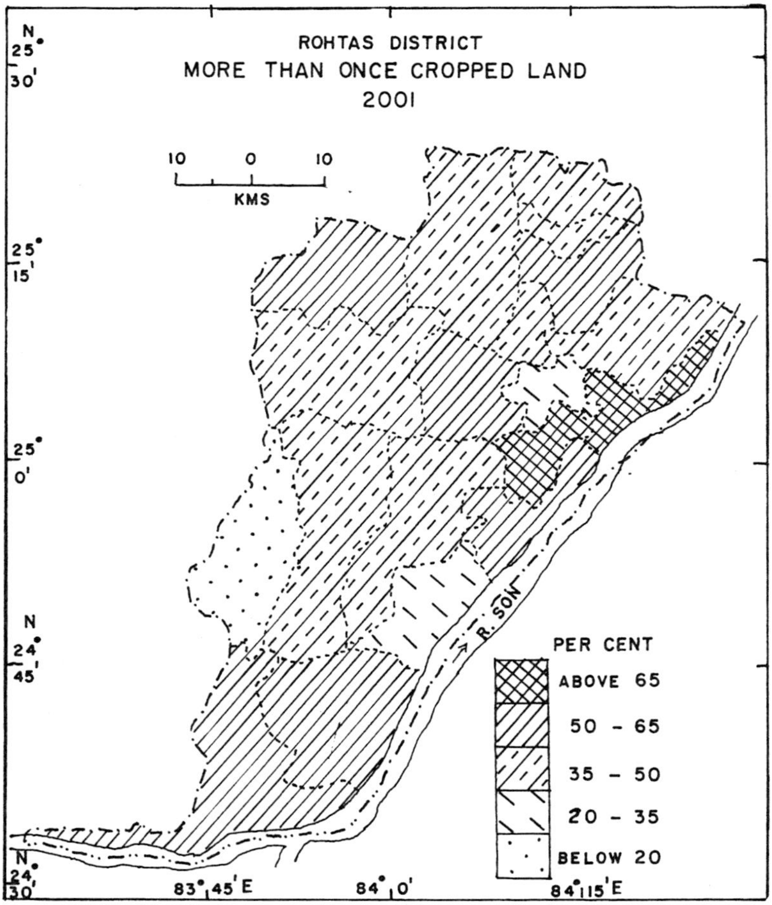
ROHTAS DISTRICT
MORE THAN ONCE CROPPED LAND
2001
10 0 10
KMS
N 25° 30'
25° 15'
25° 0'
N 24° 45'
N 24° 30'
83° 45' E
84° 0'
84° 15' E
R. SON
PER CENT
ABOVE 65
50 - 65
35 - 50
20 - 35
BELOW 20

Fig. 3.7

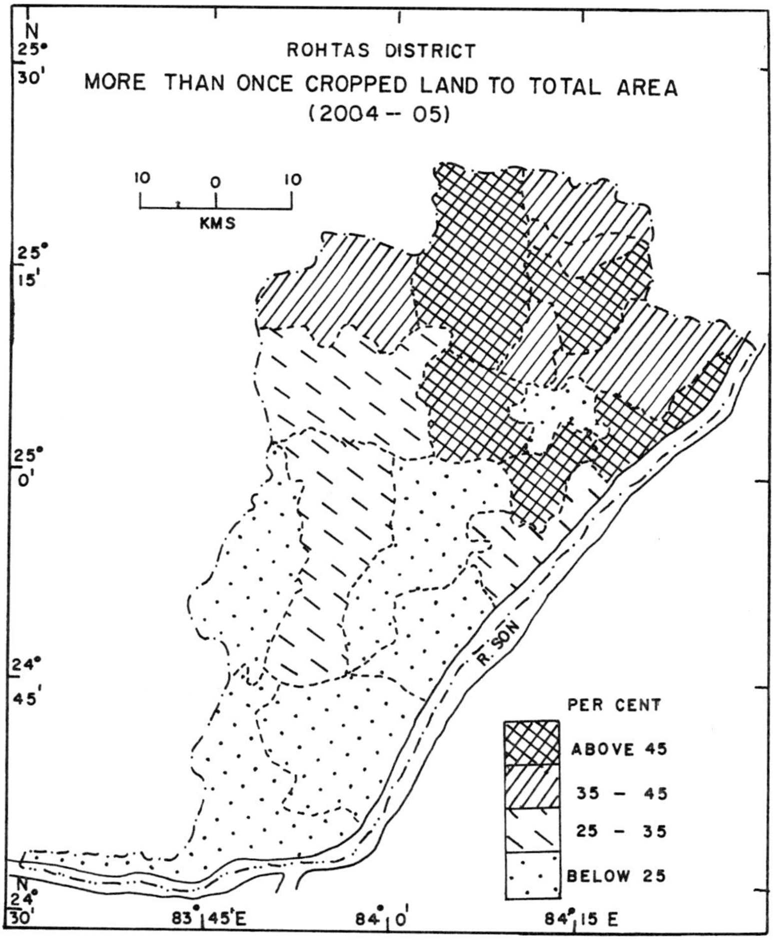
ROHTAS DISTRICT
MORE THAN ONCE CROPPED LAND TO TOTAL AREA
(2004 -- 05)
10 0 10
KMS
N 25° 30'
25° 15'
25° 0'
24° 45'
N 24° 30'
83° 45' E
84° 0'
84° 15 E
R. SON
PER CENT
ABOVE 45
35 - 45
25 - 35
BELOW 25

Fig. 3.8

3. **Poor Agricultural Region** : It comprises only two block Rohtas and Nauhatta of Rohtas district. The land of these blocks is equally distributed between plains and hills. The underground water table is low. The rainfall is not sufficient to raise crops in plain area. The soil is alkaline (reh) in plain areas. It has therefore, 12.85% in Rohtas and 33.89% in Nauhatta under net sown area. The percentage of more than once cropped land to net sown area and total area is also low i.e. 23.57% and 3.02% (Rohtas) respectively. The second important land use class in this region is forest and barren lands which account for 72.57 per cent (Rohtas) and 23.48 per cent (Nauhatta) of the area. The third important category of land use is land put to non- agricultural uses. Fallow land also occupies a conspicuous position is land use and account for 7.99% and 2.12% of the area. This is mainly because of the low fertility of the area.

It will be seen that the agricultural regions have a close relationship with physical and population regions.

References :

1. Sinha, V.N.P. (1976) : Socio-Economic Setting, Chotanagpur Plateau, K.B. Publications, New Delhi, p. 27.
2. Enyedi, G. (1971) : The Land of Hungary and Its Agricultural Utilisation : Studies in Applied and Regional Geography, Edited by Md. Shafi and Mehdi Raza, Aligarh, p. 249.
3. Jha, G.P. (1978) : Perspective in Land Utilisation Problems, Population and Agricultural Land Use in Kamla Balan Plain, Unpublished Ph.D. Thesis, p. 40.
4. Vink, A.P.A. (1975) : Land Use in Advancing Agriculture, Springerveriok, Berlin, New York, p.1.
5. Ibid.
6. Prasad, S.N. (1980) : Land Use ; Land Use in Ranchi District, Unpublished Ph.D. Thesis, p. 75.
7. Singh, R.P. and Kumar, A. (1970) : Monograph of Bihar

(Land Use), Bharti Bhawan, Patna, p. 32.

8. Ibid, p. 32.
9. Sinha, V.N.P. (1976) : Op. Cit, p. 28.
10. Singh, R.P. and Kumar, A. (1970) : Op. Cit., p. 33.
11. Dayal, P. (1953) : Bihar in Maps (Land Use), Kusum Prakashan, Patna - 3, p. 42.
12. Sinha, V.N.P. (1976) : Op. Cit., p. 28.
13. Stamp, L.D. (1952) : Land For Tomorrow, The Underdeveloped World, Chapter Iv, Food for All, pp. 41-45.
14. Chang, Jen-her (1968) : The Agricultural Potential of the Humid Tropics, The Geographical Review, Vol. 58, No. 3, pp. 331-361.
15. Survey and Settlement Report, Hazaribagh, 1917, p.6.
16. Dayal, P. (1953) : The Agricultural Harvests, Bihar in Maps, Kusum Prakashan, Patna-3, p. 48.
17. Singh, R.P. & Kumar, Anil (1970) : Land Use, Monograph of Bihar, Bharti Bhawan, Patna-1, p.44.
18. Mohammed, Ali (1978) : Sources of Variation in Agricultural Productivity, Situation of Agriculture, Food and Nutrition in Rural India, Concept publishing Company, Delhi, p. 20.
19. Namboodiri, N.V. : Economic Times, September 23, 1976.
20. Mohammed, Ali (1978) : Op. Cit., p. 21.
21. Shah, S.L. : Growing Regional Disparities through Agricultural Development, Balanced Regional Development, Indian Economic Conference, Patna, p. 98.

4

Chapter

Population Growth

GROWTH OF POPULATION :

Population geographers have traditionally been concerned with the analysis of trends and pattern of growth in world population.[1] The term growth of population is regarded as the change in the size of population inhabiting a territory during a specific period of time, irrespective of the fact whether the change is positive or negative.[2] This change can be measured both in term of absolute numbers and percentage. Any changes in population size of an area over a certain period of time is expressed in the form of rate of growth per annum.[3] The population growth is controlled by the relative balance of mortality, fertility and migration,[4] which are in turn influenced by size groups of factors : biological, environmental, economic, social, political and technological.[5] According to Harrison and Boyce three main demographic forces influence the patterns of population dynamics : natural increase/decrease, distributional inertia and human mobility. The importance of human mobility has increased immensely at a local scale whereas other demographic forces influence the pattern of population dynamics on a world scale.[6] According to Verma, the natural increase or decrease depends upon the age structure, marriage pattern, economic level, socio-religious beliefs and values.[7] A population containing large number of young people will have higher birth rate than a population consisting more of infants and old people.[8]

S. A. Qazi and Navaid Shabir Qazi estimate fertility,

mortality and mobility are the three basic components of population change at any place. The determinants of fertility are significantly wide. These may be attributed to biological, social and political factors. Biological race, fecundity, physical and mental health have been considered important. The demographic factors like age composition, sex, degree of urbanization, duration of marriage, working and non-working state of females play a significant role.[9]

Pearl affirms that the rate of growth is a function of the size of population already attained.[10] Under such conditions, because of the broad, base, even a low rate of population growth would add a large population to the region or the country each year.[11] Chandna estimates that demographic dynamism is a function of the growth of its population. Population growth is an index of its economic development and most of the other population characteristics are intimately related with the growth patterns experienced by the region and derive their meaning and significance from it.[12]

POPULATION GROWTH DURING 1901-2001 :

The trend of population growth, in a region provides a fundamental basis for the evaluation of its resource utilization. The past and current trend of population growths are the reliable indicators for future demographic trend. The socio-economic growth of a region in related with number and quality of its inhabitants.[13]

The decadal variation in population of Rohtas district in given below : -

Table - 4.1
Trend of Population Growth in Rohtas District (1901-2001)

Census Years	Persons	Decade variation in %
1901	539635	-
1911	544374	+0.87
1921	538903	-1.00

1931	589565	+9.40
1941	690220	+17.07
1951	826278	+19.71
1961	1018636	+23.28
1971	1279891	+25.64
1981	1574615	+23.02
1991	1917416	+21.77
2001	2450748	+27.81

Source : District Gazetteers of Shahabad (1966), District Census Hand Book (1981) and Census Office Patna (1991-2001).

The above table no. 4.1 portrays the pattern of population growth since 1901. The pattern of population growth may be classified as low, moderate and high. Low population growth has remained before two year 1931. In the year 1921 the population has rather decreased in comparison to the previous year. The situation has remained because of various diseases which prevailed in the study area. Between 1931 to 1951 the growth of population was moderate i.e. between 10 per cent to 20 per cent. After 1951 the growth of population in Rohtas district has become faster. It has reached to about 28 per cent in 2001. It has, however, remained slightly lower in the year 1991 i.e. 21.77 per cent. Probable causes, for such growth of population in the study area are attributed to illiteracy, early marriage, lack of using family planning techniques, poverty, out-dated concepts of earning, livelihood and incere. Through more children in the family which is applicable in case of poor families.

Block wise Population Growth (1991-2001) :

Table no. 4.2 exhibits the fact that the growth of population both in absolute number of persons, percentage and annual growth during 1991-2001.

Table - 4.2
Blockwise Population Growth (1991-2001)

Sl. No.	Name of Blocks	Total population (1991)	Total population (2001)	Persons absolute	Percent variation in decade	Annual Growth (%)
1	Sheosagar	110332	144176	+33844	+30.67	+3.06
2	Kargahar	200205	299132	+98927	+49.41	+4.94
3	Kochas	-	-	-	-	-
4	Sasaram	266835	296229	+29394	+11.01	+1.10
5	Chenari	81287	107273	+25986	+31.96	+3.19
6	Nokha	137683	197227	+59544	+43.24	+4.32
7	Sanjhauli	-	-	-	-	-
8	Karakat	142748	179195	+36447	+25.53	+2.55
9	Bikramganj	150990	184925	+33935	+22.47	+2.24
10	Suryapura	-	-	-	-	-
11	Nasriganj	138150	180166	+42016	+30.41	+3.04
12	Rajpur	-	-	-	-	-
13	Dinara	175032	192291	+17259	+9.86	+0.98
14	Dawath	114314	92987	-21327	-18.65	-1.86
15	Rohtas	88499	168835	+80336	+90.77	+9.07
16	Tilouthu	-	-	-	-	-
17	Dehri	248127	332448	+84321	+33.98	+3.39
18	Akorhi Gola	-	-	-	-	-
19	Nauhatta	63214	75864	+12650	+20.01	+2.00

Note : Combined Population figure in 6 new blocks (Kochas, Sanjhauli, Suryapura, Rajpur, Tilouthu, Akorhi Gola)

Source : Census of India, 1991 and 2001 & self computation.

FERTILITY PATTERN :

Fertility measures the rate at which a population adds to itself by births.[14] Moreover, fertility is an actual reproductive performance in a population. It is the actual occurrence of live births which differs from fecundity which denotes the physiological ability or potential to reproduce. The former refers to the number of children a women has born ; the lather, to the number she is biologically capable of having.15 On the whole fertility is a complex process responsible for the biological maintenance of society. It is one of the most important dynamics of population change. An in depth study of birth rate and death rate is essential in the present state of planning for India's development. They are particularly important now where the country has launched a programme to reduce the birth rate as expeditiously as possible. Consequently, it constituted an essential aspect of demographic study.[16] In broader perspective the population of an area is largely influenced by fertility trends. Hence the study of fertility has been gaining increasing importance in recent periods.

Table 4.3
Fertility Trends in Rohtas District 2001-08 (Figures in Persons)

Years	Rohtas District
2001	2195
2002	2113
2003	3590
2004	7419
2005	15707
2006	14839
2007	9027
2008	17474

Source : Department of Statistics, Old Secretariate, Patna.

Table no. 4.3 shows the picture of fertility pattern in the area under study. The area under study has gone through vast changes in its fertility pattern. It is attributed with a high birth rate (fig 4.1).

Table no. 4.3 reveals that the fertility in the study area is high. The fertility rate in the district was 2195 persons in 2001 which increase to 17474 persons in 2008, in the time span of eight years. In present time the district recorded higher birth rates. This has happened account of the lower literacy rate and unconsciousness of the people towards the family planning programmes launched by the government to check the higher fertility.

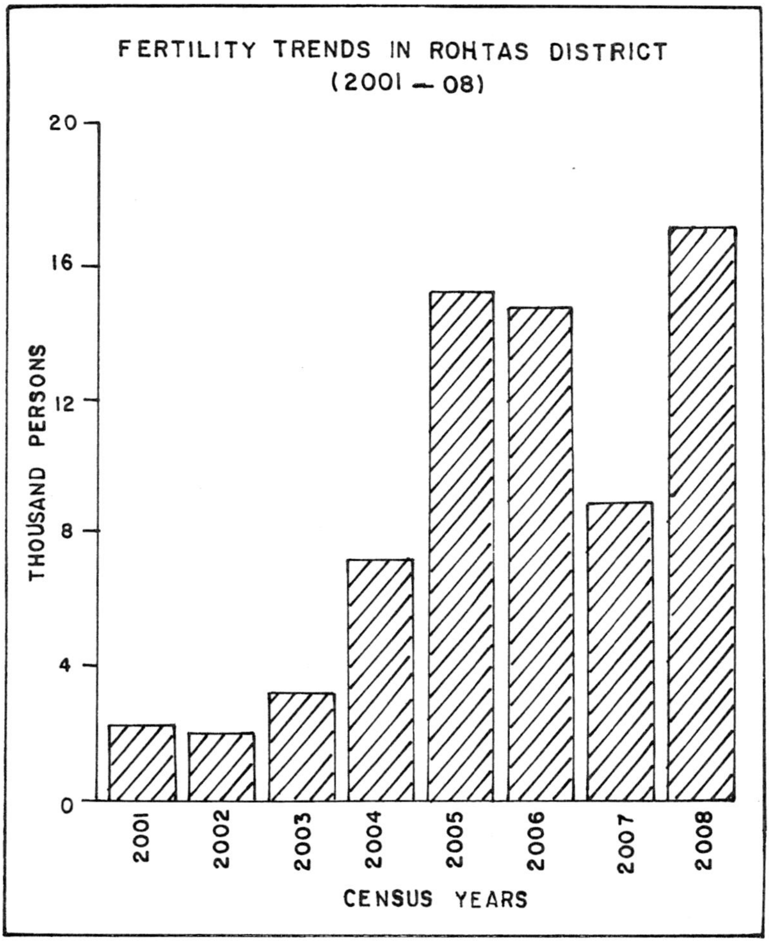
FERTILITY TRENDS IN ROHTAS DISTRICT
(2001 – 08)
THOUSAND PERSONS
20
16
12
8
4
0
2001
2002
2003
2004
2005
2006
2007
2008
CENSUS YEARS

Fig. 4.1

Causes for High Birth Rate in Rohtas District :

There are several reasons for continued high birth rate in the area under study. The important reasons are stated below :-

1. The Social and Religious Customs
2. Marital Status
3. High Mean Duration
4. Environmental Cause
5. Economic Factor
6. Low Level of Literacy
7. Age Structure
8. Sex Structure
9. High Death Rate
10. Low Level of Family Planning Practice
11. Religious Factor.

MORTALITY PATTERN :

Mortality refers to the occurrence of deaths in a particular region within a definite period of time. It contrasts with fertility by being more stable and predictable and less prone to mysterious fluctuations. It is closely interlinked. Generally death control is more acceptable than birth control. The decline in mortality has consequently been more widespread than the decline in fertility which is particularly responsible for such feared "population explosion". Indeed it is one of the most important features of the recent history of mankind. In view of the demographic significance of mortality and its manifold social and economic effects, geographers must pay due attention to it.

Mortality is one of the most important dynamics of population change.[17] It is also an essential variable having impact on fertility, population structure, population growth and many other socio-economic variables. The increase in population of a particular region depends not only upon the fertility alone, but also upon the mortality. It plays a significant role in the growth of population in a region. In an area with high birth rate and low death rate, the population will grow by leaps and bonds. On the contrary, in an area where death rate is high and birth rate is low, the population is bound to be declining. Wars, epidemics and economic depression are reflected in an increased death rate, while a low death rate is an index of economic prosperity and application of scientific knowledge to the problems of health.[18] It is an index of the resisting power of the community in times of economic distresses and natural calamities. Therefore, an in depth study of mortality is most essential in the present state of planning for India's development.[19]

Throughout its modern history the lulls spurts in district population have been governed not by fluctuations in the birth rate but also by wide variations in the death rate. Major catastrophic-famine, food shortage and epidemics took a heavy toll of life and kept population size within the limits of subsistence.[20] The control of such calamities opened a way for heavy upsurge of population in recent year. In fact uptil how many diseases have not been controlled completely. Cholera, small pox, tuberculosis, dietary malnutrition, diarrhoea and typhoid still prevail to take a toll of life of rural poverty striken and illiterate population. So in this sense the area under study is still a death ridden area and they are fundamentally[21] a death-striken people. Some improvements are however visible in this direction.

Table no. 4.4 clearly gives a picture of mortality trends in Rohtas district from the period 2001-2008 (fig. 4.2).

Table 4.4
Mortality Trends in Rohtas District (2001-08)

Years	Rohtas District (in persons)
2001	1493
2002	1918
2003	3121
2004	3421
2005	6172
2006	5477
2007	4003

2008	4849

Source : Department of Statistics, Old Secretariate, Patna.

Causes of High Death in Rohtas District :

Various causes, responsible for heavy mortality in the study area, are as fallows :

1. Malnutrition
2. Endemic and Epidemic Causes
3. Lack of Health and Medical Facilities
4. Unfavourable Environment
5. Social and Religious factors
6. Economic Factors
7. Low Level of Literacy

MOBILITY PATTERN :

Man is, by nature, a mobile creature and mobility is a fact of life. Mobility is an act of movement. It is a sufficiently broad term to include all population movements even the movement to fetch water from a nearby well and intercontinental movements over several thousand kilometres. Migration is sometimes used in this broad general sense. Most definitions of migration, however, refers to permanent change of residence.[22] It is largely the result of purposeful behaviour.[23] In general, people believe that be migrating, they can improve their condition and that of their family. Mobility, thus, indicates a system of social and economic change and can be regarded as a form of human adjustment to economic, environmental as well as social problems.[24] Each movement provides an important network for diffusion of ideas and information.[25] Therefore the mobility of man has increased fitfully with technical and economic progress.[26] Increased mobility has enabled increased migration.[27] Population increased when immigration exceeds emigration. Thus, mobility, indeed, one of the dynamic constituents of population change.

The study of migration concerns different disciplines. Scholars of these disciplines have analysed this social

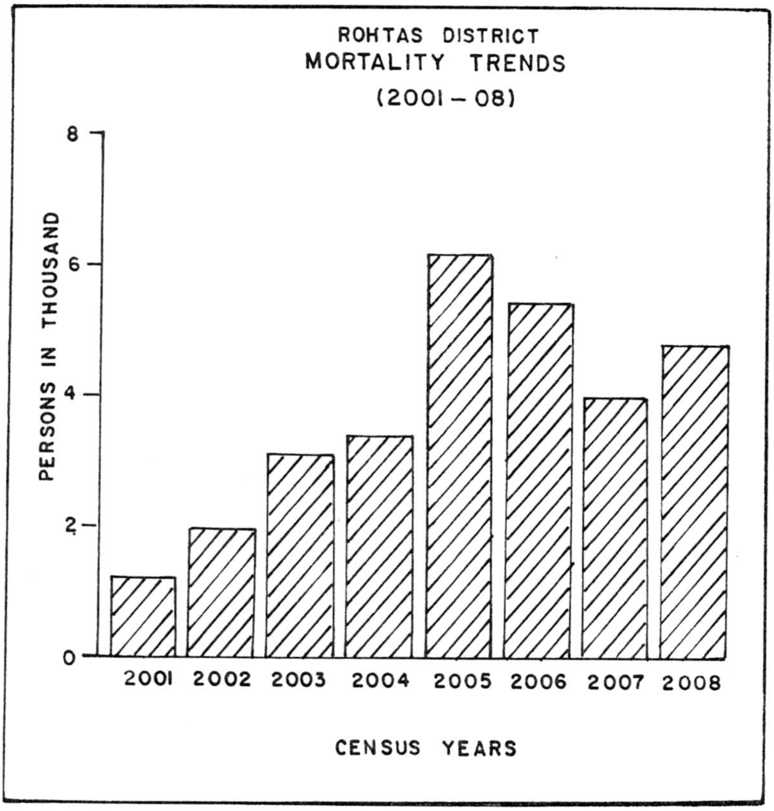
ROHTAS DISTRICT
MORTALITY TRENDS
(2001 – 08)
PERSONS IN THOUSAND
8
6
4
2
0
2001 2002 2003 2004 2005 2006 2007 2008
CENSUS YEARS

Fig. 4.2

phenomenon in their own way. They have classified migration considering aspects like distance, duration and period of stay, volume, etc. All these approaches have influenced the typology of migration to a considerable extent. Fairchild classified migration into invasion, conquest, colonisation and immigration. Later on Isaac modified his classification as free and forced migration. Again free migration got subdivided into refugee, solve and population transfer. Kant classified migration into two categories. On the basis of duration migration may be classified into accidental or temporary, permanent and periodic and definite migration. Temporary and short term migration and permanent migration are the two extreme types of migration. In between these two types of migration, there are various forms of migration.

Some scholars have classified migration like seasonal, temporary, non-seasonal, re-current, continuous and permanent. Some scholars have classified migration according to distance and direction like internal, external, national, international, etc. Similarly migration is classified as rural to rural, rural to urban, urban to urban and urban to rural. Gould and Prothero[28] considered space and time for classification of migrations. The two elements were subdivided into the following groups on the basis of space. Gould (1976) classified migration into rural to rural, rural to urban, urban to urban and urban to rural. One the basis of time mobility of man got classified into daily, periodic, seasonal, long term, irregular and permanent. Thomas[29] (1968) considered immigration as a necessity for the diffusion of skills specially in developing countries.

The district of Rohtas has also recorded some important migration types- labour migration from rural to rural, rural to urban, marriage migration etc. Marriage migration is a common feature. Females migrate from place of birth to place of husband but migration of labourers from rural areas to different places specially Punjab, Haryana, Delhi, etc. has been important during recent years. Rural -urban migration has also become equally important.

No doubt scholars of different disciplines have categorized migration in their own way but in the present study data concerning types of migration have been processed as seasonal labourers, rural or urban migrants, rural to industrial centres and others. The table 4.5 reveals number of out migrants and its types in the selected villages.

Table - 4.5
Types of Mobility

Villages	T8otal Population	No. of out-migrants	Seasonal labourers	Rural to urban	Rural to industrial centres	Others
Jogia	900	63	41	8	11	3
Turki	815	48	21	7	14	6
Gopalpur	1707	79	60	5	11	3
Auraiya	502	47	32	9	5	1
Kaithi	1763	95	59	12	16	8
Dumaria	347	24	11	3	8	2

Source : Based on Field Work by Scholar.

POPULATION GROWTH IN PHYSICAL REGIONS :

Table no. 4.6 exhibits the growth of population both in absolute number of persons, percentage and annual growth during 1991-2001 in physical regions of Rohtas district.

The table- 4.6 clearly explains that three physical regions exhibit speedy growth of population in Rohtas district. In 1991 Northern Low Plain, Central High Plain and Southern Higher Plain respectively stand for 511710, 1200626 and 101131.88 population which has increased in 2001 by 701358.50, 1504690.50 and 132824.49 population respectively. In the Northern Low Plain of Rohtas district maximum annual growth of population was recorded i.e. 3.70 per cent. Reasons for excessive population growth in these three physical regions are intensive agriculture, high production developed irrigational facilities, plain fertile land and trends of rapid urbanization, etc. In the Central High Plain specially in district headquarter Sasaram, Dehri and Nokha urban population has increased rapidly. Besides in Bikramganj, Nosriganj and Dawath and others blocks the rural population has also increased expressively. On the other hand low population growth has been recorded in the Northern Hilly Area and Southern Hilly area during 1991 to 2001. In these regions population has increased to 4517.76 and 3423.82 respectively. Due to hilly and uneven land forms many areas of these regions are isolated. In both the above mentioned regions population growth is low due to following factors; lack of plain and fertile land, lack of means of irrigation, lack of intensive farming, rural-social scenario, low literacy, less development of transport and communication, lack of medical facilities, etc. Infant mortality rate is also high in these regions. An another reason for low population growth in both the region is internal migration which is towards intensive agricultural region and urban regions.

Table - 4.6
Population Growth in Physical Regions

Physical Regions	Total Population 1991	2001	Decennial Growth Absolute (2001)	Percent (2001)	Annual Growth (%) (2001)
Northern Low Plain	511710	701358.50	189648.50	37.06	3.70
Central High Plain	1200626	1504690.50	304064.5	25.32	2.53
Southern Higher Plain	101131.88	132824.49	31692.61	31.33	3.13
Northern Hilly Area	73031.47	77549.23	4517.76	6.18	0.61
Southern Hilly Area	30901.45	34325.27	3423.82	11.07	1.10

Source : Census of India, 1991 and 2001 and self computed.

POPULATION GROWTH IN AGRICULTURAL REGIONS :

Table no. 4.7 exhibits the growth of total population both in absolute number of persons, percentage and annual growth during 1991-2001 in agricultural regions of Rohtas district.

It is clear from the above Table no. 4.7 that during 1991 to 2001 population has increased up to 3596972 persons in the total population figure in Intensive Agricultural Region. This region shows the highest growth in the study areas the annual growth recorded here is 3.10. Absolute population was 134775 in Moderate Agricultural Region in 2001. Intensive agricultural has remained the basic reason for rapid population growth in both these regions. Intensive agriculture is favoured by plain fertile land, irrigational facilities and dense population. All these factors have favoured the rapid growth of population. All six towns of Rohtas district are located in both these regions. There two have received dense population. During agricultural season labourers from the outside regions come have for work in plenty and increase population pressure temporarily. Poor Agricultural Region includes two blocks of Rohtas district which are Rohtas and Nauhatta. This region has lack of plain and fertile lands. In fact agricultural activities are limited to some regions due to the pressure of uneven landforms and dense forest areas. Intensive agriculture occurs in the basin of river Son especially in the eastern and southern parts agriculture doesn't occur to a great extant in Rohtas and Nauhatta blocks. Due to limited intensive farming absolute population growth is not very high i.e. 38860 persons but annual growth shows adequate growth which is 2.56%. North ward internal migration of labourers is an another reason for smaller size of population in this region.

Table - 4.7
Population Growth in Agricultural Regions

Agricultural Regions	Total Population 1991	2001	Decennial Growth Absolute (2001)	Percent (2001)	Annual Growth (%) (2001)
Intensive Agricultural Regions	1158373	1518070	359697	31.05	3.10
Moderate Agricultural Regions	607330	742105	134775	22.12	2.21
Poor Agricultural Regions	151713	190570	38860	25.61	2.56

Source : Census of India, 1991 and 2001, self computed.

FUTURE TREND OF POPULATION GROWTH :

Any estimate of population in future is fraught with uncertainties as there is no fixed law of population increase and also various techniques of population projection give widely varying results. The statisticians are further handicapped by the fact that neither births and deaths are properly registered in India nor migration, particularly emigration figures, and economic and social indices are reliably available. The sophisticated 'indirect' techniques of population projection which are based on correlation of population numbers and social and economic indices cannot be attempted. Among 'direct' techniques, the techniques of extrapolation is more suitable. The technique is concerned with the fitting of straight line, non linear or logistic curve to the census figures available.[30] Admittedly, this method is crude and fails to provide accurate prediction for the next year or so.[31] Further, population in India records erratic growth trend due to erratic behaviour in the pattern of rural-urban migration.

For applying extrapolation method, future population of Rohtas district has been calculated by both arithmetic and geometric progression methods. The year 1951 has been taken as the base year of population growth because this year is a cut off year. After 1951 growth of population is very fast phenomenal in character. The population growth of the district has been calculated by the following methods :

1. Arithmetic Methods :

The formula for the projection of future population by this method is :

1. Arithmetic Progression Method :

The formula for the projection of future population by this method is :

$$r = \frac{y - a}{n - 1}$$

where r = rate of population growth per year / annum.

y = present year population (2001)

a = Base year population (1951)

n = Internal of years between base year and present year.

$$r = \frac{pop.of\ 2001 - Pop.of\ 1951}{51 - 1}$$

$$r = \frac{2450748 - 826278}{50}$$

$$r = \frac{1624470}{50}$$

$r = 32489.40$

$r = 32489$ *persons per year*

Then this formula is used for getting the population

figure:

$$P = a + r\,(n\text{-}1)$$

Now, Population in 2011 A.D.

$$P = a + r\,(n\text{-}1)$$

$$= 826278 + 32489\,(61\text{-}1)$$

$$= 826278 + 32489 \times 60$$

$$= 826278 + 1949340$$

= 2772518 persons.

Population in 2021 A.D.

$$P = a + r\,(n\text{-}1)$$

$$= 826278 + 32489\,(71\text{-}1)$$

$$= 826278 + 32489 \times 70$$

$$= 826278 + 2274230$$

= 3100508 persons.

Population in 2031 A.D.

$$P = a + r\,(n\text{-}1)$$

$$= 826278 + 32489\,(81\text{-}1)$$

$$= 826278 + 32489 \times 80$$

$$= 826278 + 2599120$$

= 3425398 persons.

The method of Arithmetic Progression does not give a satisfactory result and it is, therefore, not much reliable.

2. Geometric Progression method :

Formula :

$$y = ar^{n\text{-}1}$$

Where, y = Present year population (2001)

a = Base year (1951)

r = Rate of population increase per year in constant amount.

n = Interval of years (51)

$y = ar^{n-1}$

$or,\ 2450748 = 826278 \times r^{51-1}$

$or,\ 2450748 = 826278 \times r^{50}$

$or,\ 826278 \times r^{50} - 2450748$

$$or,\ r^{50} = \frac{2450748}{826278}$$

$$or,\ r = \frac{1}{50}\left(\frac{2450748}{826278}\right)$$

$$or,\ \log r = \frac{1}{50}\ (\log y - \log a)$$

$$or,\ \log r = \frac{1}{50}\ (\log 2450748 - \log 826278)$$

$$or,\ \log r = \frac{1}{50}\ (6.38930 - 5.91713)$$

$$or,\ \log r = \frac{0.47217}{50}$$

$or,\ \log r = 0.0094434$

Now population in 2011 A.D.

$y = ar^{n-1}$

$= \log 826278 + \log r^{60}$

$= 5.91713 + (60 \times 0.00944)$

$= 5.917131 + 0.5664$

$= 6.48353$

Population (Antilog) = 3044610

= 30.44 lakh persons.

Thus population in 2021 A.D.

$y = ar^{n-1}$

$= \log 826278 + \log r^{70}$

$= 5.917131 + (70 \times 0.009443)$

$= 5.917131 + 0.66101$

$= 6.578141$

Population (Antilog) = 3785659

= 37.86 lakh persons.

Thus population in 2031 A.D.

$y = ar^{n-1}$

$= \log 826278 + \log r^{80}$

$= 5.917131 + (80 \times 0.009443)$

$= 6.672571$

Population (Antilog) = 4705071

= 47.05 lakh persons.

Table no. 4.8 shows the trend of population growth up to 2031 A.D. which has been illustrated in fig 4.3.

Table - 4.8
Population Projection for Rohtas District

Years	Actual Population	Estimated Population	
		Arithmetic Progression Method	Geometric Progression Method
1951	826278	-	-
2001	2450748	-	-
2011	-	2775618	3044610
2021	-	3100508	3785659
2031	-	3425398	4705071

Source : Census of India, 1951 and 2001, Self Computed.

In comparison to 1901 A.D. population of the district has various trends of growth. An increase of 0.87% of the district population was recorded during 1901-1911. Reasons for this was natural growth.

The decade 1911-1921 which has experienced the prevalence of plague, influenza, malaria, cholera and small pox so the total population of the district decreased by 1.00%.

Higher increase in the demographic history of Rohtas district was recorded in the decade 1961-71 and 1991-2001. During this period population increased by 25.64% and 27.81% respectively. Extension of medical facilities and immigration from adjacent areas are the main reasons for the higher increase of population.

In the decade 1951-61, 1971-81 and 1981-91 the growth of population has remained slightly lower i.e. 23.28%, 23.02% and 18.91% respectively. Such population growth is widely attributed to family welfare programs which were widely organised in the district during this periods.

In general population growth in the district has a zig-zag trend.

Harrison and Boyce state that natural change of population has probably never offered more areal variations

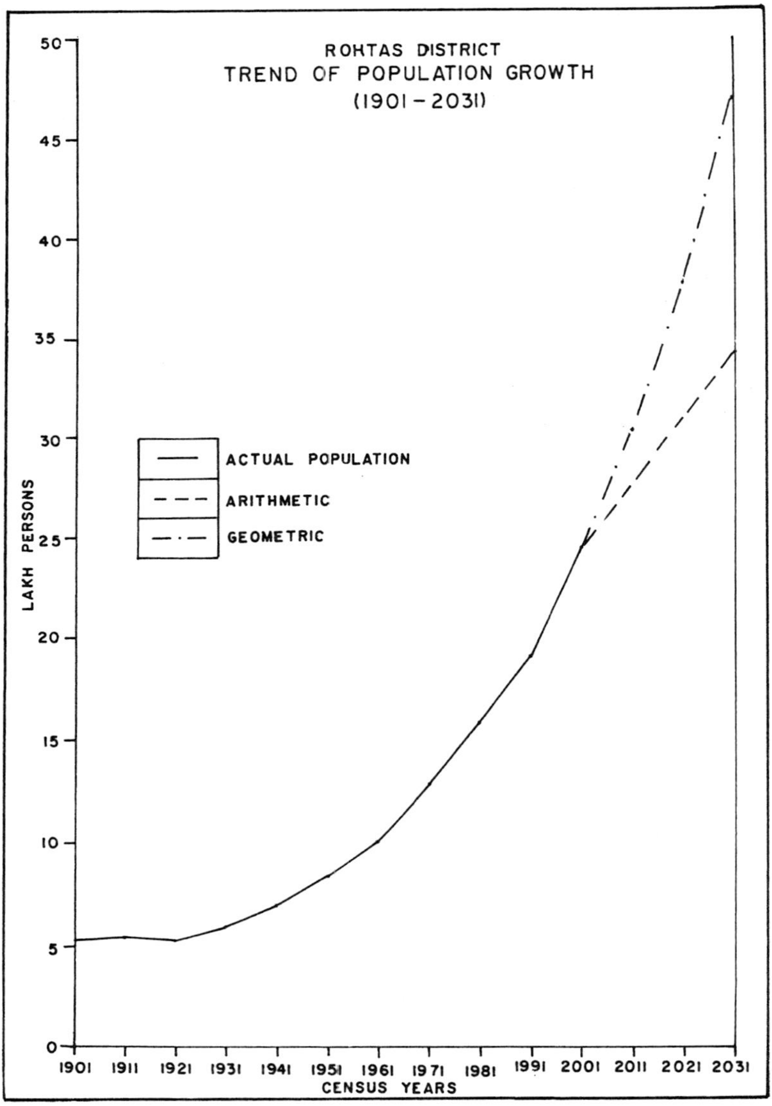
ROHTAS DISTRICT
TREND OF POPULATION GROWTH
(1901 – 2031)
ACTUAL POPULATION
ARITHMETIC
GEOMETRIC
LAKH PERSONS
0
5
10
15
20
25
30
35
40
45
50
1901 1911 1921 1931 1941 1951 1961 1971 1981 1991 2001 2011 2021 2031
CENSUS YEARS

Fig. 4.3

than at present, owing to declines in mortality and fertility at various times and rates during the nineteenth and twentieth centuries.[32] Garnier tells that in all countries of the world, the number of births every year considerably exceeds the number of deaths.[33] Negi explains that the growth has been due to a surplus of birth over deaths.[34] Hans Raj asserts that the growth of population has been tremendous on account of improved medical facilities leading to a decline in death rate and an increase in the birth rate resulting in net increase in population.[35]

References :

1. Hassan, Mohammed Izhar (2005) : Population Geography Rawat Publications, Jawahar Nagar, Jaipur, p. 74.
2. Chandra, R.C. & Sindhu, M.S. (1980) : Growth of Population, Introduction to Population Geography, Kalyani Publishers, Ludhina, New Delhi, p.31.
3. Hassan, Mohammed Izhar (2005) : Population Geography, Rawat Publications, Jawahar Nagar, Jaipur, p. 74.
4. Woods, Robert (1982) : Factors Controlling Population Growth, Theoretical Population Geography, Longman, London and New York, p. 9.
5. Sauvy, A. (1969) : General Theory of Population, London Weidenfeld and Nicolson.
6. Harrison, G.A. and Boyce, A.J. (1972) : Geographical Influences on Size, Distribution and growth of Human Population, The Structure of Human Population, Clarendon Press, Oxford, p. 25.
7. Verma, K.K. (1977) : Growth, Culture, Ecology and Population, National Publishing House, 23, Daryaganj, New Delhi.
8. Ibid.
9. Qazi, S.A. & Qazi, Navaid Shabir (2006) : A.P.H. Publishing Corporation, New Delhi, 110002, p. 57.
10. Pearl, Raymond (1939) : The Natural History of Population, Oxford University Press, Oxfords.

11. Bhende, Asha, A and Kanitkar, T. (1978) : Population Growth and Socio-economic Development in India, Principles of Population Studies, Himalaya Publishing House, Bombay, p. 478.
12. Chandna, R.C. and Sindhu, M.S. (1980) : Op. Cit, p. 31.
13. Misra, R.P. (1989) : Population and Food Supply in M.P., Northern Book Centre, New Delhi, p. 21.
14. Srivastava. O.S. (1983) : A Text Book of Demography, Vikash Publishing House, New Delhi, p. 136.
15. Sinha, V.C. (1971) : Dynamics of India's Population Growth, National Publishing House New Delhi, p. 47.
16. Determinants and Consequences of Population Trends, U.N. 1976, p. 64.
17. Mehta, B.C. (1978) : Regional Population Growth : A Case Study of Rajasthan, p. 116.
18. Sinha, V.C. (1971) : Dynamics of India's Population Growth, p. 98.
19. U.N. (1976) : Determinants and Consequences of Population Trends, p. 66.
20. Bohra, D.M. (1973) : Rates and Levels of Mortality and Fertility in Ajmer, Geographer, Vol. V, p. 25.
21. Sinha, V.C. (1979) : Op. Cit., p. 104.
22. Mahto, K. (1985) : Population Mobility and Economic Development in Eastern India, New Delhi : Inter India Publication, p. 4.
23. Mehta, B.C. (1978) : Regional Population Growth : A Case Study of Rajasthan, p. 85.
24. Clark, J.I. (1966) : Population Geography, Pergaman Press, London, p. 26.
25. Mahto, K. (1985) : : Op. Cit., p. 1.
26. Demko, G.J. (1970) : Spatial Pattern of Population Flows in Population Geography, p.1.
27. Ibid.
28. Gould, W.T.S. and Prothero, R.M. (1976) : "Population

Mobility in Tropical Africa," In Mass, R.P. and Rathborne R.J.A. (eds.), The Population Factor in African Studies, London, p. 97.

29. Thomas, B. (1968) ; Migration : Economic Aspects, International Encyclopaedia of Social Sciences, p. 10.
30. Isard, M. (1960) : An Introduction to Regional Analysis, New York, Chapter-2.
31. Wolfenden, H.H. (1984) : Population Statistics and their Complication, Estimates of Population, J.A.S.A. Vol. XXXV, p. 390.
32. Harrison, G.A. and Boyce, A.J. (1975) : Op. Cit., p. 25.
33. Garnier, J.B. (1976) : National Population Growth and its Consequences, Geography of Population, Longman, London, p. 152.
34. Negi, B.G. : Op. Cit., p. 355.
35. Raj, Hans (1982) : Op. Cit., p. 290.

5

Chapter

Population Distribution

The Rohtas district contains 24,50,748 persons (2001) and they are distributed over an area of 3839.26 sq. kms. The distribution pattern of population is not uniform in the study area. This pattern has been noticed on the basis of the spatial pattern of population in various physical regions. According to table 5.1, 30.44 per cent of the study area (Mainly Northern Plain Area) contains 35.95 per cent of population, 46.85 per cent area (The Central High Plain) accounts for 54.07 per cent of population and 22.71 per cent area (Other Physical Regions) comprises only 9.98 per cent of population in 2001. Thus the former two areas which are comparatively plain and fertile contain large size of population where as the latter is largely hilly and forested consists of small percentage of population.

Table - 5.1
Area and Population Distribution

Name of Blocks	Area in sq. km.	Area in %	Population 2001	Population in %
Dinara, Dawath, Bikramganj, Suryapura, Sanjhauli, Kochas, Rajpur, Karakat	1168.94	30.44	881049	35.95
Kargahar, Nokha, Nasriganj, Chenari, Sheosagar, Sasaram, Akorhi Gola, Dehri	1798.14	46.85	1325000	54.07
Rohtas, Tilouthu, Nauhatta	872.18	22.71	244699	9.98
Total	3839.26	100.00	2450748	100.00

Source : Self Computed from Census data.

The spatial pattern of population, further, exhibits that 87 per cent of population is distributed in rural areas and 13 per cent population dwell in urban centres of Dawath, Bikramganj, Nokha, Sasaram and Dehri.

FACTORS AFFECTING POPULATION DISTRIBUTION:

The spatial pattern of population distribution is primarily governed by ecological[1], economic[2] and historical[3] (cultural) factors to varying degrees and the level of these factors disturbs the homogeneity of distribution[4], but at a local scale it exhibits[5] its importance.[6] It has rightly been remarked that population distribution is a dynamic process. Further, the economic characteristics of an area directly influence the population pattern.

(i) Ecological Factors :- There is general agreement that the ecological conditions such as the nature and degree of fertility of soil, the configuration of the surface, climatic conditions and spatial relations affect population distribution.[7] However, there are wide differences of opinion regarding the way in which the ecological elements operate in shaping the distribution of population. Such geographers as Huntington and Taylor accept ecological elements, particularly climate as direct controlling determinants. According to Mukhergee[8], the fertility of river valleys creates and maintains the greatest density of population.

(ii) Cultural Factors :- Among the cultural variables are the types of economic activities in which the people are engaged, the techniques of production, the from of social organisation and the objectives which the society seeks to attain. Factors affecting the distribution of population also include the methods of agriculture and techniques, irrigation and transport facilities and their form of social organization.[9] According to James, any change in altitudes, objectives or technical abilities of people inhabiting an area, requires a revaluation of the significance of the land.[10]

(iii)Demographic Factors : - These include the differential birth and death rates it different areas and the currents of migration.[11] Natural change of population has probably never offered more areal variations than during the nineteenth and twentieth centuries.[12]

ANCHALWISE POPULATION DISTRIBUTION :

As such the controlling variables of population distribution are not equally distributed throughout the district and it is therefore, the spatial pattern of population distribution is not uniform. According to Table 5.2 Sasaram block has the highest (12.08%) concentration of population in the district which is spread on 8.45 per cent area of the district. In terms of area Sasaram block ranks fourth. Dehri and Dinara contain 9.65 and 7.84 per cent of population of the region which inhabit on 4.22 and 8.07 per cent of land of the district of respectively. They rank second and third in terms of population size but occupy 11th and 6th position in areal coverage. The fourth important population bearing block is Kargahar. It accounts for 7.32 per cent of population on 8.65 per cent of land of the study area. The blocks of Sasaram and Dehri are ecologically, culturally and economically better situated. They, therefore, contain exceedingly higher percentage of population in relation to their area. The headquarters of these blocks are urban centres which are indicative of their economic development and potentiality of attracting people. Bikramganj and Nokha blocks are moderately developed and their population size is commensurate with their areal size. Table 5.2 further shows that the blocks of Karakat, Nasriganj, Dawath, Sanjhauli, Rajpur and Akorhi Gola account for a larger size of population distribution (fig. 5.1).

Table 5.2
Blockwise Area and Population Distribution in 2001

Sl.	Name of Blocks	Area in Sq. km.	Area in percent of Rohtas district	Total population	Population in percent of Rohtas district
1	Sasaram	324.16	8.45	296229	12.08

2	Dehri	162.1	4.22	233835	9.65
3	Dinara	309.07	8.07	192291	7.84
4	Kargahar	331.51	8.65	179556	7.32
5	karakat	203.53	5.30	179195	7.31
6	Nokha	169.1	4.40	145762	5.94
7	Sheosagar	331.3	8.64	144176	5.88
8	Bikramganj	137.28	3.57	136703	5.57
9	Nasriganj	131.59	3.42	119556	4.87
10	Kochas	217.04	5.65	119576	4.87
11	Chenari	243.68	6.34	107273	4.37
12	Akorhi Gola	104.7	2.72	98613	4.02
13	Dawath	106.38	2.77	92987	3.79
14	Tilouthu	156.4	4.07	90210	3.68
15	Rohtas	320.85	8.35	78625	3.20
16	Nauhatta	394.93	10.3	75864	3.09
17	Rajpur	70.41	1.83	60610	2.47
18	Sanjhauli	68.2	1.77	51465	2.09
19	Suryapura	57.03	1.48	48222	1.96
Total		3839.26	100.00	2450748	100.00

Source : Self Computed from Census Data.

In all these blocks both the percentage of population and land is low but the percentage of population is much higher then the percentage of area under them. These blocks avail almost the same amenities as the blocks of Dinara and Kargahar. These blocks are plain fertile area with good irrigation and communication facilities. In other blocks of the district the land extent exceeds the population size. In blocks of Nauhatta, Rohtas and Tilouthu the population size is lower than their areal extent. These blocks are largely hilly and forested and population habitation has rarely responded to such areas. Chenari and Sasaram blocks also exhibit the presence of hills and forests within their boundaries.

Thus, the plain blocks show a greater concentration of population distribution than hilly and forested blocks of the region. The forested highlands, rugged and rocky surface are negative areas of population.[13]

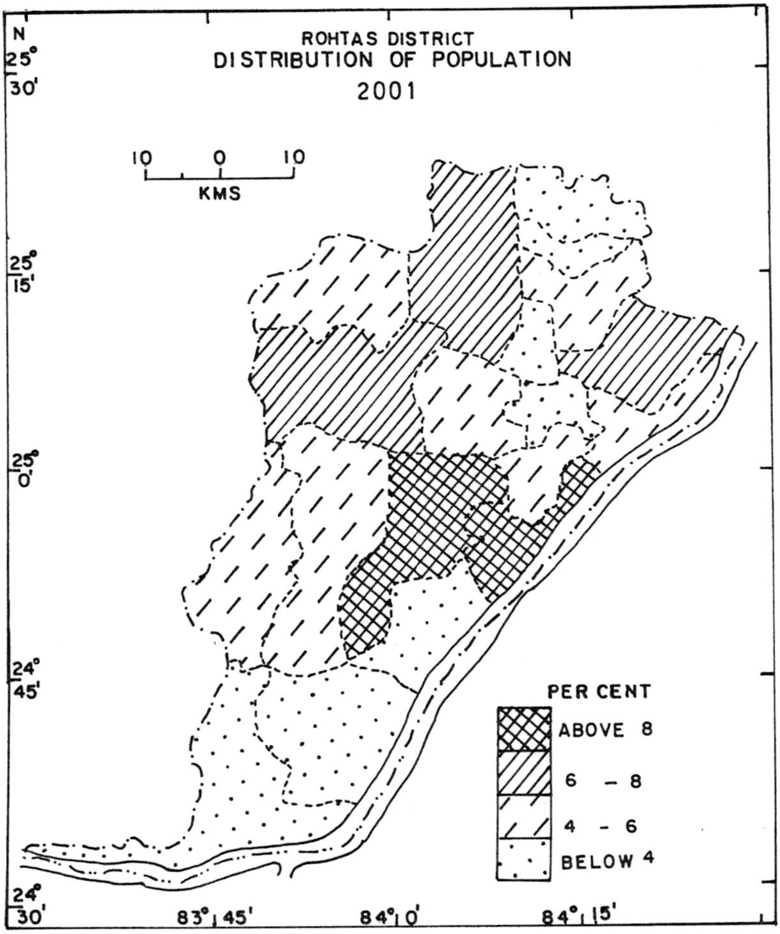
ROHTAS DISTRICT
DISTRIBUTION OF POPULATION
2001
N
25°
30'
25°
15'
25°
0'
24°
45'
24°
30'
83° 45'
84° 0'
84° 15'
10 0 10
KMS
PER CENT
ABOVE 8
6 - 8
4 - 6
BELOW 4

Fig. 5.1

POPULATION DISTRIBUTION IN PHYSICAL REGIONS :

Table 5.3 shows that the distribution of population in physical regions which is also not uniform. Three plain physical regions account for nearly 95.44 per cent of total population of Rohtas district and the rest 4 per cent of population reside in two hilly and forested regions. The plain region largely occupy the northern areas. According to Singh the gradually riging slopes of the south Ganga Plain dotted with residual hills appear as fringe of Chotanagpur highlands exhibit scantier concentration of population.[14] Population is dense towards the north in Rohtas district where the soil is fertile and a considerable area is served by irrigation, but towards the hilly south the density is very low. The percentage of area of the hilly and forested physical regions is generally larger than the percentage of population. Altogether the hilly comprise nearly 12 per cent of the study area on which 4.56 per cent of the district population resides. These areas are highly dissected and also contain rocky structure. On the other hand the plain regions contain nearly 88 per cent of total land and provide livelihood for about 95.44 per cent of total population. The Central High Plain consists of 61.40 per cent of total population occupying 46.34 per cent of total land of Rohtas district. This region exhibit flat, fertile and irrigated surface. This area also represents presence of means of transport.

Table - 5.3
Area and Population in Physical Regions in 2001

Sl. No.	Physical Regions	Area in percentage of total area of Rohtas district	Population in percentage of total population of Rohtas district
1	The Northern Low Plain	27.36	28.63
2	The Central High Plain	46.34	61.4
3	The South High Plain	14.81	5.41

4	The Northern Hilly Area	5.64	3.16
5	The Southern Hilly Area	5.85	1.4
Total		100	100

Source : Self Computed from Census Data.

POPULATION DISTRIBUTION IN AGRICULTURAL REGIONS :

Table 5.4 portrays that the distribution of population is uneven in different agricultural regions. The Intensive Agricultural Region accounts for 61.95 per cent of population on 51.33 per cent of total land of Rohtas district. This pocket contains the most fertile and irrigated agricultural fields. It also includes the urban centres of Koath, Bikramganj and Nokha. It comprises the blocks of Dinara, Dawath, Suryapura, Bikramganj, Karakat, Nasriganj, Rajpur, Nokha, Sanjhauli, Kargahar, Kochas and northern parts of Dehri. The Moderate Agricultural Region controls 30.02 percent of total land and is inhabited by 30.28 percent of total population. It is, thus, low to moderately populated with the density increasing towards the south. It consists of the blocks of Chenari, Sheosagar, Sasaram, Tilouthu and the Southern parts of Dehri. This agricultural region contains moderate surface condition i.e. physiography, drainage, climate, soils etc. The irrigation facilities are also moderate except in some parts of Chenari and Tilouthu. Poor Agricultural Region has 7.77 percent population living on 18.65 percent of total land of this district. This agricultural region consists mainly of Nauhatta and Rohtas blocks. A large part of Poor Agricultural Regions are hilly and forested and irrigational amenities are very poor. Most of the population is concentrated in relatively that pocket in this region. The areas having dissected surface and forest covered comprise a small size of population.

Table - 5.4
Area and Population in Agricultural Regions in 2001

Agricultural Regions	Area in sq. kms.	Area in percentage	Total population	Population in percentage
Intensive Agricultural Region	1970.68	51.33	1518070	61.95
Moderate Agricultural Region	1152.80	30.02	742105	30.28
Poor Agricultural Region	715.78	18.65	190573	7.77
Total	3839.26	100.00	2450748	100.00

Source : Self Computed from Census Data.

POPULATION DENSITY :

Population density refers to the population of a particular area per sq. mile or sq. kilometre[15]. The population of Rohtas district is 2450748 persons, while the area is 3839.26 sq. kms. resulting in a density of 638 persons per sq. km. in 2001. This is known as arithmetic density, a simple average. It is a crude measure and gives us a very broad picture of the actual situation. The arithmetic density is particularly misleading for regions which have only a few centres of concentrated population, the rest of the area being virtually uninhabited[16]. The regional density of population has steadily region from 333 persons per sq, kms. in 1971 to 410 persons per sq. kms. in 1981 and 499 persons per sq. kms. in 1991 (fig. 5.2).

The density of population of different blocks has been portrayed in map and by choropleth. Table 5.5 shows that the density is not uniform in all blocks. It may, however, be grouped into the following density zones

(i) Highly populated zone

(ii) Moderately populated zone and

(iii) Thinly populated zone.

(i) Highly Populated Zone :

It includes the blocks of Dehri, Dawath, Suryapura, Bikramganj, Karakat, Nasriganj, Rajpur, Nokha, Sasaram and Akorhi Gola. In these blocks the density of population ranges between 845 and 1442 persons per sq. km. respectively. It ranged from 473 to 928 and 580 to 1074 persons per sq. kms. in decadal years 1981 and 1991 respectively. Dehri block has scored the highest density (1442) in this district in 2001. All the blocks of this population zone comprise the richest agricultural lands of Rohtas district. This zone also includes the urban centres of Dehri, Koath (Dawath), Bikramganj, Nasriganj, Nokha and Sasaram towns. The richest agricultural zone combined with the presence of many urban centres have increased the number of population density in this zone.

Table - 5.5
Blockwise Density of Population in 1981,1991 & 2001

Sl. No.	Name of Blocks	Density per Sq. km. 1981	1991	2001
1	Dinara	469	566	622
2	Dawath	928	1074	874
3	Suryapura	-	-	845
4	Bikramganj	623	777	995
5	Karakat	593	701	880
6	Nasriganj	561	684	908
7	Rajpur	-	-	860
8	Nokha	473	580	861
9	Sanjhauli	-	-	754
10	Kargahar	296	365	541
11	Kochas	-	-	550
12	Chenari	265	333	440
13	Nauhatta	138	160	192
14	Sheosagar	273	333	435

15	Sasaram	638	823	913
16	Dehri	801	930	1442
17	Akorhi Gola	-	-	941
18	Rohtas	148	185	245
19	Tilouthu	-	-	576

Source : Self Computed from Census Data 1981, 1991 and 2001.

(ii) Moderately populated zone:

It spread over the blocks of Dinara, Sanjhauli, Kargahar, Kochas, Chenari, Sheosagar and Tilouthu. The density of population ranges between 435 and 754 persons per sq. km. in 2001. The range was from 265 to 469 and 333 to 566 persons per sq. km. in decadal year of 1981 and 1991 respectively. Amongst these blocks Sanjhauli shows the highest density in 2001 followed by Dinara, Tilouthu, Kochas, Kargahar, Chenari and Sheosagar. Sanjhauli is a fertile agricultural pocket. Tilouthu and Chenari blocks contain hills and forests in some parts. The plain parts of these blocks are equally fertile and suitable for good agriculture. The overall physical and cultural conditions in this zone represent moderate type. The resultant feature is density of population is, therefore, found moderate.

(iii)Thinly Populated Zone :

This zone includes the blocks of Rohtas and Nauhatta in Rohtas district. These blocks partake the characteristics of both plain as well as highland environment which influence population density accordingly. This zone exhibits only a few pockets of densely populated tract near towns.[17] The density of population ranged between 192 and 245 persons per sq. km. in 2001. It portrayed 138 and 148 persons, 160 and 185 persons per sq. km. in decadal year 1981 and 1991 respectively. In this zone Rohtas block contained the highest density in 1991 and 2001 census years. In both these blocks have hills, undulating surfaces and forests in this large parts. Consequent upon the pattern of density of population is

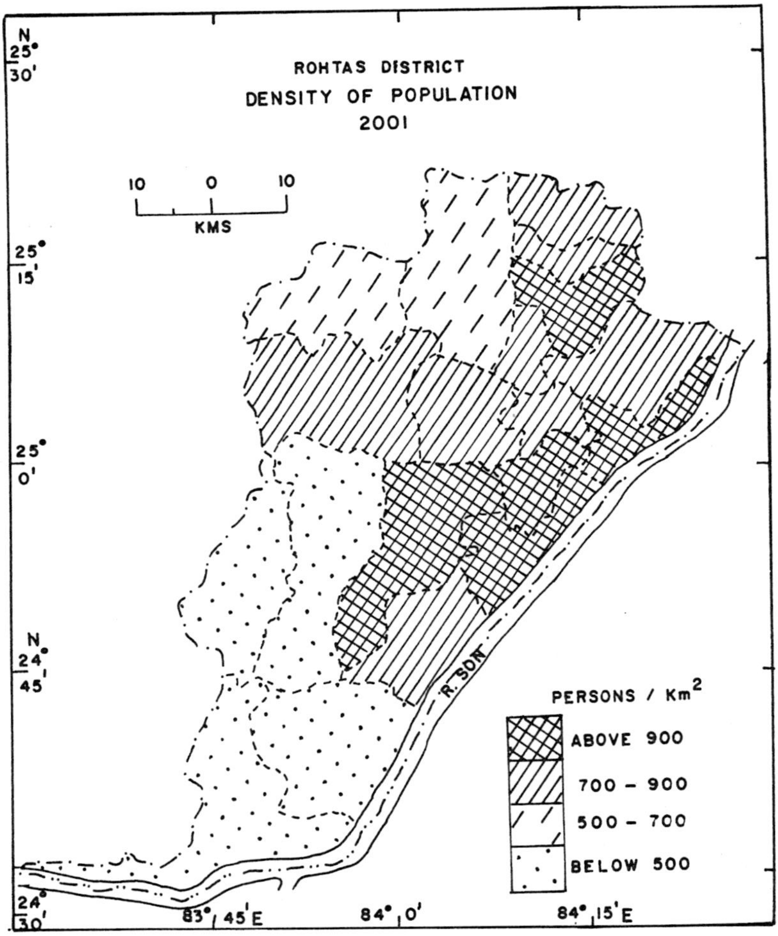
ROHTAS DISTRICT
DENSITY OF POPULATION
2001
10 0 10
KMS
N 25° 30'
25° 15'
25° 0'
N 24° 45'
24° 30'
83° 45' E
84° 0'
84° 15' E
R. SON
PERSONS / Km²
ABOVE 900
700 - 900
500 - 700
BELOW 500

Fig. 5.2

sparse. This area exhibits poor cultural and economic developments.

PATTERN OF POPULATION DENSITY IN PHYSICAL REGIONS :

The density of population is not uniform in various physical regions. Table 5.6 shows that the density per sq. km. is higher in two physical regions. These regions are northern low plain and central high plain. Population density has remained high in the central high plain throughout the three decades. This region had 557, 681 and 845 persons per sq. km. in 1981, 1991 and 2001 respectively. The northern low plain had 405, 487 and 667 persons per sq. km. in 1981, 1991 and 2001 respectively. These two physical regions have the facilities of canals irrigation, plain fertile soil, high water table, etc. These areas also represent the presence of other cultural facilities.

Table - 5.6
Density of Population (per sq. km.) in Physical Regions

Sl. No.	Physical regions	1981	1991	2001
1	Northern Low Plain	405	487	667
2	Central High Plain	557	681	845
3	Southern Higher Plain	234	288	368
4	Northern Hilly Area	33	42	59
5	Southern Hilly Area	80	95	102

Source : Self Calculated from Census Data.

Other physical regions are sparsely to moderately populated. Southern higher plain is moderately populated. This region is dotted with hills but plain pockets are fertile and have irrigational facilities. The physical regions of northern hilly area and southern hilly area are thinly populated. These areas are largely hilly and forested. The population is mainly concentrated in plain parts of these regions.

All physical regions do not have the same physical and

socio-economic conditions and consequently they display an uneven growth of population density. Table 5.7 exhibits that the variation of population density follows the absolute density of population. It has remained high in densely populated physical regions and low in thinly populated areas. The most highly populated regions of the central high plain and the northern low plain exhibit the greatest density variation in persons i.e. 165 and 180 per sq. km. between decadal periods of 1991-2001 respectively. The southern higher plain shows the next highest density variation. The thinly and moderately populated regions exhibit a lower variation of density. The highly populated regions contain agricultural pockets which are definitely responsible for the greater variation of population density. On the other hand the hilly and forested physical regions have adverse conditions for human habitation and subsequently the density of population and density variation are lower.

The higher percentage of density variation in hilly and forested physical regions my be due to the fact that even a little change of population makes a big increase in percentage because the size of population is small. A higher birth rate in these areas may be on account of large illiteracy of the people.

Table - 5.7
Variation of Population Density in Physical Regions

Sl.	Physical regions	Variation in persons 1981-91	Variation in persons 1991-2001	Variation in Percent	
				1981-1991	1991-2001
1	Northern Low Plain	82	180	20.31	37.06
2	Central High Plain	123	165	22.21	24.21
3	Southern Higher Plain	54	79	23.14	27.56
4	Northern Hilly Area	8	16	25.75	39.6
5	Southern Hilly Area	15	7	19.68	7.17

Source : Self Calculated from Census Data.

The plain and fertile physical regions are marked by

higher density variation because of the higher natural growth. This happen because these areas contain large size of population. Large population has higher multiplying capacity of population.

PATTERN OF POPULATION DENSITY IN AGRICULTURAL REGIONS :

There is an uneven pattern of density of population in various agricultural regions. The disparity has been increasing with the progress of time. Table 5.8 shows that intensive agricultural region has higher density of population which has further increased from 488 to 773 during 1981-2001. This region occupies the plain and fertile areas of Rohtas district. There areas avail the facilities of canal irrigation, high water-table, transport and communication etc. The presence of urban agglomerations of Kowath (Dawath), Bikramganj, Nasriganj and Nokha have also contributed to a higher density of population in this region.

Table - 5.8
Population Density in Agricultural Regions

Agricultural Regions	1981	1991	2001
Intensive Agricultural Region	488	593	773
Moderate Agricultural Region	440	539	674
Poor Agricultural Region	150	181	216

Source : Self Calculated from Census Data.

Second agricultural region is moderate agricultural region which exhibits a growth of density from 440 in 1981 to 674 in 2001. This region comprises the blocks which are partly hilly and the population has mainly gravitated to the agricultural pockets having fertile soil, irrigation facilities and high water-table.

Poor agricultural region has a low density of population. Here the density of population varies from 150 in 1981 to 216 in 2001. This region comprises Nauhatta and Rohtas blocks. These blocks are largely hilly and forested which has adversely affected the population habitation. So the population density is low in this region of the district.

Table 5.9 shows that the plain and fertile agricultural region i.e. Intensive agricultural region has embraced the greatest variation of population density both in terms of persons and percentage during 1991-2001. However the percentage growth was somewhat lower during 1981-91. Moderate agricultural region exhibited a variation of 22 and 25 per cent population during the decades of 1981-91 and 1991-2001 respectively. This agricultural region witnessed the second highest variation of density both in persons and percentage. Poor agricultural region occupies third position in the variation of persons and percentage of density. Half of the area of this region is hilly and forested. This agricultural region has small size of population inhabiting on small size of land. The variation of population density has therefore not decrease with the prepress of time. Other contributing factors may be higher birth rate and death rate because of prevalence of illiteracy in this area of the district.

Table - 5.9

Variation of Population Density in Agricultural Regions

Agricultural Regions	Density variation in persons		Density variation in percentage	
	1981-91	1991-01	1981-91	1991-01
Intensive Agricultural Region	105	180	21	30
Moderate Agricultural Region	99	135	22	25
Poor Agricultural Region	31	35	20	19

Source : Self Calculated from Census Data.

Thus, the population distribution in Rohtas district has been attempted on various levels and it has been arrived at that the spatial pattern of population in Rohtas district is uneven in its various parts. A variety of physical, economic and cultural factors are responsible for the development of such pattern of population in the study area. Broadly the plain and fertile regions have got high concentration of population while hilly and forested areas contain small size of population.

References :

1. Negi, B.S. : Op. Cit., p. 362.
2. Sinha, R.B. (March, 1981) : "Demographic Structure and Typology of Population Resource : A Case Study of Siwan District (Bihar), Indian Geographical Studies, research Bulletin no. 16, Geographical Research Centre, Patna-5, India, p. 35.
3. Negi, B.S. : Op. Cit., p. 362.
4. Singh, R.B. : Op. Cit., p. 35.
5. Negi, B.S. : Op. Cit., p. 362.
6. Harrison, G.A. and Boyce, A.J. (1975) : Op. Cit., p. 25.
7. Negi, B.S. : Op. Cit., p. 362.
8. Mukherjee, M. The Political Economy of Population, pp. 112-113.
9. Negi, B.S. : Op. Cit., p. 368.
10. James (1949) : A Geography of Man, p. 27.
11. Negi, B.S. : Op. Cit., p. 370.
12. Harrison, G.A. and Boyce, A.J. : Op. Cit., p. 25.
13. Singh, R.P. and Kumar, Anil (1970) : Distribution of Population Monograph of Bihar, Bharti Bhawan, Patna, p. 102.
14. Singh, R.P. and Kumar, A. (1970) : Op. Cit., p. 102.
15. Bhende, Asha A. and Kanitkar, T. (1978) : Measures of Population Distribution, Principles of Population Studies, Himalaya Publishing House, p. 392.
16. Ibid, pp. 392-393.
17. Thakur, B. (1980) : Urban Settlements- Eastern India : Entropy Changes and Pattern Analysis, Concept Publishing Co., New Delhi, p. 100.

6

Chapter

Population Composition

SPATIAL PATTERN OF SEX RATIO :

The sex ratio, an indicator of the relative number of males and females in a population is a basic measure in demography.[1] It is important because it has serious bearing on the labour supply, marriage rate, fertility and such other social problems like prostitution, polygamy, etc.[2] Table 6.1 shows that excess of male over female is the characteristic of urban landscape[3], in decadal years 1981, 1991 and 2001. In the rural areas of Rohtas district the sex ratio also exhibits the same pattern but it is relatively better. The combined urban and rural sex ratio also portrays the same pattern of sex ratio. The difference, however, is small. In Bihar state, the sex ratio is the number of females per 1000 males. The most probable cause for relatively higher female ratio in rural areas and preponderance of males in urban areas of Rohtas district is the out- migration of males from rural areas to towns and to neighbouring districts in search of employment.[4]

Table - 6.1
Sex Ratio (Female per 1000 males)

	1981	1991	2001
Urban	839	876	884
Rural	920	897	913
Combined Urban & Rural	909	894	909

Source : Self Computed from Census Data.

Table - 6.2
Blockwise Sex Ratio (Female per 1000 males)

Sl. No.	Name of Blocks	1981	1991	2001
1	Kochas	-	-	898
2	Dinara	911	895	913
3	Dawath	942	901	925
4	Suryapura	-	-	934
5	Bikramganj	915	903	907
6	Karakat	944	923	928
7	Nasriganj	934	909	927
8	Rajpur	-	-	924
9	Sanjhauli	-	-	910
10	Nokha	937	908	916
11	Kargahar	916	886	898
12	Chenari	909	893	905
13	Nauhatta	901	909	919
14	Sheosagar	917	881	917
15	Sasaram	893	888	893
16	Akorhi Gola	-	-	908
17	Dehri	857	878	892
18	Tilouthu	-	-	915
19	Rohtas	890	865	908

Source : Self Computed from Census Data.

Table 6.2 further provides detailed insight in to spatial and temporal pattern of sex ratio. It shows that the females per 1000 males have remained generally low in blocks which form fertile agricultural belts such as Kochas, Kargahar. In these blocks the male persons do not go outside for jobs because the fertile fields provide plenty of work and potentialities for livelihood. Sasaram and Dehri blocks also exhibit low sex ratio. High urbanisation is the main factor for low sex ratio. In other blocks either female population is close to the male population is excess of the male population in the same decennial livelihood and the male workers are forced to emigrate elsewhere for employment (fig. 6.1).

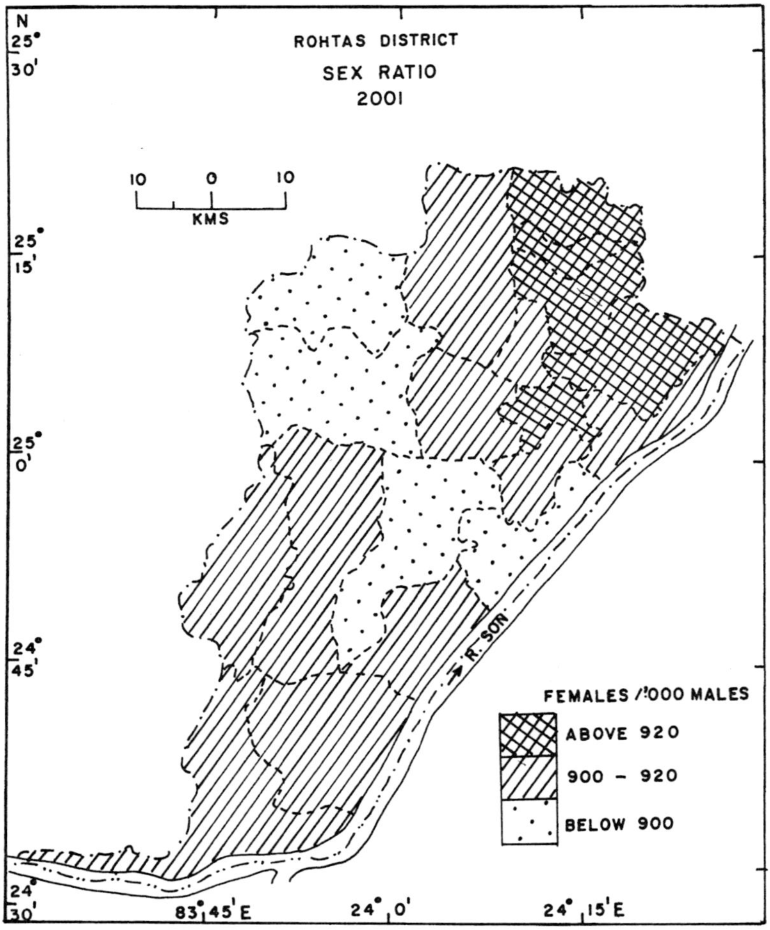
ROHTAS DISTRICT
SEX RATIO
2001
10 0 10
KMS
N
25° 30'
25° 15'
25° 0'
24° 45'
24° 30'
83° 45' E
24° 0'
24° 15' E
R. SON
FEMALES /1000 MALES
ABOVE 920
900 - 920
BELOW 900

Fig. 6.1

Table 6.3 shows the spatial and temporal pattern of male-female ratio in percentage. The percentage of female population is generally low in fertile agricultural blocks and high in blocks of relatively poor agriculture. Altogether the female sex ratio in % has lower both spatially and temporally. The above stated phenomena may be observed with the close inspection of the table no. 6.3. The female percentage, however, has always remained higher in comparison to other parts of Bihar state. It explains that Rohtas district either provides better nourishment and love for women folk or does not provide facilities for livelihood. The latter is obviously the correct explanation, as it leads to male out- migration.

Table 6.3

Blockwise Sex Structure (in Percentage)

Sl. No.	Name of Blocks	1981 Male	1981 Female	1991 Male	1991 Female	2001 Male	2001 Female
1	Kochas	-	-	-	-	2.57	2.30
2	Dinara	4.81	4.39	4.81	4.31	4.10	3.74
3	Dawath	3.22	3.04	3.13	2.82	1.97	1.82
4	Suryapura	-	-	-	-	1.01	0.95
5	Bikramganj	4.01	3.67	4.13	3.73	2.92	2.65
6	Karakat	3.94	3.72	3.87	3.57	3.79	3.51
7	Nasriganj	3.72	3.47	3.77	3.43	2.53	2.34
8	Rajpur	-	-	-	-	1.28	1.18
9	Sanjhauli	-	-	-	-	1.90	1.00
10	Nokha	3.68	3.45	3.76	3.41	3.10	2.84
11	Kargahar	5.38	4.93	5.53	4.90	3.85	3.46
12	Chenari	2.14	1.95	2.23	2.00	2.29	2.08
13	Nauhatta	1.81	1.63	1.72	1.57	1.61	1.48
14	Sheosagar	2.99	2.74	3.50	2.69	3.06	2.81
15	Sasaram	6.93	6.19	7.37	6.54	6.38	5.70
16	Akorhi Gola	-	-	-	-	2.10	1.91
17	Dehri	7.31	6.26	6.88	6.50	5.04	4.49
18	Tilouthu	-	-	-	-	1.92	1.75
19	Rohtas	2.37	2.11	2.47	2.14	1.68	1.52

Source : Self Computed from Census Data.

LITERACY :

The United Nations has defined literacy as the ability of a person to read and write with understanding a short simple statement in his every day life.[5] According to the census 1971, a person who can both read and write with understanding in any language is to be taken as a literate.[6] One of the important indicators of social development is the level of literacy and educational attainment, a high level of which is considered to be an important factor in the process of modernization.[7] The wealth of a nation lies not only in the material resources at its command but also in the energy, technological level, initiative and the moral fibre of the people.[8] This is why the development of human resources was recognised as one of the basic objectives of the country since 1957.[9]

The district under study is marked by a high level of literacy. It has remained at 32.55, 48.52 and 61.29 per cent of total population in the decadal years 1981, 1991 and 2001 respectively. But, it is recorded more than the state of Bihar as a whole (47.53%) in 2001. More depressing than the slow progress of general literacy is the position of literate women in the district. This accounts to only 8.24, 14.14 and 21.64 per cent of total population in the census years 1981, 1991 and 2001 respectively. In Bihar state the female literacy out of total population has remained at 33.47 per cent in 2001. The lower percentage of female literacy in the region may be one of the major reasons for many of our problems relating to socio-economic development.[10] The male literacy in the same decennial years, has remained at 22.31, 34.37 and 39.65 per cent respectively. It is 60.32 per cent in Bihar as a whole in 2001. Thus the literacy percentage both among the males and females is 47.53 than in Bihar State (fig. 6.2).

The chief reasons for the high level of literacy are comparatively good infra- structural development, awareness of people's and socio-cultural developments as well as increase in no. of schools & allied educational facility in the district during last decades.[11]. The excessive illiteracy among females is the product of the thinking masses who perceive

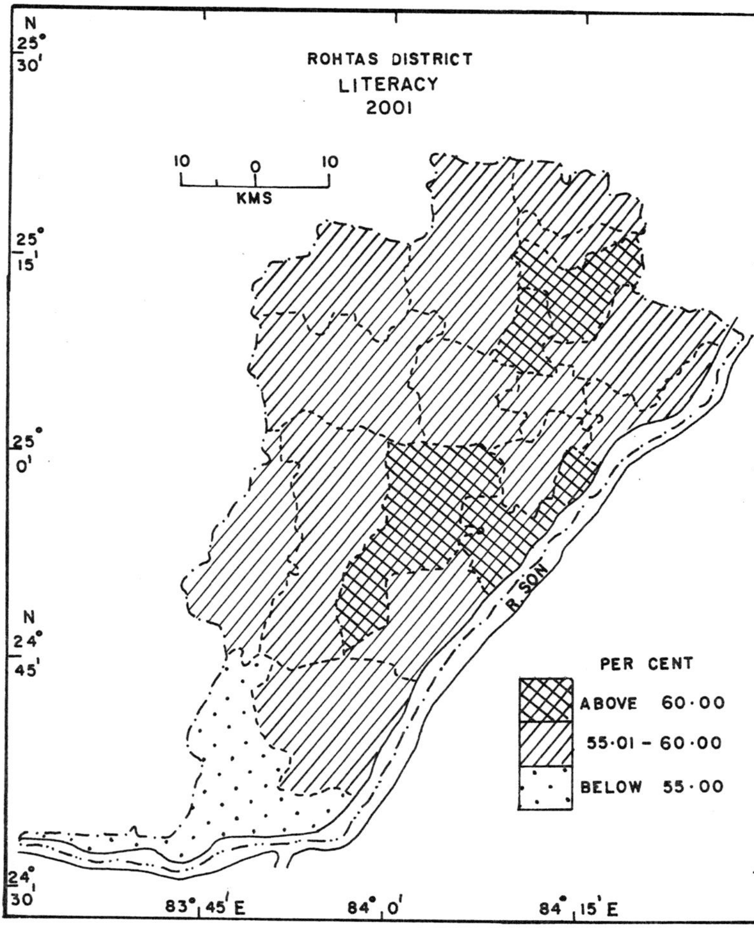
ROHTAS DISTRICT
LITERACY
2001
10 0 10
KMS
N
25°
30'
25°
15'
25°
0'
N
24°
45'
24°
30'
83° 45' E
84° 0'
84° 15' E
R. SON
PER CENT
ABOVE 60·00
55·01 - 60·00
BELOW 55·00

Fig. 6.2

an ideal female as a dutiful home bird[12]. Secondly women in general enjoy a relatively low status in the society. Thirdly, not only the educational institutions for girls are few and far between but also the number of female teachers ready to work in rural areas has been inadequate until recently. Fourthly girls are not allowed much mobility[13] and it is rare that a female child is sent to a school in only the adjoining village. Fifthly early marriage takes away girls from schools even before they become literate. Sixthly the people in general have a feeling that the ultimate home of the girl is her husband's abode and an investment in her education will not bring any economic benefit to her parents[14] lastly, the educated girls are to be married to educated persons and educated persons demand higher dowry these days.

Spatial and Temporal Pattern of Literacy :

Table 6.4 exhibits that out of total literate persons 79.59, 81.08 and 83.29 percent is constituted by rural literates and 20.41, 18.92 and 16.71 percent are urban literates in the decennial years 1981, 1991 and 2001 respectively. During the same period the percentage of literacy of female has remained constant in case of urban literates and the same has increased in rural literates. The percentage of male literates has however, decreased in both urban and rural literates.

Table 6.4
Percentage of Literacy (Urban and Rural) Out of Total Literate Persons

	1981	1991	2001
Urban	20.41	18.92	16.71
Male	13.68	11.97	9.99
Female	6.73	6.95	6.72
Rural	79.59	81.08	83.29
Male	61.24	58.89	54.69
Female	18.35	22.19	28.60

Source : Self Computed from Census Data.

Table 6.5 shows that the percentage of literate persons

out of total population in rural areas i.e. 28.42, 45.88 and 59.23 and in urban areas i.e. 50.29, 64.38 and 74.14 in decennial years 1981, 1991 and 2001 respectively. In both rural and urban areas the literacy of males and females has increased but the rate of change in female literacy has been higher than among the males. The rate of literacy is also increasing more in rural areas than in urban areas. The above explanation thus attracted that rural people are actively participating in get them educated.

Table 6.5
Percentage of Literacy (Urban and Rural) Out of Total Urban and Rural Population Separately

	1981	1991	2001
Urban	50.29	64.38	74.14
Male	62.08	63.25	59.81
Female	36.19	36.74	40.18
Rural	28.42	45.88	59.23
Male	42.14	72.63	65.66
Female	13.45	27.37	34.34

Source : Self Computed from Census Data.

Table 6.5 also explains that during the recent decades people have witnessed a great change even in traditional agrarian societies. The gap between the male and female literacy rates is decreasing rapidly. The opening of a large number of schools in rural areas with increasing number of female teachers and the increasing male literacy figures have in themselves stimulated advancement in the field of female literacy. Besides, education for females is increasingly becoming a matrimonial necessity.

Table 6.6 further explains that literacy has increased with the progress of time among both male and female persons in all blocks of Rohtas district. Despite thus, female literacy during 2001 is high in some blocks like Sasaram (3.11%), Dehri (2.57%), Kargahar (1.57%), Dinara (1.51%) and Karakat (1.54%) low female literacy rate is found in Suryapura (0.37%),

Rajpur (0.49%), Sanjhauli (0.47%) and Nauhatta (0.42%) blocks. Other blocks have female literacy above 0.5 percent of total population. Male literacy is also high in those blocks where female literacy is high. Male literacy during 2001 is very high in Sasaram (5.02%) and Dehri (4.22%) blocks and very low in Suryapura (0.74%), Rajpur (0.96%), Nauhatta (0.97%) and Sanjhauli (0.88%) blocks. Literacy is more in plain agricultural blocks because the people of these blocks are better able to meet financial requirements needed for education. The percentage of literacy is very low in hilly and forested blocks and some those blocks made after 1991 i.e. Suryapura, Rajpur and Sanjhauli blocks. The aforesaid explanation truly correspond with the cultural and economic pattern of the study area.

Table - 6.6
Blockwise Literacy Level in Percentage Out of Total Population of Rohtas District in Percent

Sl. No.	Name of Blocks	1981 Male	1981 Female	1991 Male	1991 Female	2001 Male	2001 Female
1	Kochas	-	-	-	-	1.87	1.01
2	Dinara	1.93	0.67	2.98	1.11	3.03	1.51
3	Dawath	1.45	0.49	2.15	0.81	1.48	0.78
4	Suryapura	-	-	-	-	0.74	0.37
5	Bikramganj	1.97	0.66	2.77	1.16	2.33	1.29
6	Karakat	1.89	0.57	2.61	0.98	2.94	1.54
7	Nasriganj	1.76	0.56	2.54	1.03	1.92	1.04
8	Rajpur	-	-	-	-	0.96	0.49
9	Sanjhauli	-	-	-	-	0.88	0.47
10	Nokha	1.68	0.59	2.39	0.96	2.29	1.21
11	Kargahar	2.09	0.78	2.52	1.45	2.90	1.57
12	Chenari	0.80	0.24	1.31	0.45	1.57	0.81
13	Nauhatta	0.63	0.15	0.81	0.24	0.97	0.42
14	Sheosagar	1.21	0.32	1.86	0.64	2.25	1.19
15	Sasaram	2.95	1.37	4.94	2.40	5.02	3.11
16	Akorhi Gola	-	-	-	-	1.61	0.84
17	Dehri	4.21	1.55	5.04	2.36	4.22	2.57
18	Tilouthu	-	-	-	-	1.38	0.75

19 Rohtas	0.91	0.29	1.45	0.55	1.18	0.63
Total	22.31	8.24	34.31	14.14	39.54	21.64

Source : Self Computed from Census Data.

Table 6.7 exhibits that the percentage variation of literacy calculated out of total population is greater in the rural areas than in the urban areas. The same trend is found in case of male literacy variation female literacy variation is, however larger in case of urban literacy. Altogether the percentage of variation is positive both in case of male and female (both in urban and rural literacy). Percentage variation of literacy have however, become quit large during 1991-2001.

Table 6.7
Percentage Variation of Literacy (Urban and Rural) Out of Total Urban and Rural Population Separately

	1981-1991	1991-2001
Rural Literacy	+13.29	+31.77
Male	+8.23	+17.66
Female	+4.94	+14.03
Urban Literacy	+15.60	+29.31
Male	+7.98	+15.32
Female	+7.62	+13.99

Source : Self Computed from Census Data.

In spite of the aforesaid facts there is need of faster development of literacy in rural areas where about 87 per cent of the population resides. A skilful and proper utilization of land resources requires literate persons who can understand, appreciate and adopt modern beneficial and progressive techniques of land utilization.[15]

SCHEDULED CASTES :

According to table no. 6.8 scheduled castes share 17.44, 17.31 and 18.13 per cent of total population of Rohtas district in 1981, 1991 and 2001 respectively. The scheduled caste population is distributed over the entire district. It is, however, more concentrated in the blocks of Sasaram and Kargahar which share 1.92 and 1.58 per cent of the scheduled caste population of Rohtas district. Individually each six blocks namely Dinara, Karakat, Nokha, Chenari, Sheosagar and Dehri shared more than 1 per cent of the population of scheduled caste in 1981, 1991 and 2001. In rest blocks of the district the percentage of scheduled caste is at. Suryapura (0.30%) and Rajpur (0.40%) blocks represent the lowest percentage of scheduled caste population in 2001. Table 6.8 however, shows that the percentage of scheduled caste population has increased in almost blocks of Rohtas district in 1981, 1991 and 2001 (fig. 6.3).

Table - 6.8
Blockwise Scheduled Caste Population in Percentage Out of Total Population of Rohtas District

Sl. No.	Name of Blocks	1981	1991	2001
1	Kochas	-	-	0.89
2	Dinara	1.60	1.62	1.49
3	Dawath	0.93	0.88	0.58
4	Suryapura	-	-	0.30
5	Bikramganj	1.26	1.27	0.92
6	Karakat	1.33	1.27	1.31
7	Nasriganj	1.16	1.14	0.76
8	Rajpur	-	-	0.40
9	Sanjhauli	-	-	0.37
10	Nokha	1.22	1.26	1.04
11	Kargahar	2.03	2.04	1.58
12	Chenari	1.03	0.94	1.14
13	Nauhatta	0.68	0.66	0.60
14	Sheosagar	1.18	1.22	1.29
15	Sasaram	2.20	2.22	1.92
16	Akorhi Gola	-	-	0.90
17	Dehri	2.01	1.95	1.29
18	Tilouthu	-	-	0.76
19	Rohtas	0.81	0.84	0.59
Total		17.44	17.31	18.13

Source : Self Computed from Census Data.

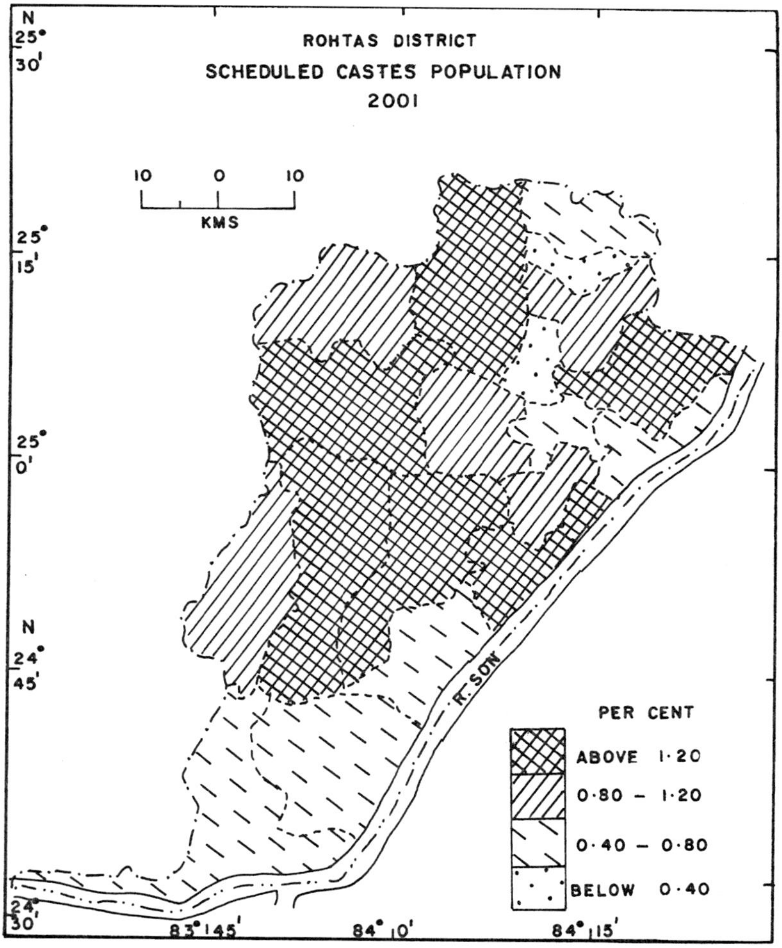
ROHTAS DISTRICT
SCHEDULED CASTES POPULATION
2001
10 0 10
KMS
N
25° 30'
25° 15'
25° 0'
N
24° 45'
24° 30'
83° 45'
84° 10'
84° 15'
R. SON
PER CENT
ABOVE 1·20
0·80 – 1·20
0·40 – 0·80
BELOW 0·40

Fig. 6.3

Table 6.9 exhibits that in majority of blocks, scheduled caste population shares between 15 to 22 per cent of total population of respective block. Only Chenari block in 1981 and 1991 and Akorhi Gola and Chenari blocks in 2001 contained more than 22 per cent of their population as scheduled caste population Dehri block has the lowest percentage of scheduled caste population. Table 6.9 further indicates that the percentage of scheduled caste persons has increased in a majority of blocks except in Nasriganj, Nokha, Sasaram and Dehri between 1991 and 2001.

Table - 6.9
Blockwise Scheduled Caste Population in Percentage Out of Total Population of each Block

Name of Blocks	1981	1991	2001
Kochas	-	-	18.29
Dinara	17.40	17.80	19.05
Dawath	14.84	14.88	15.39
Rural	13.12	13.02	12.65
Urban	1.72	1.86	2.75
Suryapura	-	-	15.06
Bikramganj	16.36	16.11	16.59
Rural	14.51	14.21	14.06
Urban	1.85	1.90	2.53
Karakat	17.23	17.07	17.90
Nasriganj	16.16	15.79	15.53
Rural	15.25	14.85	15.53
Urban	0.91	0.94	-
Rajpur	-	-	16.32
Sanjhauli	-	-	17.36
Nokha	17.05	17.52	17.46
Rural	17.05	15.98	15.59
Urban	-	1.54	1.87
Kargahar	19.57	19.58	21.52
Chenari	25.16	22.11	25.67
Nauhatta	19.66	19.97	19.58
Sheosagar	20.62	21.19	22.00
Sasaram	16.78	15.93	15.89

Rural	14.21	13.42	12.81
Urban	2.57	2.51	3.08
Akorhi Gola	-	-	22.40
Dehri	14.84	15.05	13.51
Rural	11.18	11.52	8.79
Urban	3.66	3.53	4.72
Tilouthu	-	-	20.70
Rohtas	18.03	18.12	18.43

Source : Self Computed from Census Data.

The total variation of scheduled caste persons out of total population in the district has been recorded as +3.64 and +5.86 per cent during 1981-91 and 1991-2001. This shows a higher natural growth of these persons. However, their number is not uniformly distributed all over the district. These people are primarily landless labourers but some of them have their traditional occupations. They perform useful functions in the society and constitute an essential element in population geography. They are, however looked down upon by the society in general. This is certainly a disgraceful act often witnessed even in the present society.

Towns have plenty of jobs for scheduled caste population from lanes to lawns and promising to the core of farm and factory. They are represented from primary school to universities performing all laudable duties of true citizens.[16]

SCHEDULED TRIBES :

These people share only 0.96, 1.03 and 1.04 per cent of the total population of the district in 1981, 1991 and 2001 respectively. They are found mainly in Nauhatta, Sasaram and Rohtas blocks. These blocks account for 0.37, 0.15 and 0.26 per cent in 1981, 0.37, 0.13 and 0.26 per cent in 1991 and 0.34, 0.19 and 0.23 per cent in 2001 of the total population under scheduled tribe. Thus, the tribal people are mainly distributed in hilly and forested blocks of the district.

The total variation of scheduled tribe population in relation to total population of the district has increased only

+0.30 and +0.31 per cent during 1981-91 and 1991-2001 respectively.

OCCUPATIONAL STRUCTURE :

In any population there are very few individuals to whom the universal need for work does not apply.[17] The earning of bread in most of the societies is, however, primarily the male responsibility.[18] That is why attempts have been made to describe the male workers. Table 6.10 comprises that the percentage of male workers in the total working force in all blocks of Rohtas district is larger in comparison to female workers. The percentage of participation of male and female has, however, remained uneven in many blocks and the district as a whole during the decadal years 1981-2001.

The extent of females participation in work in any area depends primarily upon the status which they enjoy in the society; the extent to which they are allowed mobility, the economic exigencies necessitating their participation in work; the availability of suitable jobs for females and the desire on the part of the females to avail themselves of these opportunities.[19]

Similarly, disparities also exist in the proportion of working population among urban and rural areas. The size of working force in rural areas is relatively large in comparison with the urban areas.[20] Both child and female participation in economic activities in rural areas are relatively high as compared to urban areas.[21] There also exists an unescapable causal relationship between the age of a person and his potentially as a worker. The age group of 15-60 years is the most active in the region.[22]

Table 6.10 also describes that the proportion of workers is larger in those blocks which have a bigger population size.

Occupational Categories of Working Force :

Man's accomplishments are largely written in his occupational structure.[23] It holds immense significance as it

Table - 6.10
Blockwise Working Force

Sl. No.	Name of Blocks	1981 % of total workers of Rohtas district	1981 Percentage of workers to total workers Male	1981 Percentage of workers to total workers Female	1991 % of total workers of Rohtas district	1991 Percentage of workers to total workers Male	1991 Percentage of workers to total workers Female	2001 % of total workers of Rohtas district	2001 Percentage of workers to total workers Male	2001 Percentage of workers to total workers Female
1	Kochas	-	-	-	-	-	-	5.00	3.92	1.08
2	Dinara	9.65	8.19	1.46	9.64	7.97	1.67	8.77	6.55	2.22
3	Dawath	6.30	5.33	0.97	5.93	5.09	0.84	3.51	2.99	0.52
4	Suryapura	-	-	-	-	-	-	1.72	1.53	0.19
5	Bikramganj	7.97	6.76	1.21	7.36	6.41	0.95	4.96	4.2	0.76
6	Karakat	7.24	6.48	0.76	7.36	6.23	1.13	7.40	5.82	1.58
7	Nasriganj	7.26	6.33	0.93	7	6.09	0.91	4.86	3.81	1.05
8	Rajpur	-	-	-	-	-	-	2.84	2.06	0.78
9	Sanjhauli	-	-	-	-	-	-	2.12	1.71	0.41
10	Nokha	7.24	6.19	1.05	7.54	6.15	1.39	6.30	4.80	1.50
11	Kargahar	10.02	8.94	1.80	10.53	8.85	1.68	7.86	5.97	1.89

12	Chenari	4.89	3.8	1.09	4.54	3.67	0.87	4.63	3.47	1.16
13	Nauhatta	4.06	3.19	0.87	3.90	2.88	1.02	3.66	2.60	1.06
14	Sheosagar	6.49	5.24	1.25	6.44	5.06	1.38	6.18	4.70	1.48
15	Sasaram	12.04	10.81	1.23	14.12	11.53	2.59	11.04	9.02	2.02
16	Akorhi Gola	-	-	-	-	-	-	4.26	3.24	1.02
17	Dehri	12.59	11.81	0.78	11.15	10.34	0.81	8.38	7.11	1.27
18	Tilouthu	-	-	-	-	-	-	3.63	2.82	0.81
19	Rohtas	4.25	3.93	0.32	4.48	3.87	0.61	2.88	2.44	0.44
	Total	100.00	87.00	13.00	100.00	84.14	15.85	100.00	78.76	21.24

Source : Self Computed from Census Data.

reveals : (i) whether a country's economy is agricultural, industrial or semi-industrial; (ii) its level of economic development and (iii) the direction which the entire process of planning a country could follow.[24]

Rohtas district is largely rural and agricultural in character. Table 6.11 shows that the cultivators and agricultural labourers dominate the occupational structure in the district. The proportion of cultivators has, however, decreased and the percentage of agricultural labourers has remained variable. These two workers are of basic primary categories. Household workers are small in size. Other workers and marginal workers are however, in population in study area.

Table - 6.11
Occupational Structure

Sl. No.	Categories of Workers	1981	1991	2001
1	Cultivators	41.18	39.18	29.91
2	Agricultural Labourers	31.71	35.50	21.85
3	Household Industry	2.15	1.44	2.58
4	Other Workers	19.43	17.56	18.86
5	Marginal Workers	5.53	6.32	26.80
	Total	100.00	100.00	100.00

Source : Census Data and Self Computation.

Table 6.12 further shows that the primary workers portray a decreasing trend in majority of blocks. It explains that the people are diverting their interest from the fields. The probable causes are uncertainly of rainfall, inadequate irrigational facilities, undesirable law and order situation, etc. (fig. 6.4).

It would be seen that in almost blocks where there is no presence of urban and hilly pockets there blocks have as much as 31 per cent of the workers engaged in agricultural and the proportion of workers in other categories exhibits little significance. In the district as a whole, 21.44 per cent workers belong to all other categories including industrial workers and 26.80 per cent are marginal workers (2001). Marginal workers are mostly under employed or seasonally employed. The pattern of workers is the same in almost all blocks except in urban areas where the proportion of cultivators is less and that of other workers somewhat higher. This is but natural and no significant variation can otherwise be discerned (fig 6.5).

Table - 6.12
Blockwise primary Occupational Structure (Figures in Percentage)

Sl. No.	Name of Blocks	1981		1991		2001	
		Cultivators	Agricul- Agricul- labourers	Cultivators	Agricultural labourers	Cultivators	Agricultural labourers
1	Kochas	-	-	-	-	42.97	25.68
2	Dinara	47.97	36.90	48.20	36.31	36.00	25.67
3	Dawath	50.7	33.12	47.55	37.52	41.11	24.38
4	Suryapura	-	-	-	-	48.04	25.03
5	Bikramganj	46.06	35.63	45.58	29.03	31.65	22.35
6	Karakat	51.06	32.78	44.57	40.3	31.11	26.16
7	Nasriganj	41.31	36.45	35.86	46.01	24.39	17.87
8	Rajpur	-	-	-	-	31.92	25.70
9	Sanjhauli	-	-	-	-	40.45	19.14
10	Nokha	47.76	38.44	39.93	40.87	30.57	28.42
11	Kargahar	49.73	35.47	47.05	39.93	39.62	26.06
12	Chenari	39.74	37.68	42.58	34.25	34.88	32.45
13	Nauhatta	33.54	27.96	33.60	40.82	19.62	22.00
14	Sheosagar	41.37	36.19	39.78	39.85	32.62	27.77
15	Sasaram	34.09	22.81	29.75	26.16	16.74	15.75
16	Akorhi Gola	-	-	-	-	27.47	22.11
17	Dehri	26.29	20.00	29.4	28.39	16.94	10.78
18	Tilouthu	-	-	-	-	31.83	19.89
19	Rohtas	28.30	30.94	29.4	35.38	18.29	19.39

Source : Self Computed from Census Data.

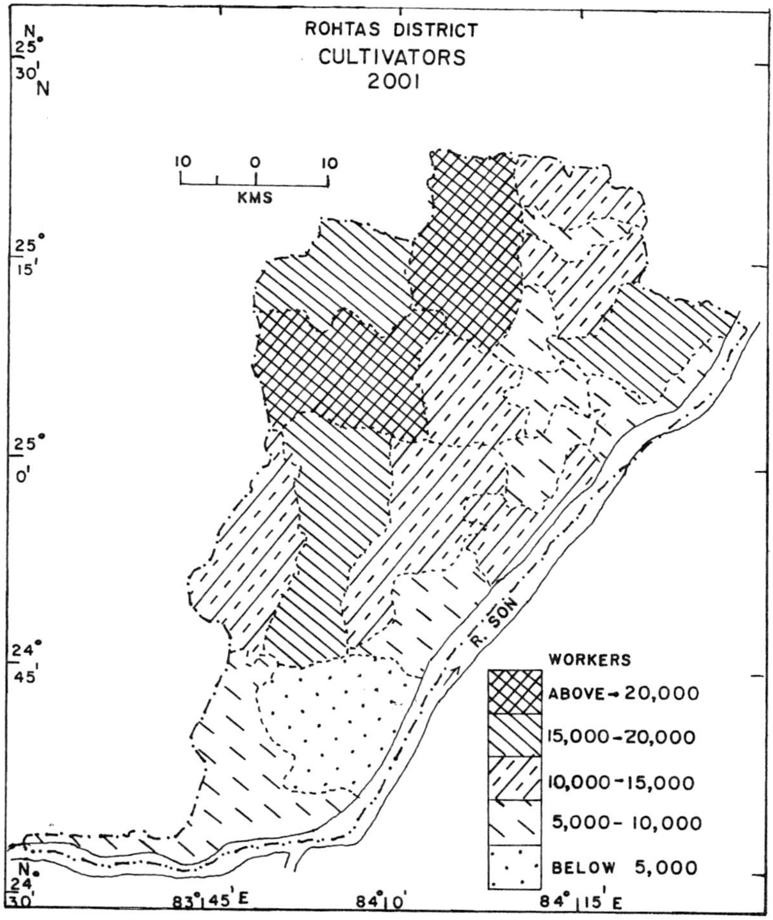
ROHTAS DISTRICT
CULTIVATORS
2001
10 0 10
KMS
R. SON
WORKERS
ABOVE→20,000
15,000-20,000
10,000-15,000
5,000- 10,000
BELOW 5,000
N 25° 30' N
25° 15'
25° 0'
24° 45'
N 24° 30'
83° 45' E
84° 0'
84° 15' E

Fig. 6.4

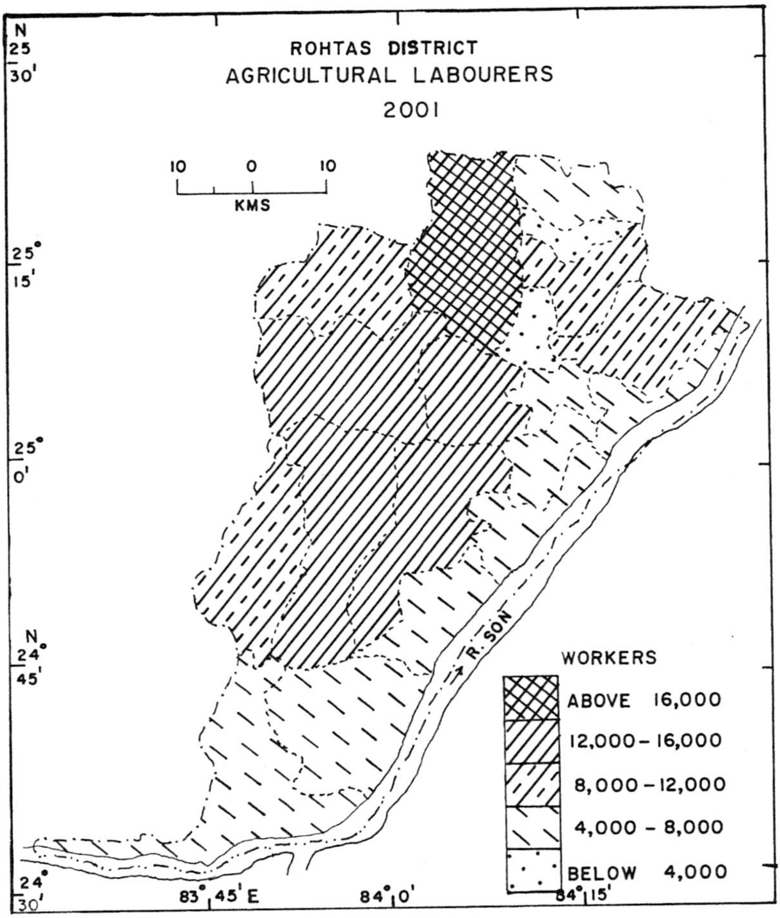
ROHTAS DISTRICT
AGRICULTURAL LABOURERS
2001
10 0 10
KMS
N 25 30'
25° 15'
25° 0'
N 24° 45'
24° 30'
83° 45' E
84° 0'
84° 15'
R. SON
WORKERS
ABOVE 16,000
12,000 - 16,000
8,000 - 12,000
4,000 - 8,000
BELOW 4,000

Fig. 6.5

POPULATION REGIONS :

Rohtas district does not exhibit uniform distribution of demographic variables in its different parts. It has therefore divided in population region. The variables which are considered for establishing the population region are : density of population, literacy and sex ratio. The choropleth maps of these variables were superimposed upon one another and the boundaries for population regions were determined by sieve technique. The boundaries are drawn where maximum number of lives representing different demographic variable have coincided. The population regions so distinguished are :

(1) Densely Populated Region

(2) Moderately Populated Region and

(3) Sparsely Populated Region

Densely Populated Region :

It comprises the blocks of Dinara, Dawath, Suryapura, Bikramganj, Sanjhauli, Karakat, Nasriganj, Rajpur, Nokha, Akorhi Gola, Dehri and Sasaram. This region lies in the north-east part of Rohtas district. It contains approximately 67 per cent of total population of the region on 48.02 per cent of total land of the study area. This region represents the highest population density i.e. above 600 persons per sq, km. This area has also got the highest percentage in literacy i.e. between 45.47 to above 55 per cent. The sex ratio is, however, low i.e. below 934 females per thousand males. The probable reason for higher density of population and higher literacy may be attributed to better economic and cultural conditions of the region. This area has uniform plain and fertile agricultural land and is well irrigated by canals system. This region also contains all the townships of Rohtas district. The region obtains moderate to high rainfall. The causes of low sex ratio may be the inclusion of male dominated urban population and poor nourishment to females particularly in rural areas (fig. 6.6).

Moderate Populated Region :

This region spreads over the blocks of Kochas, Kargahar, Chenari and Sheosagar. This region occupies the western part of Rohtas district. It comprises 22.47 per cent population of the Rohtas district on 29.26 per cent area of the district. In most of the areas the density of population ranges between 400 to 550 persons per sq. km. The region has medium to high fertile land. It receives medium rainfall. The water table is at low to moderate depth. There is, however, arrangement of canal irrigation in all blocks. The literacy is between 43 and 50 per cent. The townships are for off and are not well linked by means of transport and communication. The female ratio per thousand male varies from 898 to 917. It shows that the sex ratio is slightly adverse.

Sparsely Populated Region :

It comprises the blocks Tilouthu, Rohtas and Nauhatta. It lies in the southern part of the Rohtas district. It approximately embraces 10 per cent of total population of the Rohtas district who on 28 per cent of total land of the district. This region is conspicuous by its low density of population and low percentage of literacy in the whole of the district. The population density varies between 192 to 576 persons per sq. km. The literacy ranges between 36 to 47 per cent. Nearly half of this region is hilly and forested. The soil is infertile and the water table is generally low. Eastern part of Nauhatta and Rohtas blocks and northern part of Tilouthu block contain fertile soils. A large percentage of people of this population region are concentrated in this part of the region. This part of the region is irrigated by wells and the water table is available at higher level. This sub-region as a whole receives good rain but it facilities only the paddy harvest which is continued foothills area only. The number of male population is generally low all over this region. The male members have out migrated in search of jobs and earning livelihood for their family members.

Thus, the above analysis clearly demonstrates the spatial

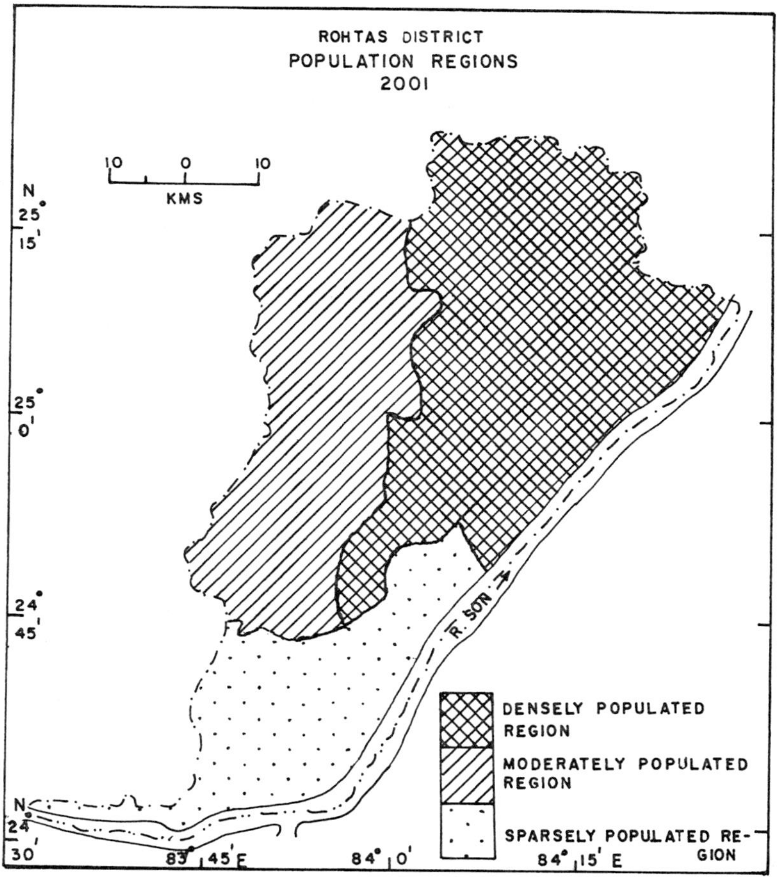
ROHTAS DISTRICT
POPULATION REGIONS
2001
10 0 10
KMS
N 25° 15'
25° 0'
24° 45'
N 24° 30'
83° 45' E
84° 0'
84° 15' E
R. SON
DENSELY POPULATED REGION
MODERATELY POPULATED REGION
SPARSELY POPULATED REGION

Fig. 6.6

pattern of population and also shows its relationship with physical and economic factors such as relief, soil, water table, rainfall, land use etc., prevailing in the district.

References :

1. Harrison, G.A. & Boyce, A.J. : Op. Cit.
2. Punit, A.E. (1978) : Population, Social systems in Rural India, Sterling Publishers, Pvt. Ltd., New Delhi, p. 37.
3. Singh, R.P. and Kumar, A. (1970) : Op. Cit.
4. Singhal, G.D. (1981) : Some Features of Population Geography of New Gaya District, Indian Geographical Studies, Research Bulletin no. 16, March, geographical Research Centre, Patna- 5, p. 24.
5. Kiser, Clyde, C. (1968) : The Aging of Human Populations, mechanism of Chango in Charles B. Mam (ed.), Population and Society, Boston Houghton Miffin Company, p. 364.
6. Bhende, Asha A. and Kanitkar, T. (1978) : Op. Cit., p. 186.
7. Ibid, p. 183.
8. Singh, M. (1969) : "Land Utilisation in North Eastern Uttar Pradesh," Unpublished Ph.D. Thesis, p. 106.
9. Chopra, P.N. (ed.) (1975) : The Gazetteer of India, Vol. III, Economic Structure and Activities, New Delhi, p. 140.
10. Bhende, A. A. and Kanitkar, T. (1978) : Op. Cit., p. 187.
11. Sinha, V.N.P. (1976) : Op. Cit., p. 47.
12. Krishan, G. and Shyam, M. (1973) : "Spatial Perspective on Progress of Female Literacy in India : 1901-71," Pacific View Point, Vol. 14, p. 204.
13. Chandna, R.C. and Sidhu, M.S. (1980) : Op. Cit., p. 99.
14. Ibid.
15. Singhal, G.D. : Op. Cit., p. 24.
16. Singh, R.P. and Kumar, A. (1970) : Op. Cit.
17. Garnier, J.B. (1966) : Op. Cit., p. 285.
18. Mehta, S. (1967) : India's Rural Female Working Force

and Occupational Structure, 1961-A Geographical Analysis, Indian Geographer, Vol. 12, No. 1 & 2, p. 50.

19. Chandna, R. C. (1967) : Op. Cit., p. 47.
20. Chandna, R.C. and Sidhu, M.S. (1980) : Op. Cit., p. 109.
21. Clarke, John I (1972) : Population Geography, Pergamon Press Oxford, pp. 88-89.
22. Chandna, R.C. and Sidhu, M.S. (1980) : Op. Cit., p. 109.
23. Singh, R.P. and Kumar, A. (1970) : Op. Cit. p. 11.
24. Chandna, R.C. and Sidhu, M.S. (1980) : Op. Cit., p. 110.

7

Chapter

Sample Villages

The author has visited different parts of the study area with study point of view. On account of varied observations in various parts of the Rohtas district, the author has collected voluminous of data associated with physical, cultural and economic set up these data and has attempted to authenticate with the help of sample villages. The general pattern, thus, found in the villages are correlated with the general pattern of the respective physical unit from where the village concerns. These villages are chosen from different physical units which are of average size in respect of population and agricultural land in respective physical units.

VILLAGE : TURKI

This village lies is Chenari block which forms the part of Central High Plain. This village thus, lies in moderately populated region. Agriculturally this village represents the area of Moderate Agricultural Region.

Turki village is 6 kms. away from the block headquarters and 21 kms. off the railway station. Here only primary school is available. There are good doctors in the village. Drinking water is available through wells and hand pumps. There is regular supply of electricity in the village. It is connected by an unmetalled road which links the block headquarter. This village consists of 656 (2001) population. The village area spreads over 168.35 hectares of land. Apart from above facilities, this village has got plain and fertile soils over its large area. The above factors are, thus, responsible for the cultivation of every type of harvest here.

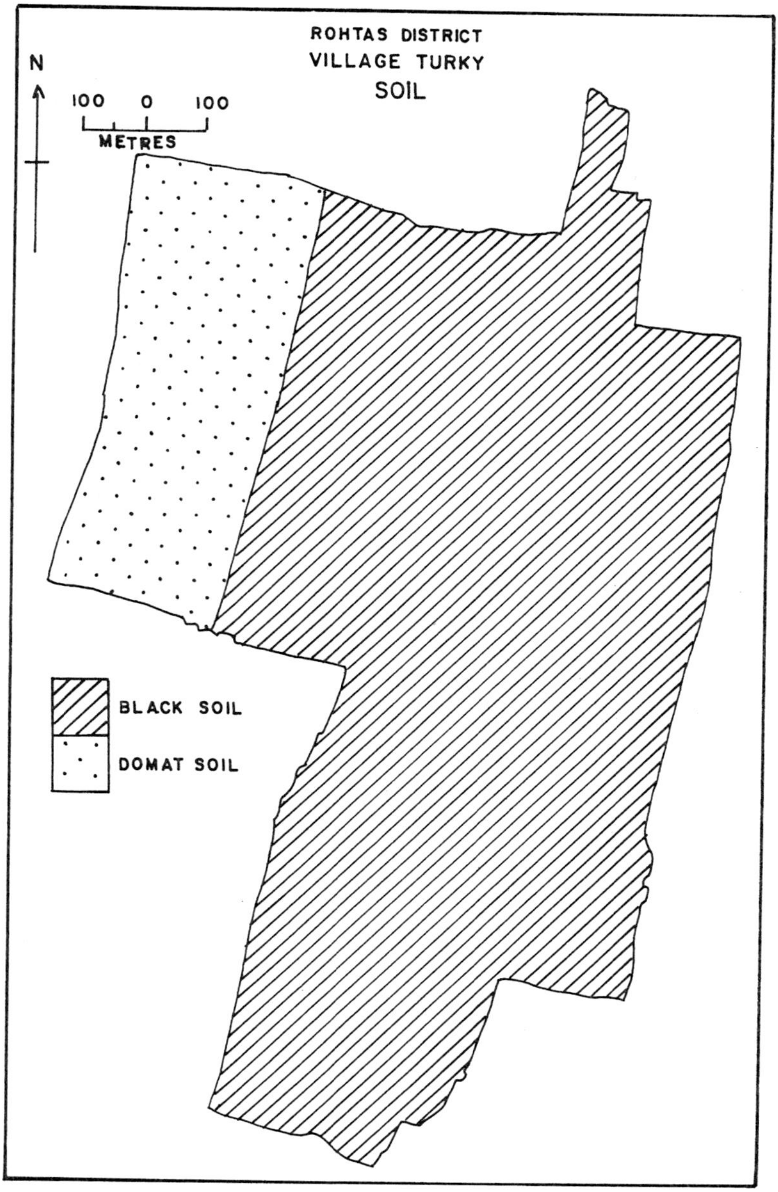
ROHTAS DISTRICT
VILLAGE TURKY
SOIL
N
100 0 100
METRES
BLACK SOIL
DOMAT SOIL

Fig. 7.1

LAND PROFILE :

As this village extends over a large area its whole area is not even in physical appearance and has been categorised in three categories i.e. upland, intermediate land and lowland. The upland is usually known as Did-land. This area contains nearly 30 per cent of land of the village. It is generally useful for the extension of settlements. Turki village is situated in its northern part. On this land there is triple to multiple cropping. Cash crops are generally grown here. In this part of the village there are facilities of fertile soils and irrigation. The general slope of this area is from south to north.

The intermediate land spreads over 50 per cent of land of the village. As this land contains fertile plain tracts it has become the main source of agricultural harvests. Rabi, Bhadai and Garma crops are raised here respectively. The general slope of these parts is from north to south.

The lowland is found in extreme northern parts of the village and comprises nearly 20 per cent area of Turki village. Such lands have same limitation in proper utilization because these lands remain under water particularly in the months of rains. Here, there are, however, practice of two harvests i.e., Rabi and Aghani because of the facilities of fertile soils and irrigation. The general slope of the area is like the general slope of other categories of land.

This village contains some orchards which roughly cover the areas of upland and stand for nearly 5 per cent land of the village.

Soils of the village are domat and black. Black soil is the most important soil in the village. It extends over large part of village. This soil is useful for raising many crops in this village. North-west area of the village contains domat soil (fig. 7.1).

The above said discussion, of course, provides clear cut information about the physical condition of the village Turki. These conditions are usually found in villages Central High

Plain. These characteristics have been revealed when the scholar visited the area as a part of field survey. The similar character of soils and climatic conditions are found in this village as is observed in entire Central High Plain. Thus, the physical conditions of the village are comparable with the physical conditions of the Central High Plain.

CULTURAL SETTING :

Population Characteristics : Turki village comprises 815 persons and of which 415 are males and 400 are females in April 2008. Thus, there is 50.92 per cent male and 49.08 per cent female in this village. Large population in this village is working population. This is thus, helpful in prosperity. The percentage of the same is, however, discouraging in case of female population. Children and old persons comprise nearly 12 per cent of female population. Nearly 39 per cent population in the village is of scheduled castes.

The village has got primary school where 158 students (2008) obtain education. Male students are 74 and female students are 84. The village is connected with a main road. The villages get better yield from fields. On account of above factors, there are 331 literate persons in the village out of which 200 are males and 131 are females in 2001. The percentage of female literates is, however, low than that of male population.

In the present research, attempt has also been made to study the working population. Nearly 19 per cent population in this village is working population and 81 per cent is nonworking. Out of working population nearly 23 per cent are cultivators, 40 per cent agricultural labourers and 20 per cent engaged in other works.

Table 7.1
Caste Pattern in Turki Village, 2008

(in Percentage)

Sl. No.	Castes	Total Population	Male	Female
1	Koeri	58.90	30.80	28.10

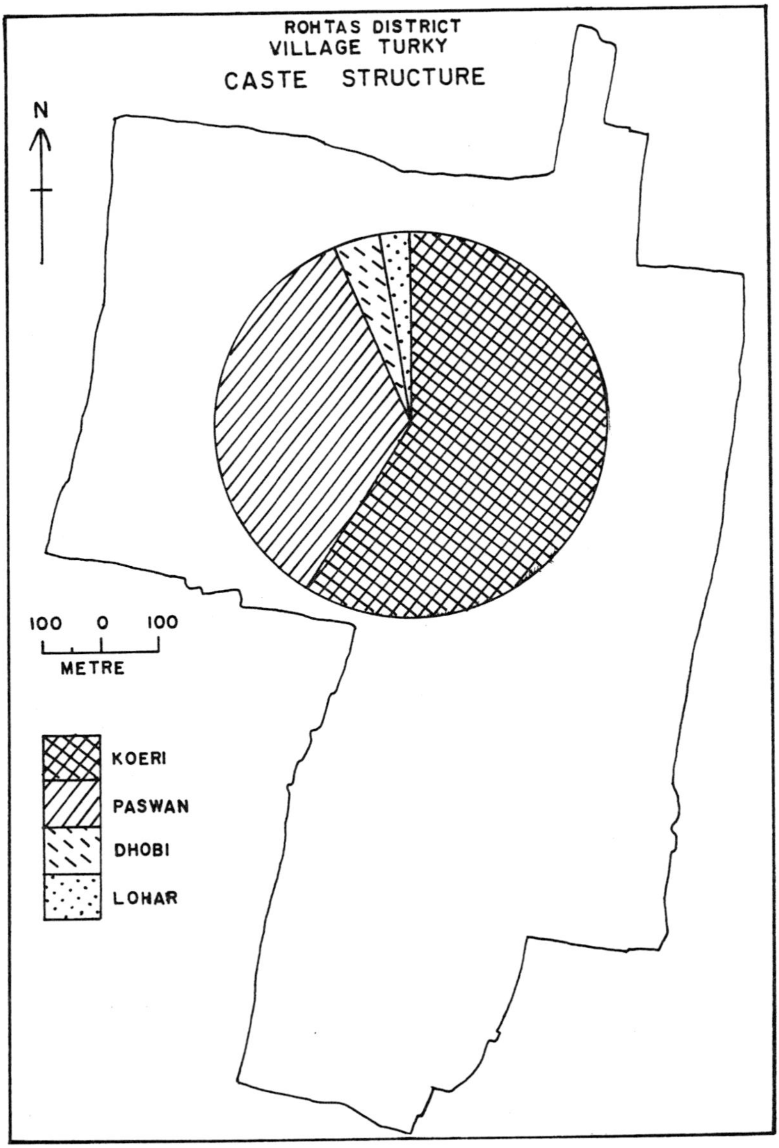
ROHTAS DISTRICT
VILLAGE TURKY
CASTE STRUCTURE
N
100 0 100
METRE
KOERI
PASWAN
DHOBI
LOHAR

Fig. 7.2

2	Paswan	35.22	17.42	17.80
3	Dhobi	3.55	1.47	2.80
4	Lohar	2.33	1.22	1.11
	Total	100.00	52.75	47.25

Source : Field Survey.

The author has also attempted to investigate the population in terms of its caste structure. The village population is dominated by Koeri caste. It represents 58.90 per cent population of the village followed by Paswan 35.22 per cent, Dhobi 3.55 per cent and Lohar 2.33 per cent (fig. 7.2).

Other Cultural Characteristics :- Attempts have also been made to know the position of agricultural implements used in fields and its associated works. Here there are 4 tractor, 11 harvesters, 9 diesel and 18 electric pumping sets. The above pattern of agricultural implements, thus, explains that the farmers are skilled particularly in agricultural works. The agricultural situations in this village are, therefore, very good.

The village is linked with an unmetalled road. The block headquarter is hardly 6 kms away from the village. Drinking water is available through wells and hand pumps. Electric is available for domestic and agricultural purposes.

It is clear from the above mentioned facts that cultural settings of Turki are similar to the moderate population region of Rohtas district. Average population density of this region is 490 persons per km^2 while population density of Turki village is 390 persons per km^2. This population region contains 23.62 % of total working population while Turki contains about 19 per cent of total working population which is similar to total working population of this population region. Thus various population characteristics found in Turki village are comparable with that the moderate population region.

LAND USE :

Land use pattern in the village shows that Net Sown Area is on 85 per cent of land of the village, followed by other cultivable land 6 per cent, fallow land 5 per cent, settlement and others 4 per cent. The above pattern of land use, therefore, explains that the percentage of N.S.A. is high because this village contains fertile soils and has got irrigation facilities (fig. 7.3).

In this village the irrigation to fields is made available with the help of tubewells, diesel pumping sets and rain water. The former two methods of irrigation are, however, important.

The presence of above amenities in Turki village has encouraged four harvests in fields. These harvests are Aghani, Rabi, Bhadai and Garma. Aghani harvest is taken from nearly 60 per cent land of N.S.A. followed by Rabi 100 per cent, Bhadai 10 per cent and Garma 5 per cent. Aghani and Rabi crops are grown on all classes of land. Bhadai crops are grown on upland and intermediate land. Garma crops are also done on upland or intermediate lands. Under these harvests a number of crops are grown which are evident from the table 7.2 given below.

Table - 7.2
Cropping Pattern in Turki Village, 2008

Crops	Percentage of total cultivated land	Yield per bigha monds
Paddy	50	30
Wheat	36	10
Pulses	6	6
Maize	5	4
Vegetable	2	350
Other Crops	1	15

Source : Field Survey.

Paddy is the most important crop in Aghani harvest of

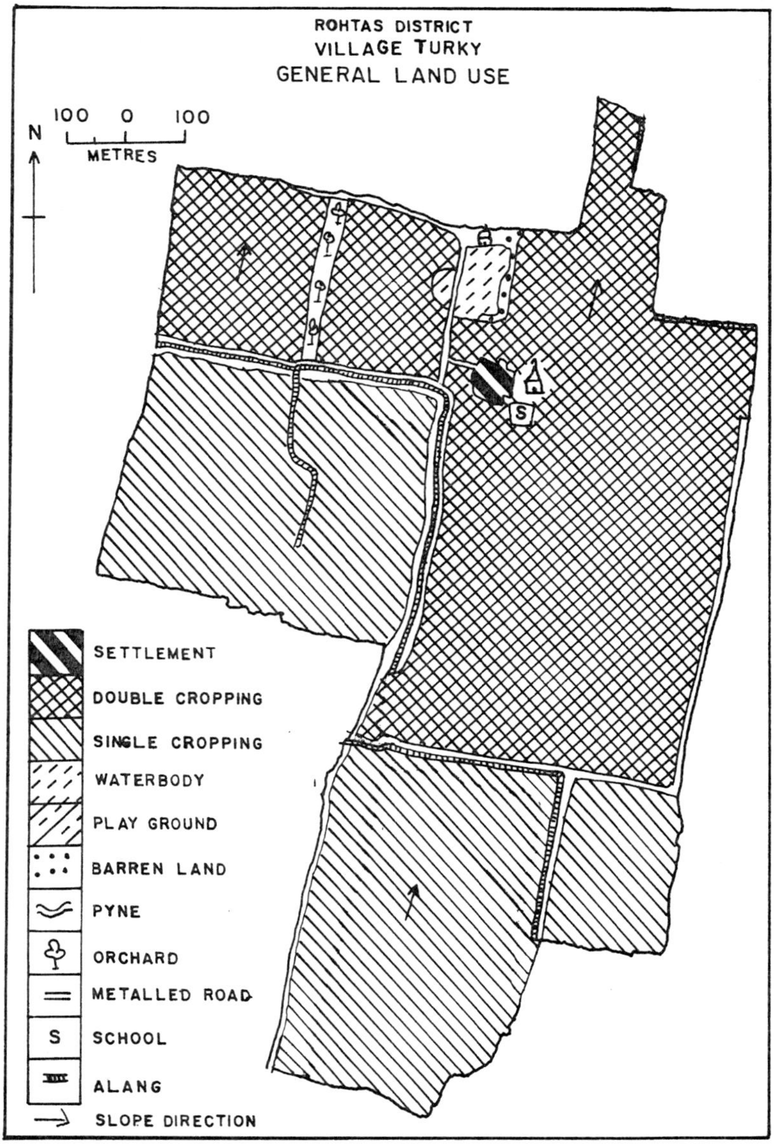
ROHTAS DISTRICT
VILLAGE TURKY
GENERAL LAND USE
N
100 0 100
METRES
SETTLEMENT
DOUBLE CROPPING
SINGLE CROPPING
WATERBODY
PLAY GROUND
BARREN LAND
PYNE
ORCHARD
METALLED ROAD
S SCHOOL
ALANG
SLOPE DIRECTION

Fig. 7.3

the village. It is done on 50 per cent of the total cultivated land and per bigha yield of the same is 30 monds. The comfortable situations of paddy are governed by fertile soil, irrigation facilities, rainfall etc.

Wheat is the second important crop in the village, which is grown on nearly 36 per cent of its total cultivated land and per bigha yield of the same is 10 monds. The above farmer do not pay much attention to grow wheat because their livelihood requirement as being fulfilled by good harvest of paddy.

Other crops in this village are insignificant. There collectively stand for 14 per cent of its total cultivated land. Pulses and maize are cultivated on 3 per cent of land. The yield of these crops is moderate to high.

The pattern of agriculture in the village, thus, explains the facts that the harvest pattern is dominated by Aghani and Rabi crops. Their areal percentage, out of total cultivated land, is very high. Other harvests also contain significant size of land in the village. Paddy in Aghani and wheat in Rabi harvests are important crops. These two crops dominate the cropping pattern because these crops form part of staple food for people and abundant facilities are available for cultivating these crops. Other important crops in this village are pulses and maize. The farmer two crops are grown on nearly almost N.S.A. which occurs in all classes of land.

Thus we see that the land use pattern of village Turki is altogether of moderate type and represents the general pattern of agriculture found in moderate agriculture region.

VILLAGE : GOPALPUR

Gopalpur village is located in Dinara block and forms a part of northern low plain. It comes under Densely Populated Region and Intensive Agricultural Region.

This village is surrounded by Kunr-Rampur in north, Khairhi-Chilharua in south, Mathiya-Dihra in west and

Shahpur in east. It is situated at 3.5 kms away from block headquarters and 20 kms of Bikramganj Railway Station. There are only primary schools as educational centre. There are, however, presences of Allopathic Doctor. Regular Electric supply is available for domestic and agricultural purposes. Irrigation is available by canal also. As this village contain fertile black soil, a number of crops in different harvests are grown here. Double cropping system is common. The agricultural products are, thus, the main source of livelihood for a large size of population in the village. It is a large village and contains 1707 persons. It spreads over an area of 378.28 hectares.

LAND PROFILE :

The landscape of the village may be classified in to three categories-upland, intermediate land and lowland. The upland is situated near the settlement. The upland hardly contains 20 per cent area of the village and slopes from south-west to north-east. It contains fertile soil and a number of crops are raised here.

The intermediate land spreads over 65 per cent land of the village. It slopes from south-west to north-east. The soils are fertile here. On account of above factors, many crops are grown here.

The lowland areas are found along the eastern part of the village. It contains nearly 15 per cent land of the village. Here soils are also black. The main crops, thus raised are rice, wheat and maize.

Here the drainage is found in form of pynes and canals. Pynes are, however, numerous in the southern parts of the village.

Soil in this village is totally black but fertility content is favourable over large areas.

Above mentioned facts give general information about physical condition. The land profile of this village is similar to the land found in northern low plain particularly with respect to the soil and climatic conditions.

POPULATION CHARACTERISTICS :

Gopalpur village consists of 1707 persons out of which 934 are male and 773 are female. Thus, male persons stand for 54.71 per cent and female stands for 45.29 per cent of total population. Out of male population 3.65 per cent are old persons, 8.29 per cent are children and 42.77 per cent are working persons. Out of female population, 3.81 per cent are old, 7.82 per cent are children and 33.66 per cent are working persons. Thus, the percentage of male and female population is comparable. Combined together nearly 58.82 per cent population is non-working and 41.18 per cent are working persons. Thus, workable population is sufficient to obtain livelihood for rest of population in the village. This village has got nearly 19 per cent of its population as scheduled castes.

As this village is far away from any transport system, it has not got even a middle school. Only primary schools are here where nearly 206 students obtain education. Literate persons in the village are 50.86 per cent. Most of them have obtained education at Dinara and Sasaram. They have obtained the same because the economic condition of people is good. They grow a number of crops in their fields. Most of literate persons are matriculates. Female literates are, however, very small.

An attempt has also been made to examine the pattern of working population in the village. It has been found that nearly 41 per cent persons are working. Out of this nearly 77 per cent are main workers and 23 per cent are marginal workers. Out of total population, non workers are nearly 59 per cent. Thus, the per cent of working population shows that it is not favourable for agriculture.

The author has also studied the cast structure in the village. Yadav comprises nearly 25 per cent population of the village. Koeri contains nearly 15 per cent population followed by Chamar 11.95 per cent, Kanu 9.25%, Muslim 8.49 %, Dusadh 6.90%, Bramhan 6.26% and other castes 16.92 per cent. In all these castes sex ratio is comparable except in Yadav and Koeri castes (fig. 7.4).

Table - 7.3
Caste Pattern in Gopalpur Village in Percentage, 2008

Sl. No.	Caste	Total Population	Male	Female
1	Yadav	25.24	14.00	11.24
2	Koeri	14.99	8.08	6.91
3	Chamar	11.95	6.61	5.34
4	Kanu	9.25	4.92	4.33
5	Muslim	8.49	4.27	4.22
6	Dusadh	6.90	3.39	3.51
7	Bramhan	6.26	4.26	2.00
8	Other Castes	16.92	9.18	7.74
	Total	100.00	51.39	48.61

Source : Field Survey.

Other Cultural Characteristics :- The author has also studied the pattern of use of agricultural implements. In this village there are 7 tractors 4 husking machines and 9 diesel pumping sets. The above pattern of agricultural implements, thus, explains that the farmers are economically sound.

The village is linked with an unmetalled road. There are facilities of drinking water through wells and hand-pumps. Electricity is irregularly available. There is also a dispensary in this village.

It is clear that the population attributes of Gopalpur village are similar as are found in Densely Population Region as a whole population density of Gopalpur village is 451 persons per km2 which is very high. This region contained 66.15 per cent of total working population while Gopalpur village contains 411 of working population.

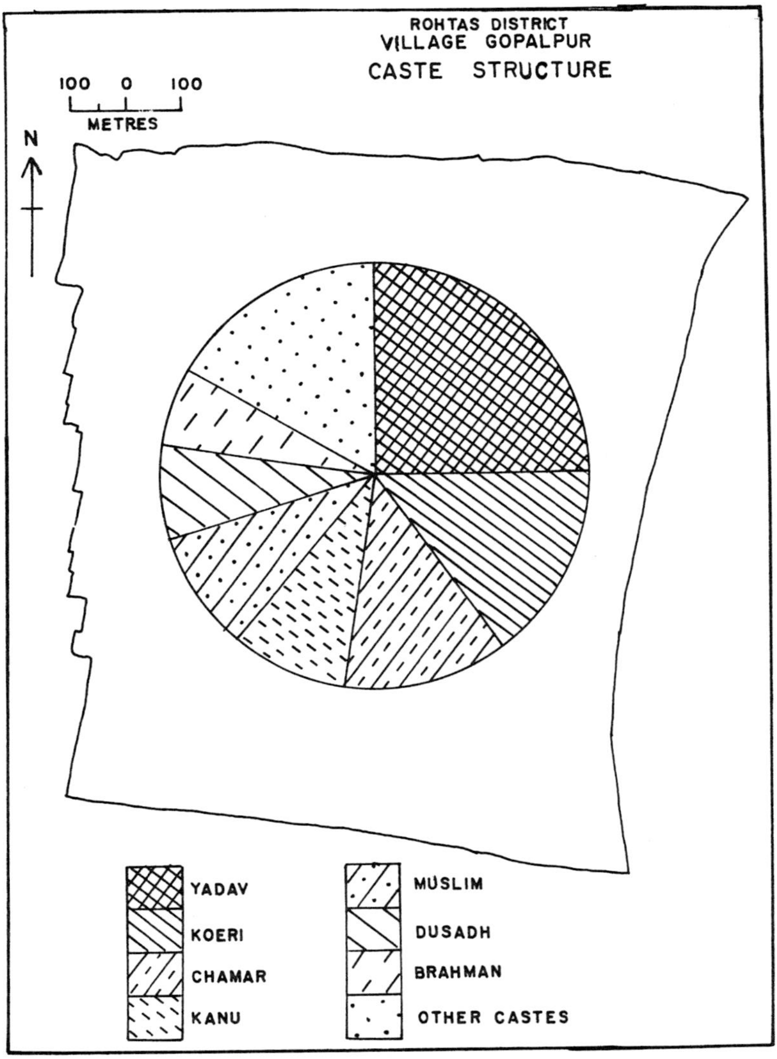
ROHTAS DISTRICT
VILLAGE GOPALPUR
CASTE STRUCTURE
100 0 100
METRES
N
YADAV
KOERI
CHAMAR
KANU
MUSLIM
DUSADH
BRAHMAN
OTHER CASTES

Fig. 7.4

LAND USE :

Land use pattern in this village shows that Net Sown Area covers nearly 83 Sown of its total land followed by other cultivable lands 6 per cent, fallow land 5 per cent, settlement 2 Per cent and waste land and pasture 4 per cent. Thus, the pattern of land use explains that the percentage of NSA is very-very high, because the soils found here are fertile. There are also irrigation facilities by canals. In this village irrigation in fields are made available with the help of only canals (fig. 7.5).

On account of above facilities in this village the pattern of agriculture developed is satisfactory. From fields two harvests are taken i.e. Aghani and Rabi. Total agricultural lands are double cropped area. Aghani harvest is done on 100 per cent of its NSA flowed by Rabi 100 per cent. Aghani and Rabi crops are grown on all classes of land. Under these harvests mainly two crops are grown which are given in table no. 7.4 below. The same table also explains the pattern of yield.

Table - 7.4
Cropping Pattern in Gopalpur Village, 2007-08

Crops	Percentage of total cultivated land	Yield per katha in kgms
Paddy	50	80
Wheat	48	40
Other crops	2	120

Source : Field Survey.

Paddy is the most important crop in Gopalpur village. It is done on 100 per cent of its total cultivated land during Aghani cropping period. In paddy yield is 80 kgms per katha. Thus, the cultivation of paddy is good. It has become possible because, the irrigation for paddy is available from canals. Soil is the village are fertile also.

Wheat is the second important crop. It is practised on 48

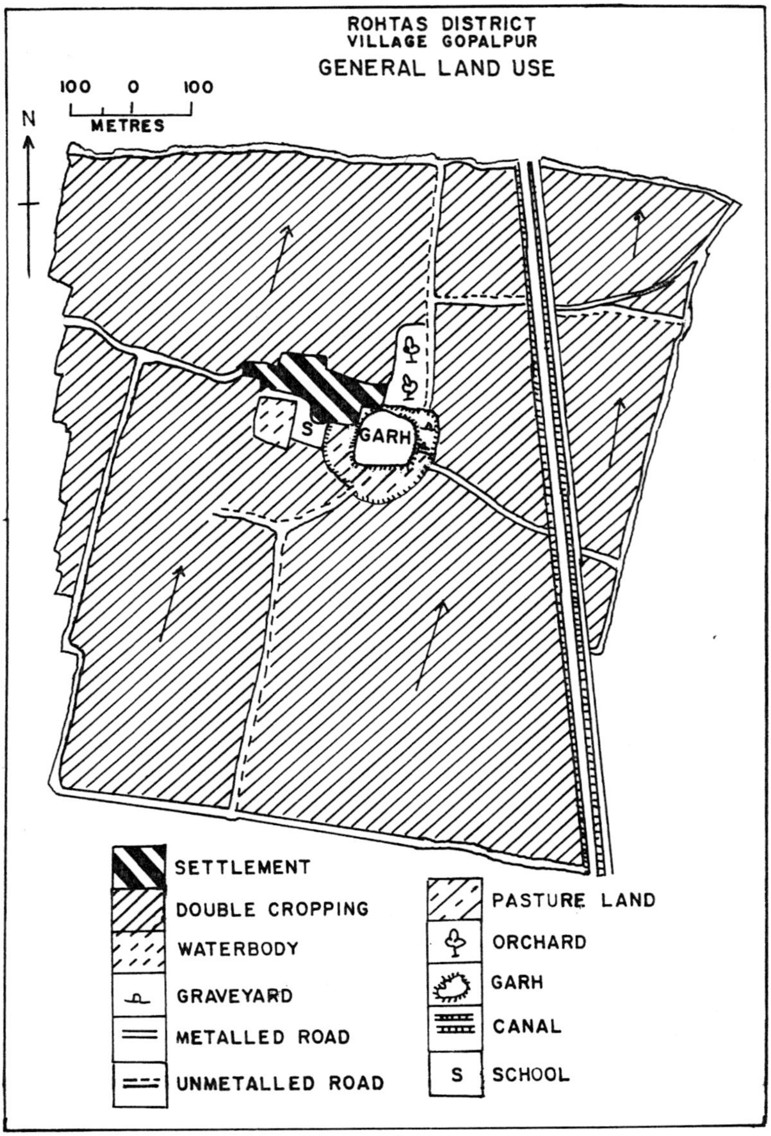
ROHTAS DISTRICT
VILLAGE GOPALPUR
GENERAL LAND USE
100 0 100
METRES
N
S
GARH
SETTLEMENT
DOUBLE CROPPING
WATERBODY
GRAVEYARD
METALLED ROAD
UNMETALLED ROAD
PASTURE LAND
ORCHARD
GARH
CANAL
S
SCHOOL

Fig. 7.5

per cent of its total cultivated land. Per katha yield of wheat is 40 kgms. Thus, the situation of wheat is comfortable in this village.

Other crops grown in this village are pulses, maize, oilseeds vegetables etc. Amongst all these crops maize in significant. It covers 2 per cent cultivated area of the village. per katha yield of pulses in 15 kgms.

Thus the pattern of agriculture in Gopalpur village describes that the harvest pattern is dominated by Aghani and Rabi crops. Their areal percentage and their yield are comparatively higher. Paddy in Aghani and wheat in Rabi harvests are important crops. These two crops cover nearly 98 per cent cultivated land and their yield is higher. These two crops, of course, are staple food for bulk of population in the village.

The author has studied that agricultural as well as other cultural and economic situation in varied classes of people are completely different types. The middle and poor class people need help even for their livelihood. There are also necessity of fertilizer, irrigation and good seeds in fields. Regular supply of electricity and a school up to high school are must for education in the village.

Land use pattern of Gopalpur village shows that it is very high and it comes under Intensive Agriculture Region. Agricultural density of this village is 5.43 persons / hectares. Which is due to irrigational facility and other agricultural facilities. Thus Gopalpur village truly represents the character of intensive agricultural region.

VILLAGE : KAITHI

Village Kaithi is located in Tilouthu blocks and is a part of Southern High Plain. It lies in Low Population Region and Moderate Agricultural Region.

This village is situated at 6 kms from block headquarters and 30 kms far off the railway station in Dehri. As this village lies far from the any transport system except an unmetalled road, it has, therefore developed little cultural and economic facilities. Here there are only primary and middle schools. Irregular electricity is available for domestic and agricultural purposes only. The land of the village is fertile which helps in raising a good number of crops in agricultural area. Single to double cropping system is common. This village consists of 1763 persons. The village has got 167.54 hectares of land. The main source of livelihood for a large size of population is based on agricultural produces.

LAND PROFILE :

The landscape of Kaithi village may be classified in to Upland, Intermediate land and Low land. The upland area is found in south-eastern parts and consists of 25 per cent of total area. It is the land on which this village has developed. This land is known as Dih land and it is very fertile. It is, thus, noted for raising a number of crops. It is the area where the extension of houses in village is possible. The slope of this area is from south-west to north-east.

The Intermediate land lies in north and west of upland areas and comprises nearly 50 per cent area. The general slope of the area is from south-west to north-east. It is the area which in true sense fetches the residing population in the village. It is a fertile plain area and grows a number of crops by different harvests.

The Low lands areas are found in northern part of this village and stand for nearly 25 per cent of total area of the village. The slope of this part of the village is from west to east. This part remains under water for many months of rainy days. It is, therefore, noted for Rabi crops only.

Soil in this village is totally Domat. It is also a fertile soil. During field survey it was found that soils, slope and climatic conditions are similar as are generally found in South High Plain. Thus the characteristics found in this village are similar to its physical region.

CULTURAL SETTING :

Population Characteristics :- As this village has got medium to low cultural and economic amenities, it is a medium size village in respect of population. It contains 1763 persons of which 891 are males and 872 are females. Thus male and female stands for 50.53 and 49.47 per cent of total population respectively. Out of male population 31 per cent are working, 16 per cent are children and 7 per cent are old persons. In case of female population, 29 per cent population is working and 15 and 4 per cent population are children and old persons respectively. Thus, the percentage of male and female population in this village is comparable to each other except the percentage of old persons i.e. exceedingly high in case of male population. The percentage of working population is, however, high-both in males and females which are helpful in supporting the livelihood of children and old persons. Nearly 32 per cent population in this village is scheduled caste.

As this village has got primary and middle schools only and is not connected with a metalled road, the pattern of literate persons is not very good. It has got 31 per cent of its population as literate persons out of which 25 per cent is female literates. There are 248 students in primary school and 150 students in middle school.

Table - 7.5
Caste-wise Population Pattern in Percentage, 2008

Sl. No.	Castes	Total Population	Male	Female
1	Yadav	24.00	11.63	12.37
2	Rajput	20.6	10.78	9.82
3	Chamar	18.71	10.2	8.51
4	Paswan	13.31	6.51	6.80
5	Bania	10.38	4.65	5.73
6	Others	13.00	6.76	6.24
	Total	100.00	50.53	49.47

Source : Field Survey.

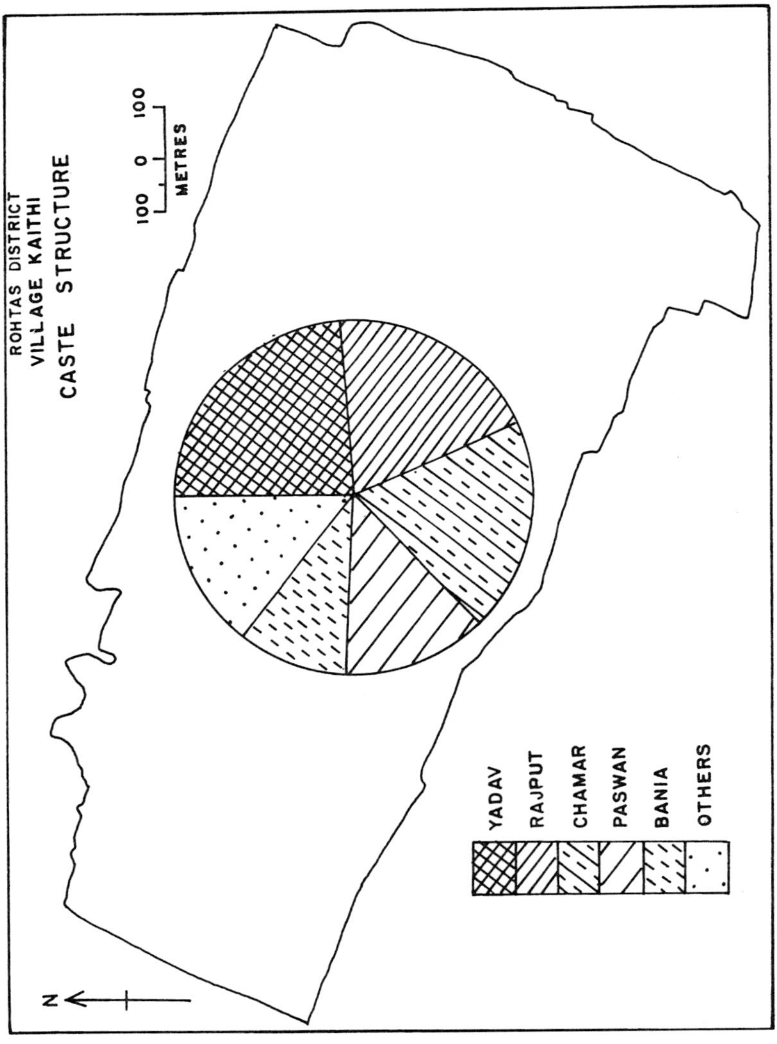
ROHTAS DISTRICT
VILLAGE KAITHI
CASTE STRUCTURE
100 0 100
METRES
YADAV
RAJPUT
CHAMAR
PASWAN
BANIA
OTHERS
N

Fig. 7.6

In this village there are 76.76 per cent main workers and 23.24 per cent marginal workers.

The author has also studied caste wise percentage of male and female population which can be seen in table 7.5.

The table no. 7.5 shows that Yadav population stands for nearly ¼th population of the village. Individually other castes hardly contain over 10 per cent population. Male and female population is almost uniform in all castes. The percentage of female is, however, a little high in case of Paswan and Bania (fig. 7.6).

Other Cultural Characteristics :- The author has also studies the pattern of use of agricultural implements. In this village there are 5 tractors, 3 husking machines and 13 diesel pumping sets. The above pattern of agricultural implements, thus, explains that the farmers are conscious towards cultivation.

The village is linked with an unmetalled road. Drinking water facilities are available in form of wells and hand-pumps. Irregularly Electricity is available here.

Population characteristics of Kaithi is not similar to the population region. Its population density is 1049 persons per km^2, which is very high. Reasons for such a high population density are- fertile land, good irrigational facilities, literacy and social awareness.

LAND USE :

The land use pattern in the village is dominated by Net Sown Area. Net Sown Area covers nearly 65.78 per cent land of the village followed by area not able for cultivation 22%, waste land and pasture 5.22% and settlement and other 7% (fig. 7.7).

On the Net Sown Area almost harvests are done. Out of total cultivated land Rabi harvest is practised on 50 per cent followed by Aghani 40 Per cent and Bhadai 10%. The area under Rabi harvest is, however, higher because irrigation

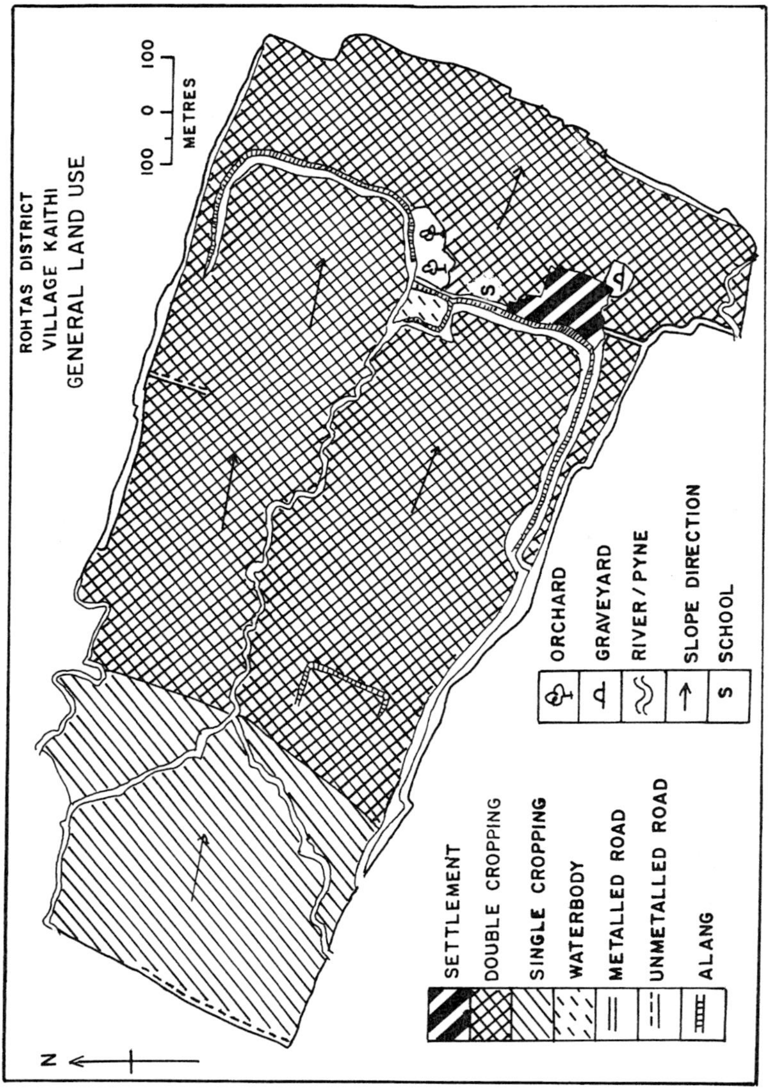
ROHTAS DISTRICT
VILLAGE KAITHI
GENERAL LAND USE
100 0 100
METRES
N
SETTLEMENT
DOUBLE CROPPING
SINGLE CROPPING
WATERBODY
METALLED ROAD
UNMETALLED ROAD
ALANG
ORCHARD
GRAVEYARD
RIVER / PYNE
SLOPE DIRECTION
SCHOOL
S

Fig. 7.7

system is well developed. A number of crops are raised in different harvests because of many facilities. This village contains domat soil in its entire area. Water table in summer goes down to 55 feet followed by winter 35 feet and rainy season 5 feet. There is also supply of regular electricity for agricultural purposes.

The table no. 7.6 presents the facts that the total cultivated area under paddy is also larger. Other important crops are wheat and pulses in respect of cultivable area and yield. Maize, vegetables and others crops combined together comprise nearly 15 per cent of total cultivated land. Thus, distribution of agriculture land in the Kaithi village shows a great diversity. Agriculture also faces problems like irrigation, non availability of good seeds, fertilizer, pesticides etc.

Table - 7.6
Cropping Pattern in Kaithi Village , 2007-08

Crops	Area in percentage of total cultivated land	Yield per katha in kgms
Paddy	38.28	37
Wheat	36.10	28
Maize	5.41	35
Pulses	10.83	17
Vegetables	1.80	200
Other Crops	7.58	20
Total	100.00	

Source : Field Survey.

Kaithi comes under Moderate Agricultural Region but due to high population density and favourable agricultural facilities its agricultural density is 16 persons / hectares. Thus this village comes under Moderate Agricultural Region in spite of that it has favourable land use.

VILLAGE : AURAIYA

Auraiya village is situated in Chenari block and comes

under the area of Northern Hilly Region. It represents Moderate Agricultural Region and Moderate Population Region.

The village is at the height of nearly 800 feet from sea level and is located on Kaimur Hills. It is surrounded by the villages of Pachoura and Bhunda Dih in north, Phulwaria in south, Marpa in east and Bhurkura in west. The Chormara river bisects this village. There is no any mean of transportation to reach the village. The sole mean is to go on foot passing through narrow hilly streets which is locally termed as "Ghat". Goods of daily use are carried by ox. This village is nearly 15 kms away from the block headquarters and 30 kms. away from the railway station in Kudra. As a result the village shows a little economic and cultural development. There is an Anganbari centre where 40 children's study in five class. The village has no electricity. Drinking water is made available by well. On account of the aforesaid inadequate facilities, the farmers obtain single Aghani harvest over their land. Double harvest system is being practised around the village land only. There is, however, high yield of Aghani crop which forms the main source of sustenance to farmers. The village has got a total area of 611.47 hectares and 502 persons.

LAND PROFILE :

Based on the details of surface features, the landscape of Auraiya village may be put in to two categories. The categories, thus, obtained are hilly area and plain area. The hilly areas are found over north, south and east parts of the village. This area comprises rugged and undulating surface and represents nearly 70 per cent area of the village. These are the areas where there are no settlements and agricultural practices are also absent.

The plain area stands for nearly 30 per cent land of the village and extends over its middle and western parts. In this area some settlements are found and growing some crops under different harvests. The Chormara river passes through this area from east to west.

The general slope of the village is from north to south, south to north and east to west. Bunds are present in plain areas only. Soil of this village is totally red soil.

To sum up the land profile and other associated features of the village are identical to the general physical set up the Northern Hilly Region.

CULTURAL SETTINGS :

Population Characteristics : - Auraiya village contains smaller cultural and economic facilities even of it is a large size village in regard to population size. It comprises 502 persons which is represented by 264 males and 238 females. Male population, thus, contains 52.60 per cent and female population stands for 47.40 per cent of total population. Out of total population 50 per cent are working population, 42.04 per cent are children's and 7.96 per cent are old persons. Nearly 34 per cent population in this village belong to scheduled tribe.

As such Auraiya village has got only a Anganbari centre and also lies for from block headquarter and any transport system, more than 88 per cent population is illiterate. There are 9.16 per cent male and 2.78 per cent female literate in the village. Thus, literacy pattern in Auraiya village closely reflects the general pattern of literacy found in the block as a whole.

In the present study, attempts have further been made to examine the pattern of workers this village. There are 40.56 per cent main workers, 57.83 per cent non-workers and 1.61 per cent marginal workers. It shows that a large size of population is associated with agriculture.

The author has also examined caste-wise percentage of male and female population in Auraiya village. The table no. 7.7 comprises the same and portrays that the percentage of both male and female in each caste is unevenly represented.

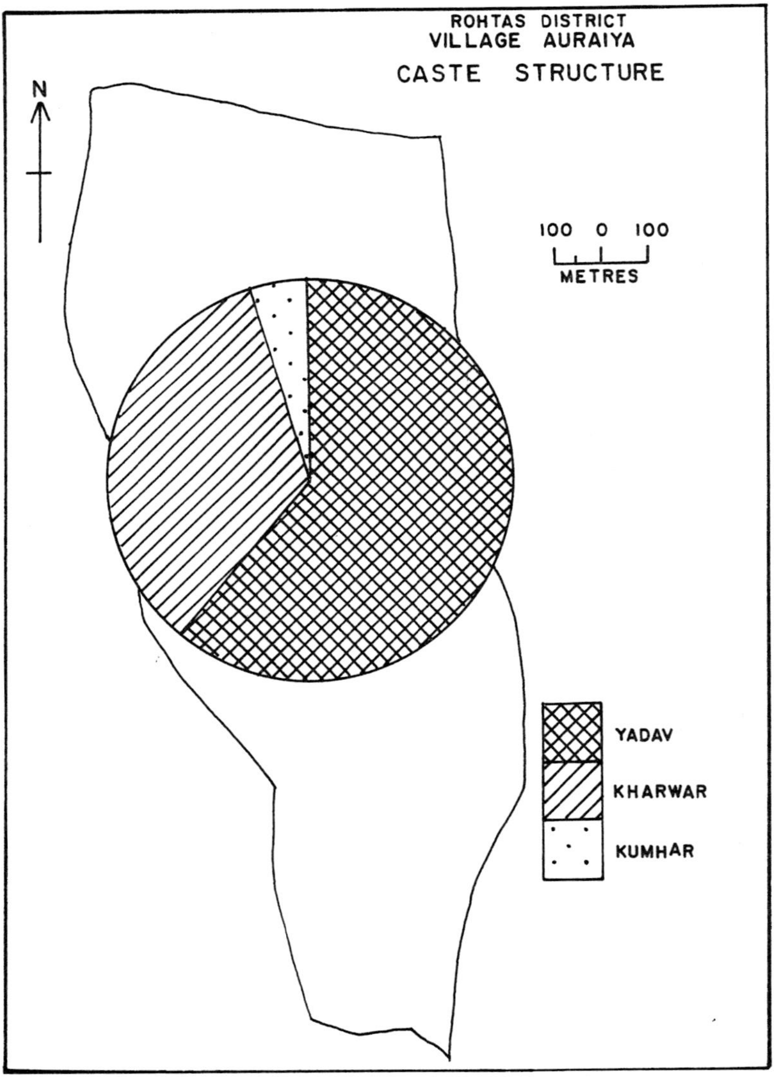
ROHTAS DISTRICT
VILLAGE AURAIYA
CASTE STRUCTURE
N
100 0 100
METRES
YADAV
KHARWAR
KUMHAR

Fig. 7.8

It is, however, the male population is larger than female population in Yadav community (fig. 7.8).

Table - 7.7
Caste-wise Population Pattern in Percentage, 2008

Sl. No.	Castes	Total Population	Male	Female
1	Yadav	61.36	32.88	28.48
2	Kharwar	34.60	17.33	16.73
3	Kumhar	4.58	2.39	2.19
	Total	100.00	52.60	47.40

Source : Field Survey.

Population density of the village is lower than average of the area. It is only 82 persons per km^2. It is due to its location in hilly region and due lack of various facilities.

LAND USE :

The land use pattern is dominated by forest. It occurs on 88.68 per cent land of the village. Net Sown Area is however, on only 5 per cent land of the village followed by 3.90 per cent area under not available for cultivation and 2.42 per cent area occupied by settlement and others. Thus, very low area of the village has been under agriculture (fig. 7.9).

The agricultural lands are used under two harvests i.e. Aghani and Bhadai. Aghani crops are grown on nearly 50 per cent of total cultivated land and other 50 per cent lands are used under Bhadai crops. This village does not provide suitable conditions for raising Rabi crops. Conditions available are not congenial for the production of wheat in particular. Thus, Aghani and Bhadai crops are main source of livelihood in the village. Agriculture is based on rain water. Water table goes down to more than 50 feet during summer season. In rainy season the water table remains only 10 feet below the surface of the earth sources of drinking water are 2 hand pumps and 4 wells.

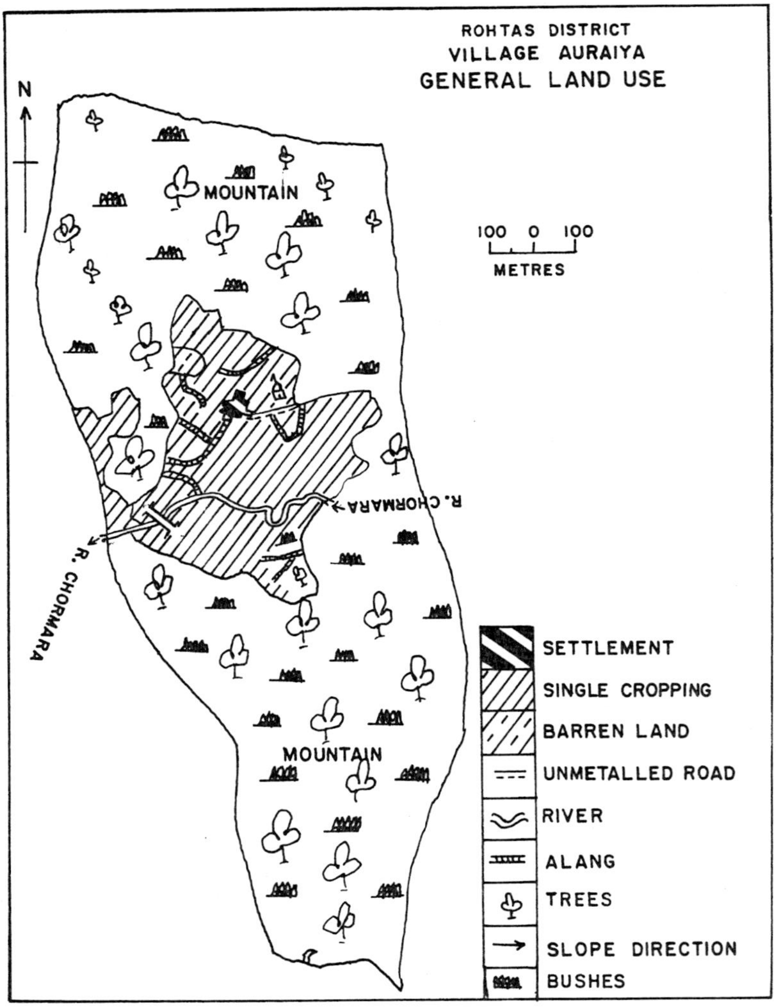
ROHTAS DISTRICT
VILLAGE AURAIYA
GENERAL LAND USE
N
MOUNTAIN
100 0 100
METRES
R. CHORMARA
R. CHORMARA
MOUNTAIN
SETTLEMENT
SINGLE CROPPING
BARREN LAND
UNMETALLED ROAD
RIVER
ALANG
TREES
SLOPE DIRECTION
BUSHES

Fig. 7.9

Table - 7.8
Cropping Pattern in Auraiya Village, 2007-08

Crops	Area in percentage of total cultivated land	Yield in kg per katha
Paddy	50.00	37
Maize	33.33	10
Millet	12.50	9
Others	4.17	7
Total	100.00	

Source : Field Survey.

The above table no. 7.8 explains that paddy is the most important crop among crops grown in this village. Its yield is also greater than other crops. Maize and Millets are other important crops in respect of total cultivated area. Thus, the above pattern of crops portray that the Aghani crops are comparatively in better portion than Bhadai crops. Aghani crops are grown on more than 50 per cent of total cultivated lands in the village.

The main problems associated with agriculture in the village are lack of plain and fertile land, non availability of fertilizer better seeds and irrigation, etc.

Auraiya village comes under Moderate Agricultural Region. It has a huge pressure of population on its farm land due to lack of net sown area. Its agricultural condition is undeveloped due to lack of plain and fertile land and lack of modern facilities in farming.

The afforested information's associated with Auraiya village gathered by the author, thus, represents the general pattern of various parameters found in the Northern Hilly Region.

VILLAGE : DUMARIA

Dumaria village lies in Nauhatta block and forms the area of Southern Hilly Area. This region is agriculturally poor and has sparse population.

This village is situated on foothill of Kaimur hill. It is surrounded by Pipardih village in the north and Lohara village in the south. Chaphla and Banua village bounds Dumaria village from east and west respectively. During some years back a narrow gauge railway line was passing through the northern part of this village. At the present time it is not found here. This village lies 4 kms. away from the block headquarters of Nauhatta and 65 kms away from Dehri railway station. As this village is located in nearly Kaimur hill, it has no metalled road. As a result economic and cultural aspects are poorly represented in this village. It also lacks the facilities of education, irrigation, market of good shops and doctors. Electricity is available only for domestic purposes. Drinking water is made possible through wells and hand pumps. This village has, got a small size of land i.e. 75.27 hectares. The population in the village is only 347 persons. The main source of livelihood of population is agriculture. The agriculture is, however, poorly developed. Single harvest is common over NSA of the village.

LAND PROFILE :

Even if this village contains a small size of land, the whole area is apparently not uniform in physical out look. The northern and southern parts of this village are hilly and present un-uniform landscape. Middle part of the village area is plain where village itself is locates and agricultural works are done. The hilly area spreads over nearly 50 per cent land of the village. Here nearly 12 per cent land is found under forest. The general slope is from north to south and south-east to north-west respectively.

The plain areas are found in centre and south-west parts of the village. It covers nearly 50 per cent area of the village. Of course, such lands are the basis of agriculture in this village. Aghani and Bhadai crops are generally raised on such lands. Here the farmers practice little rotation of crops. The general slope of this area is from north to south and east to west (fig. 7.10).

Drainage in this village is in form of pynes. Pynes follow the general slope. Soils of the village are generally affected by hilly and forested area. Consequently the soils found in this village appear reddish in look.

From above mentioned facts it is clear that the land profile found in Dumaria village truly represents the physical conditions present in Southern Hilly Region. Its slope, climate, soils, landform, etc are also similar as is generally available in this region. The scholar has found aforesaid characteristics during filed survey.

CULTURAL SETTING :

Population Characteristics :- Dumaria village has got poor cultural and economic amenities. It is a small size village and has got small size of population. It contains only 347 persons of which 179 are males and 168 are females. Thus male and female stand for 51.59 and 48.41 per cent of total population respectively. In the Dumaria village the entire population has scheduled tribe and belongs to only one caste i.e. Oraon. Out of male population about 5 per cent are old persons, 32 per cent working persons and 14 per cent belong to children. In case of female population, old persons are 6 per cent, working persons nearly 31 per cent and children stand for 12 per cent. Thus the percentage of male and female population is comparable. The age structure of population is, however, not even. A good size of population is non- working population. The percentage of the same is rather larger in case of female population. Dumeria village has, however, a comfortable percentage of working population.

As Dumaria village has got only a primary school, nearly 75 per cent population is illiterate. There are 22.61 per cent male and 2.40 per cent female literates in the village.

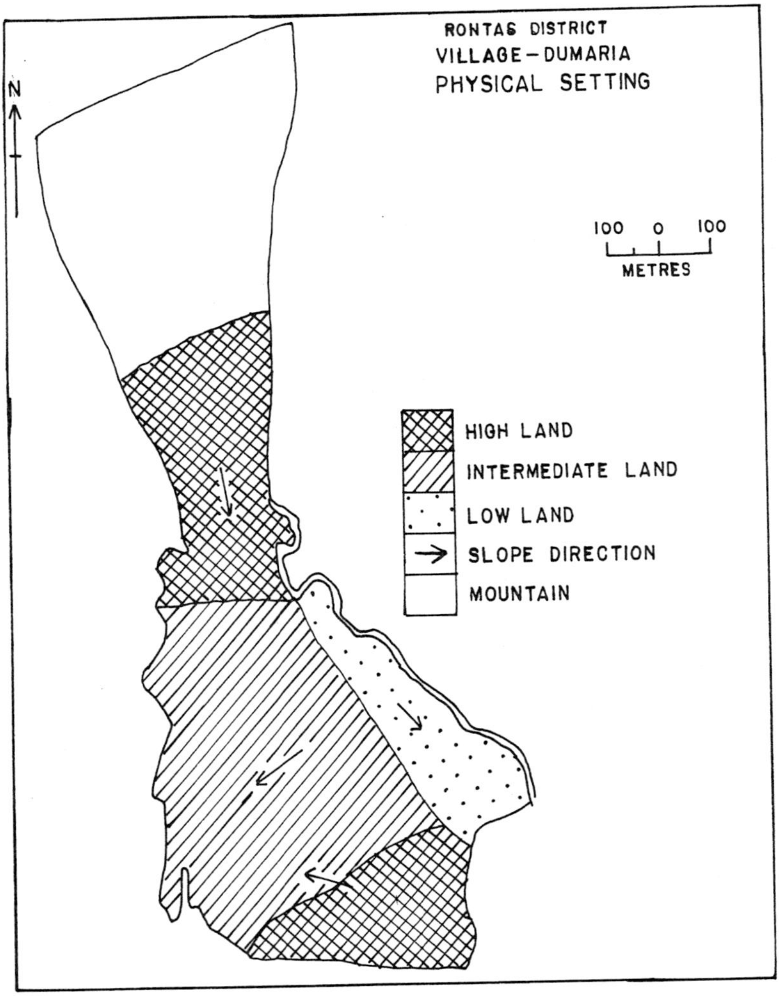
RONTAS DISTRICT
VILLAGE-DUMARIA
PHYSICAL SETTING
N
100 0 100
METRES
HIGH LAND
INTERMEDIATE LAND
LOW LAND
SLOPE DIRECTION
MOUNTAIN

Fig. 7.10

Table - 7.9
Oraon in Dumaria Village in percentage, 2008

Sl. No.	Caste	Total population	Male	Female
1	Oraon	100.00	51.59	48.41
	Total	100.00	51.59	48.41

Source : Field Work.

The present research has also attempted to study the working population. Altogether nearly 54 per cent population of this village is working population. Out of this working population nearly 45 per cent are cultivators, 7 per cent agricultural labourers and 3 per cent engaged in other works. Thus, a large size of population is engaged in primary occupation. The percentage of agricultural labourers is, however, exceedingly low which proves the fact that the agricultural output will not be sufficient to fetch livelihood. Thus, this situation in the village proves that the village has not got good agriculture.

Other Cultural Characteristics :- The author has also studied the technological know how which have less developed in the village. Here there are no tractors, no electric pumping sets and no diesel pumping sets. The village is linked with unmetalled road. In this village electricity is available for domestic purposes. Drinking water is obtained by hand pumps and wells. Irrigation is based on rainy water. In this village there is one primary school where nearly 100 students get education. Other persons obtain education in block headquarters.

Dumaria village comes under Sparsely Population Region. Population density of the village is 46 persons per km^2, which is very low than the average. As the main occupation of the village is cultivation more than 50% of population is working population.

LAND USE :

Net Sown Area in the village occurs on nearly 30 per cent

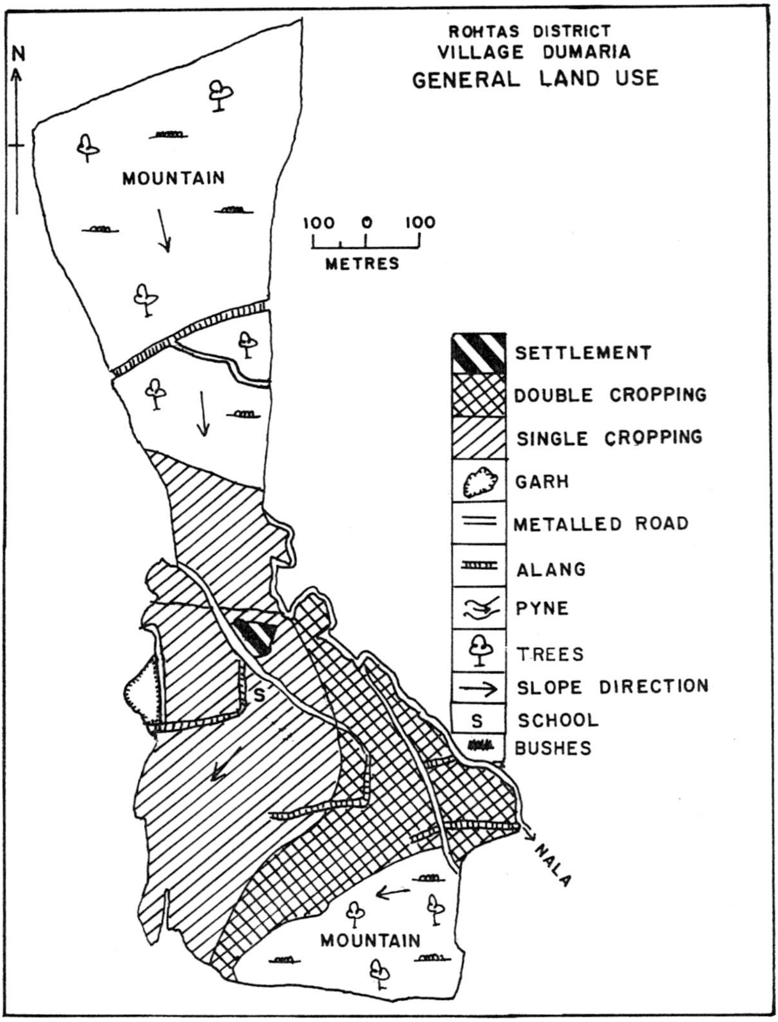
ROHTAS DISTRICT
VILLAGE DUMARIA
GENERAL LAND USE
N
100 0 100
METRES
MOUNTAIN
S
NALA
MOUNTAIN
SETTLEMENT
DOUBLE CROPPING
SINGLE CROPPING
GARH
METALLED ROAD
ALANG
PYNE
TREES
SLOPE DIRECTION
S
SCHOOL
BUSHES

Fig. 7.11

of its total area. Forest land stands for nearly 12 per cent, culturable waste 34 per cent and area not available for cultivation covers nearly 24 per cent land of the village. The above land use pattern thus explains the facts that a large part of its total area has been not suitable for cultivation. In this village the source of irrigation is rain water and wells.

Here the farmers of this village obtain two harvests on their agricultural land. These harvests are Aghani and Bhadai. About 75 per cent cultivated land is represented by Aghani crops and 25 per cent by Bhadai harvests. The irrigation of crops depends on rain water and wells (fig. 7.11).

Paddy is the main crop of Aghani harvest which is done on 75 per cent cultivated land. The yield of paddy is 15 kgms per katha. The second important crop is maize and cultivated on 20 per cent cultivated land. The yield of maize is 9 kgms. per katha. Other crops in the village are done on 5 per cent of cultivated land of the village.

Table - 7.10
Cropping Pattern in Dumaria Village, 2007-08

Crops	Area in percentage of total cultivated land	Yield per katha in kgms
Paddy	75	15
Maize	20	9
Others crops	5	8

Source : Field Survey.

The main problems in the village are lack of plain area, proper irrigation, availability of good seeds, adequate fertilizer, etc. They, therefore, need help from the government and other machineries.

Dumaria comes under Poor Agricultural Region and agriculture characteristics are also poor. Prominent reasons for the backwardness of agriculture are uneven landscape and lack of agricultural facilities. Agricultural density of the population is 15.36 persons / hectares due to which there is a great population pressure on its limited land resource.

VILLAGE : JOGIA

Jogia village comes in Bikramganj block and lies in the area of Northern Low Plain. Village Jogia comes under Densely Populated Region and Intensive Agricultural Region.

This village is 5 kms. away from block headquarters and Bikramganj railway station. Here, primary schools are available. There are good doctors in the village. Drinking water is available through wells and hand pumps. There is regular supply of electricity in the village. It is connected by a metalled road which links Bikramganj and Sasaram. Grampanchayat and playground are also available here. This village consists of 900 populations. The village area spreads over 70.82 hectares of land. Apart from above facilities, this village has got plain and fertile soils over its area. The above factors are, thus, responsible for the cultivation of every type of harvest here. The main source of livelihood for a population is, therefore, agriculture. Triple harvests are common on almost all cultivable area.

LAND PROFILE :

The landscape of Jogia village may be classified into Upland, Intermediate land and Low land. The upland area is found in southern parts and consists of 15% of total area. It is the land on which this village has developed. It is known as Dihland and is very fertile. It is generally useful for the extension of settlements. Cash crops are generally grown here. In this part of the village there are facilities of fertile soil and irrigation. The general slope of this area is from south to north.

The Intermediate land spreads over 65 per cent of land of the village. This land contains fertile plain tracts. It has become the main source of agricultural harvests. Aghani, Rabi Bhadai and Garma crops are raised here respectively. Such areas are found in middle and north-west parts of the village. The general slope of these parts is from south to north.

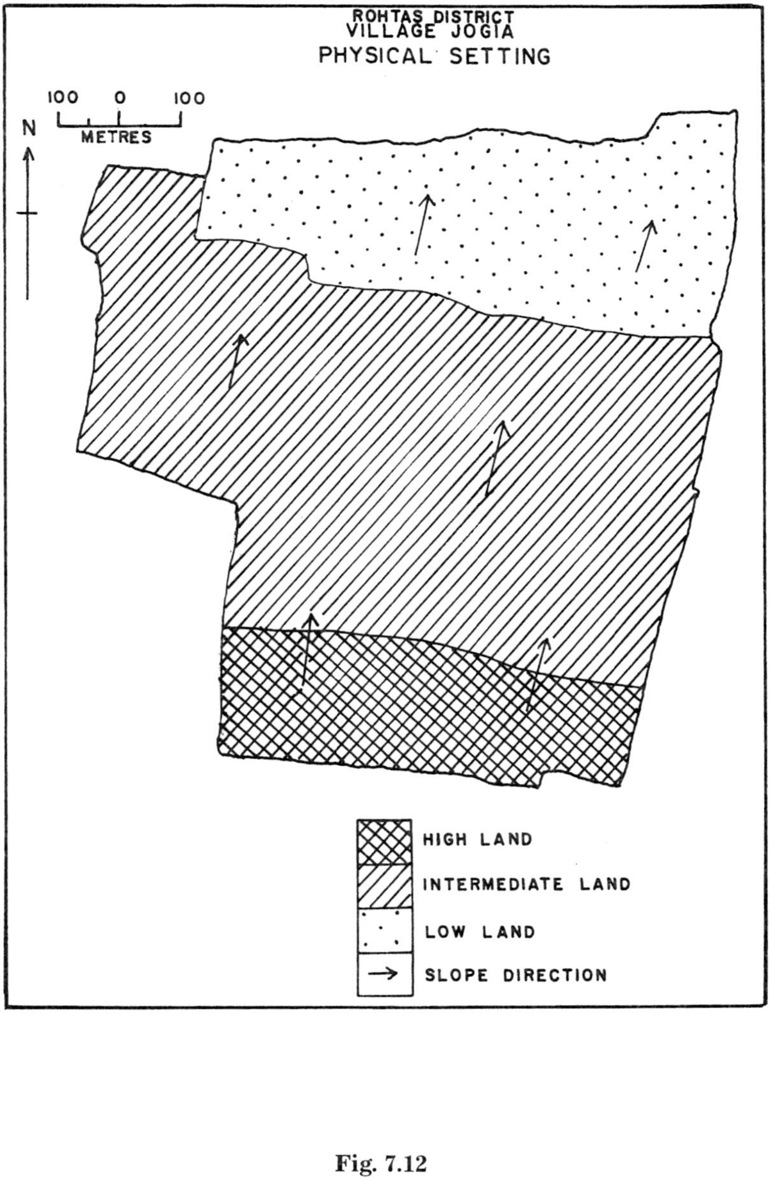
ROHTAS DISTRICT
VILLAGE JOGIA
PHYSICAL SETTING
100 0 100
METRES
N
HIGH LAND
INTERMEDIATE LAND
LOW LAND
SLOPE DIRECTION

Fig. 7.12

In this village, there is a tubewell for irrigation in the fields.

The lowland are found in extreme northern parts of the village and comprises nearly 20 per cent areas of Jogia village. Such lands have some limitation in proper utilization because these lands remain under water particularly during the months of rains. Here, there are, however, practice of two harvests i.e. Rabi and Bhadai because of the facilities of fertile soil and irrigation. The general slope of the area is like the general slope of other categories of land (fig. 7.12).

Drainage in this village is in the form of a numerous pynes. The drainage has been in co-ordination with the general slope of the village. Most of them, thus, flow from south to north.

This village contains some orchards which roughly cover the areas of upland and intermediate land and stand for nearly 5 per cent land of the village.

Soil of the village is entirely black. This soil is useful for raising many crops in the village. It is very fertile soil and multiple cropping system has been in operation on this soil.

It is thus clear from the above discussion that the parameters available in the village truly represent the conditions present in physical agricultural and population region associated with Jogia village.

CULTURAL SETTING :

Population Characteristics :- Jogia village comprises 900 persons and of which 498 are males and 402 are females. Thus, there is 55.33 per cent male and 46.67 per cent female in this village. Out of male population 3.67 per cent are old persons, 4.72 per cent are children and 46.94 per cent are working persons. In case of female population, old persons are 4.27 per cent, children and 5.31 per cent and working persons are 37.09 per cent. Thus, the percentage of male and female population is incomparable. Nearly 69 per cent population in this village is non working population. The percentage of the same is, however, discouraging in case of female population. Children and old persons comprise nearly 10 per cent of female population. Nearly 64 per cent population in the village is of scheduled castes.

The village has got primary school only where 145 students obtain education. Other persons obtain Middle and High school education in Bikramganj. The village is also connected with a main road. The villagers get better yield from fields. On account of above factors, nearly 49 per cent population of this village are literate persons. The percentage of female literates (17%) in, however, lower than that of male population (32%) out of the total population of village.

In the present research, attempt has also been male to study the working population. Nearly 31 per cent population in this village is working population. Almost working population is engaged in agriculture. As a result the pattern of agriculture workers shows that the agricultural condition in the village must be of the best quality.

Table - 7.11
Caste Pattern in Jogia Village, 2008

(in percentage)

Sl. No.	Castes	Total Population	Male	Female
1	Paswan	64.22	36.44	27.78
2	Bhumihar	23.67	11.77	11.89
3	Kamkar	7.67	4.33	3.33
4	Kanu	4.44	2.77	1.67
	Total	100.00	55.33	44.67

Source : Field Work.

The author has also attempted to investigate the population in term of its caste structure. This villages population is dominated by Paswan caste. It represents 64.22 per cent population of this village followed by Bhumihar 23.67 per cent, Kamkar 7.67 per cent and Kanu 4.44 per cent. The pattern of female population in all castes in smaller than male

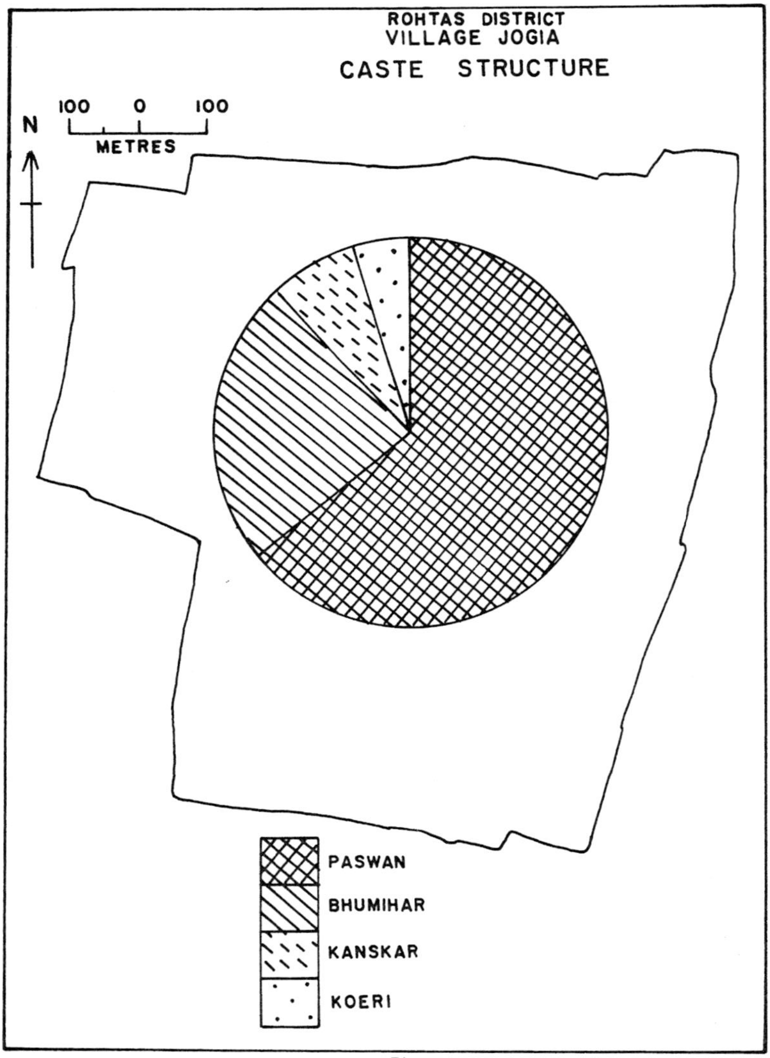
ROHTAS DISTRICT
VILLAGE JOGIA
CASTE STRUCTURE
N
100 0 100
METRES
PASWAN
BHUMIHAR
KANSKAR
KOERI

Fig. 7.13

population (fig. 7.13).

Other Cultural Characteristics : - Attempts have also been made to know the position of agricultural implements used in fields and its associated works. Here there are 6 tractors, 18 harvesters, 9 husking machines and 4 diesel and 6 electric pumping sets. The above pattern of agricultural implements, thus, explains that the farmers are literates particularly in agricultural works. The agricultural situations in this village are therefore, very good.

The village is linked with a metalled road. The block headquarters is hardly 5 kms. away from the village. Drinking water is available through wells and hand pumps. Electric is available for domestic and agricultural purposes.

Population characteristics of this village show that the demographic features are nearly the same as are found in Densely Populated Region. Population density in the village is 12 persons per hectares. Percentage of working population in the village is 46. 94. Jogia village is located in Intensive Agricultural Region. It has got almost characteristics of agriculture which are available in Intensive Agriculture Region.

LAND USE :

Land use pattern in the village is dominated by Net Sown Area. It is on 85 per cent of land of the village, followed by other cultivable land 7 per cent, fallow land 4 per cent, settlement 2 per cent and waste land and pasture 2 per cent. The above pattern of land use, therefore, explains that the percentage of N.S.A. is very high because this village contains fertile soil and has irrigation facilities. Thus, the land use pattern of Jogia village may well be compared with the land use found in tubewell irrigated western land of the district general (fig. 7.14).

In this village the irrigation of fields is made available with the help of tubewells, diesel pumping sets and rain water.

The presence of above amenities in Jogia village has

encouraged four harvests in fields. These harvests are Aghani, Rabi, Bhadai and Garma. Aghani harvest is taken from 90 per cent land of N.S.A. followed by Rabi 100 per cent, Bhadai 60 per cent and Garma 50 per cent. Aghani and Rabi crops are grown on all classes of land. Bhadai crops are grown on upland and intermediate land. Garma crops are also done on upland or intermediate land. Under these harvests a number of crops are harvested which are evident from the table no. 7.12 given below :

Table - 7.12
Cropping Pattern in Jogia Village, 2007-08

Crops	Area in percentage of total cultivated land	Yield per katha in kgms
Paddy	50	74
Wheat	35	46
Pulses	6	14
Maize	5	115
Vegetables	3	350
Other Crops	1	12

Source : Field Survey.

Paddy is the most important crop which is obtained from Aghani harvest in the village. It is done on 50 per cent of the total cultivated land and per katha yield is 74 kgms. The comfortable position of paddy is governed by the presence of fertile soil, irrigation facilities, better literacy pattern in farmers, etc. in the village.

Wheat is the second important crop in the village which is grown on 35 per cent of its total cultivated land and per katha yield of the same is 46 kgms. The above factors such as fertile soil, irrigation, economic soundness of farmers also help in practising of wheat cultivation on a large size of land with a good yield.

Other crops in this village are insignificant. They collectively stand for 15 per cent of its total cultivated land.

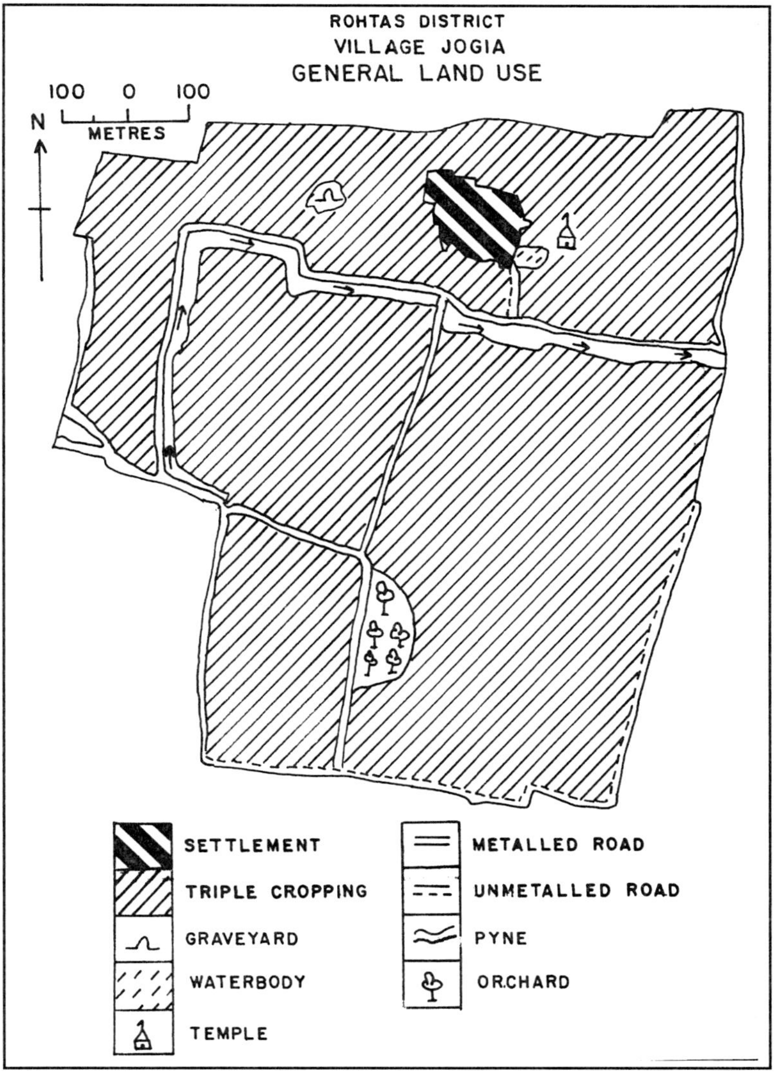
ROHTAS DISTRICT
VILLAGE JOGIA
GENERAL LAND USE
100 0 100
METRES
N
SETTLEMENT
TRIPLE CROPPING
GRAVEYARD
WATERBODY
TEMPLE
METALLED ROAD
UNMETALLED ROAD
PYNE
ORCHARD

Fig. 7.14

Pulses and maize are cultivated on 11 per cent of its total cultivated land. The yield of maize is high because of the irrigation facilities coupled with fertile soil. Pulses do not get proper regard in this village and it, therefore, gives poor yield i.e. 14 kgms. per katha.

Vegetables and other crops represent 4 per cent of total cultivated land in the village. Because of facilities stated above the yield of these crops is moderate to high.

The pattern of agriculture in the village, thus, explains the facts that the harvest pattern is dominated by Aghani and Rabi crops. Their areal percentage out of total cultivated land is very high. Other harvests also contain significant size of land in the village. Paddy in Aghani and wheat in Rabi harvests are important crops. Of course, these two crops form part of staple food for people and abundant facilities are available for cultivating these crops. Other important crops in this village are pulses and maize. The farmer two crops are grown on nearly almost N.S.A. which occurs in all classes of land.

In spite of the aforesaid favourable conditions there are necessity of good fertilizer, better irrigation facilities and good seeds in fields. Regular supply of electricity and a school up to high school are essential for sufficient agricultural also output and education in the village.

On the basis of the discussions made in above paragraphs it may be concluded that Jogia village represents the pattern of physical setting popular characteristics and agricultural attributes available around this village. Thus, the selection of Jogia village as sample village is comparable and justified.

8

Chapter

Geographical Pattern

IMPACT OF PHYSICAL FACTORS ON GEOGRAPHICAL PATTERN OF POPULATION :

The physical factors play a vital role in deciding the geographical pattern of population. We have already established that the spatial variation in parameters such as relief, slope, rainfall, soil, etc. has a close similarity and comparable to that of population distribution and density, literacy and sex ratio.

The Rohtas district can thus be studied under three geographical regions of population. The population region I may be called as Densely Population Region comprises the largest share of the population of the district. The density of population here is more than 600 persons per sq. km. It also has the highest percentage of literacy i.e. 45.47 to above 55 per cent. The sex ratio is below 934 per thousand male. The large size and high density of population are the result of plain and fertile agricultural land accompanied by a high ground water table. The fertile agricultural lands and well irrigated by canal system contain all the township of Rohtas district have naturally created prosperous economic conditions which have helped in the education of the people. The poor sex ratio may be the inclusion of urban population and poor nourishment to women particularly in rural areas.

The population region II termed as Moderate Population Region consists of a smaller percentage of total population of the district. The density of population ranges between 400 to 550 persons per sq. km. The literacy percentage varies from 43 to 50. The sex ratio is between 898 to 917 per thousand male. This population region is also plain except for a few hilly areas. The soil is of medium fertility. The ground water table is at low to moderate depth. Thus, the economic condition is poorer than that in population region I. Hence the density of population and the literacy are relatively smaller. The slightly higher sex ratio is not significant, as the conditions are not much different from the region I.

The population region III i.e. sparsely Population Region stands for the lowest percentage of total population of the district. The density of population is also low. Density varies between 191 to 576 persons per sq. km. The literacy is the poor i.e. 36 to 47 per cent. These are the result of hilly and forested topography. In a large part of this region, the soil is infertile and the ground water-table is at low depth. The rainfall, however, is higher. Thus, the physical factors except rainfall are adverse and do not favour cultivation. The population concentration is in eastern part of Nauhatta and Rohtas blocks and in northern part of Tilouthu block. The poor economic conditions of the people have adversely affected the pattern of education also. The sex ratio is high because the agricultural yield is not sufficient to provide livelihood to the people. The male population, therefore, prefer to migrate for work to urban areas or other prosperous areas of the region.

RELATIONSHIP BETWEEN POPULATION REGIONS AND AGRICULTURAL REGIONS :

Land is the most important source of livelihood for the entire population living in the district. The pattern of its use, therefore, affects the pattern of population. We have identified three geographical regions of population and agriculture which are being examined in the following paragraphs.

The population region I comprises parts of agricultural region I. The area of agricultural region I is slightly larger than that of population region I. These two type of regions however, span in the same direction i.e. from north-south to east-west and lie in the northern parts of the Rohtas district. The boundaries of these regions coincide closely in the north-south. As the agricultural region I is largely plain it has a high net sown area. The percentage of land cropped more than once and total cultivated land in all blocks is also high. The percentage of net sown area to total area in all blocks is above 60%. In many blocks, it is more than 85 per cent. Other important categories of land use are fallow land and land put to non- agricultural uses. A large percentage of total population of the district is to be found in this region leading to the highest density zone of population in the whole of Rohtas district. The literacy percentage is, also, comparatively better than in other regions of population. This has directly resulted from better economic conditions in the area. This population region contains all the towns of the Rohtas district.

The population and agricultural region II lie to the south and west of regions I. the boundaries of these regions II, however, do not coincide. This anomaly occurs because the population region II includes some parts of agricultural region I and II and spans over the mid-west parts of the Rohtas district. The boundaries of the population and agricultural regions II coincide only in the west. This anomaly also occurs because the population region II does not include the Kochas and Kargahar blocks of agricultural region II. These parts of population region II are covered by agricultural region I. The plain areas of agricultural region II have low to medium fertility. The water table is at low to moderate depth which facilitates well irrigation. The blocks of Sasaram and Sheosagar also have well canal irrigation. As a result of these natural and man made facilities, about 50 per cent of the land has been under net sown area. The area cropped more than once is about 25 per cent. Thus, the spatial pattern of agriculture is poorer than in agricultural region I. As the agricultural practice is poor in agricultural region II, the concentration of population is also more sparse than in population region I. The density of population ranges between 400 to 600 persons per sq. km. The population region II has medium percentage of literacy. There is no township in this region.

The population region III lies in the southern parts of Rohtas district. The agricultural region III includes the whole area of population region III. Population region III also comprises the hilly and forested parts of agricultural region III. The whole area of this region is, thus, hilly and forested. The percentage of net sown area is, therefore, low. The percentage of land under double cropping is also low. The ground water level is at low depth. Because of the above adverse physical conditions, the concentration and density of population are low. The literacy percentage is also poor due to poor economic conditions of the people. The sex ratio is high because the male members are forced to emigrate for earning their livelihood. Thus the density of population and literacy exhibit declining tendency with the poor pattern of agriculture.

IDENTIFYING GEOGRAPHICAL REGIONS :

The geographical region is an area which is distinct from neighbouring area in physical, economic and cultural aspects. The study area is divisible into three geographical regions. Each geographical region contains different characteristics and is separate from the neighbouring regions. For obtaining these geographical regions the author has firstly drawn choropleth maps for almost all important physical, land use and population variables. The physical regions have been determined after superimposing maps of physical variables one after another. The maps of physiography, average slope, rainfall and soil are taken for this purpose. The data of local water table has also been considered. The agricultural regions are obtained by the same process. The variables such as net sown area and land under double cropping were considered important for this purpose. The population regions have been identified after superimposition of choropleth maps of density of population, literacy and sex ratio. Finally, the geographical regions were determined by the sieve technique of superimposing maps of physical, land use and population regions. The geographical regions of the study area have thus, been primarily determined by a cartographic technique.

The three geographical regions of Rohtas district exhibit divergent characteristics from each other. Each geographical region represents all important variables of physiography, land use and population (Fig.8.1).

(i) Geographical Region I (Fertile Agricultural Plain) : It spreads over nearly 50 per cent of the total area of Rohtas district. It cover the whole of Kargahar, Nokha, Kochas, Karakat, Bikramganj, Nasriganj, Dinara, Dawath, Sanjhauli, Suryapura and Akorhi Gola and northern areas of Dehri block. Thus it spans over northern part of the district.

The whole of this geographical region is a low plain to moderates plain area and has humid climatic conditions. The soil is relatively fertile. This area is highly canalised. The local ground water level is high. This region is therefore an intensive agriculture and harvests a number of crops over large area. The percentage of land under net sown area is, thus, very high (over 80 %). A large part of net sown area is put to double cropping. The prosperous economic condition of the area has enabled the region to attract a moderate to high number of people. Thus, the density of population is high. Also this area has a high percentage of literacy because three township out of five townships of the Rohtas district lie in this region. This area has got also a good road network. The immigration of male labourers to the townships from other geographical regions has reduced the ratio of female population. As this geographical region is agriculturally prosperous it has got the representation of well built houses. The settlements are generally of compact and hamleted types. Most of the settlements contain large population size. A large number of service centres of Rohtas district are located in this region.

(ii) Geographical Region II (Undulating Agricultural Plain) :- It covers nearly 27 per cent of the total area of the Rohtas district. It is situated in central part of Rohtas district.

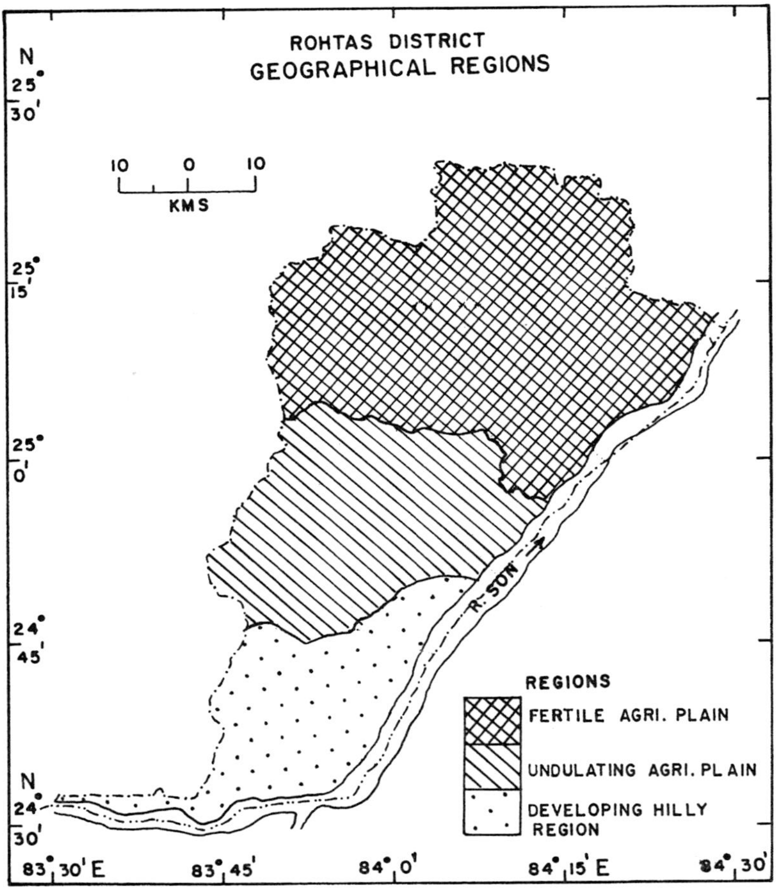
ROHTAS DISTRICT
GEOGRAPHICAL REGIONS
N
25°
30'
10 0 10
KMS
25°
15'
25°
0'
24°
45'
N
24°
30'
83° 30' E
83° 45'
84° 0'
84° 15' E
84° 30'
R. SON
REGIONS
FERTILE AGRI. PLAIN
UNDULATING AGRI. PLAIN
DEVELOPING HILLY REGION

Fig. 8.1

It includes areas of Sheosagar, Sasaram, Chenari and southern part of Dehri and northern part of Tilouthu blocks.

The entire area of this geographical region is slightly undulating and fertile. This region is relatively higher plain area. The ground water table is variable. Rainfall is normally higher than in other geographical region but more of rain occurs in hilly and forested area. Therefore, there is a gap between the percentages of net sown area in different parts of this region which varies from nearly 33 to 63 per cent. In this geographical region moderate drainage and moderates agricultural pattern are found. The percentage of net sown area is higher in relatively fertile plain and irrigationally better managed blocks. Its percentage is low in hilly and forested blocks of Sasaram and Chanari. The density of population is moderate to higher order. The percentage of literacy is high on account of better educational facilities and a better arrangement of roads which link this region with the towns of Sasaram and Dehri. The sex ratio of this area is medium to low order. This geographical region has well built houses in Dehri and Sasaram towns. The settlements are compact because of agrarian character. The number of service centres is moderate.

(iii) Geographical Region III (Developing Hilly Region) :- This geographical region spreads over the southern areas of Rohtas district and represents nearly 23 per cent of the study area. It comprises parts of Nauhatta, Rohtas and southern parts of Tilouthu blocks. Thus, this region represents the eastern part of the great Vindhyan system.

The greater part of this region is hilly and forested, except the southern and eastern areas which usually lie along the bank of Son river and exhibits wet climatic conditions. The underground water table is low. The rainfall is not sufficient to raise crops in plain areas. It exhibits poor representation of most variables of land use, population and settlement. It has a poor net of transport. The percentage of more than once cropped land to net sown area and total area is also low but the irrigation is moderate to high. The sex ratio is medium and the settlements are of dispersed type. Service centres are rarely found. This area is, thus, underdeveloped.

CORRELATIONS AND INFERENCES :

A major hypothesis of the present study is that there is a strong environmental control of cultural phenomena in Rohtas district. This has become more probable because the region under study is relatively undeveloped and has therefore, witnessed little technological modification of natural elements. However, this statement has to be objectively examined and confirmed.

In order to make a scientific analysis of physical, human and cultural elements in the region under study Pearsonian Correlation Coefficients (Product Moment Coefficient of Correlation) have been calculated between the following parameters at blocks level :-

1. Average relief
2. Annual rainfall in centimetres
3. Percentage of net sown area in total block area
4. Percentage of land cropped more than once over net sown area (intensity of cropping)
5. Population density (persons per sq. km.)
6. Irrigation

Six correlation coefficient (r) values have been found for the above six parameters and the analysis of variance (r^2) has been expressed as percentage. Also the discrete variables have been plotted on suitable scatter diagrams fitted with lines of linear regression (fig. 8.2).

Table - 8.1
Showing Significant Correlation in Rohtas District

Nature of Correlation		X Variable	Y Variable	Correl-ation (r)	Analysis of Variance (r^2 x 100)
High	1	Average relief	% NSA	-0.79	62
Medium	1	Irrigation	Pop. Density	-0.59	35
	2	Irrigation	% NSA	-0.45	20
	3	% NSA	Pop. Density	0.41	17
	4	% Double cropped	Pop. Density	0.36	13
Low	1	Average relief	Pop. Density	-0.27	7
	2	Average relief	% Double Cropped	-0.11	1.21
	3	Rainfall	% Double Cropped	-0.05	0.25

Table 8.1 shows that the there is a high correlation between average relief and NSA in % (-0.79). Since about 80 per cent of the variation in the dependent variable depends upon the variation in the independent variable in each case (fig. 8.3).

Irrigation also has a medium correlation with population density (0.59, -0.59) and NSA in % (0.56, -0.45). However, the intensity of cropping has not got high correlation with population density (0.36) and (fig. 8.4).

Relief has a low correlation with population density and intensity of cropping (% double cropped land). Thus relief, as an environmental determinant has small an immense negative effect on population density and double cropped in %. Correlation between rainfall and % double cropped is negligible (fig. 8.5).

Average relief has a high correlation with NSA in % (-0.79) and low correlation with population density and double cropped in % (-0.27 and -0.11 respectively). At the same time the rainfall and irrigation has a medium correlation with

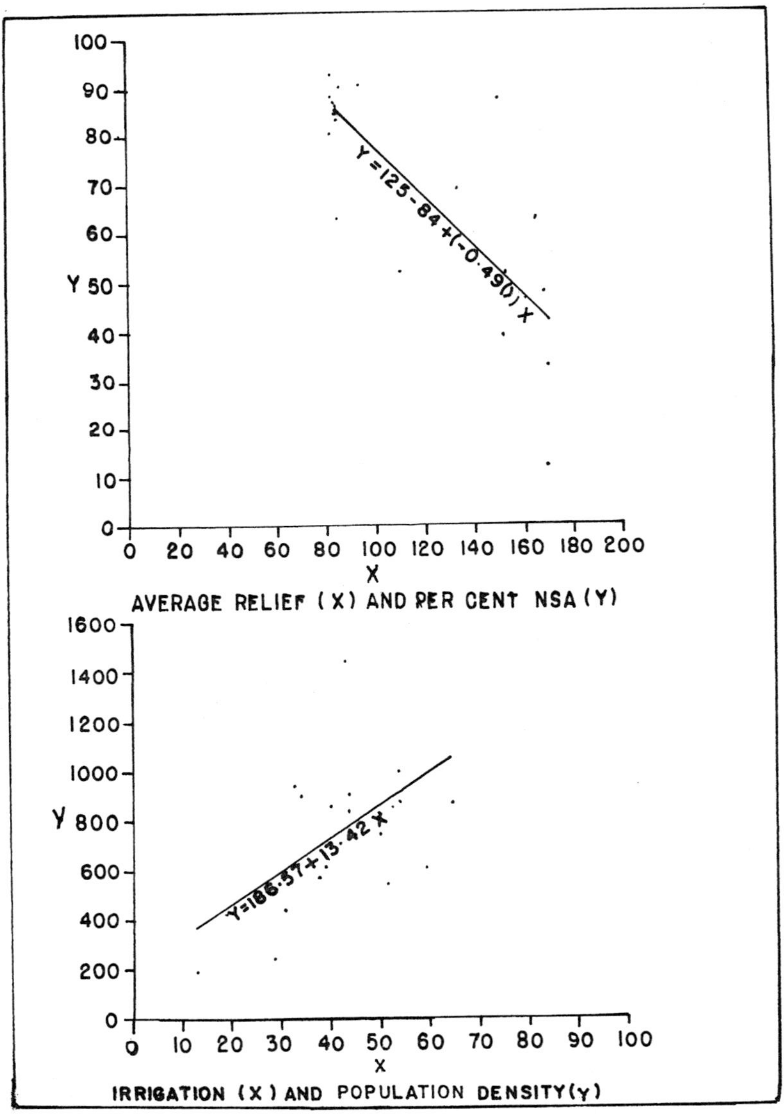
Y
X
Y = 125·84 + (-0·49(1)) X
0
20
40
60
80
100
120
140
160
180
200
10
30
50
70
90
AVERAGE RELIEF (X) AND PER CENT NSA (Y)
Y=186·57+13·42 X
1600
1400
1200
1000
800
600
400
200
IRRIGATION (X) AND POPULATION DENSITY (Y)

Fig. 8.2

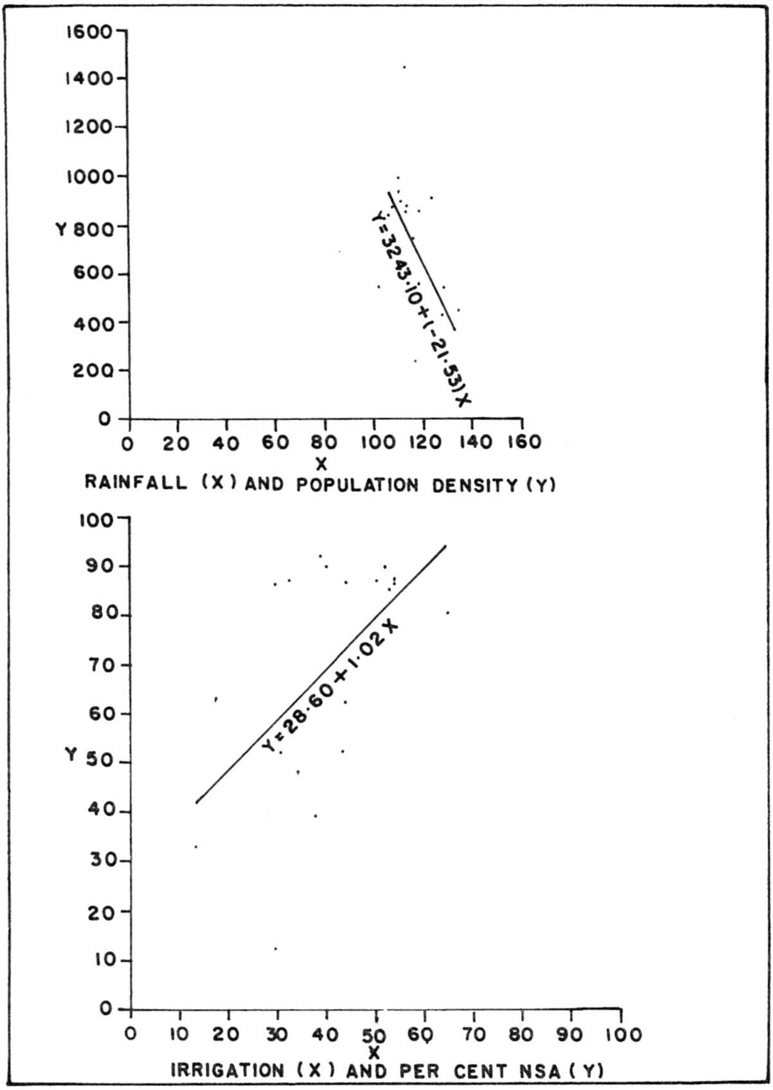
1600
1400
1200
1000
Y 800
600
400
200
0
0 20 40 60 80 100 120 140 160
X
Y=3243·10+(-21·53)X
RAINFALL (X) AND POPULATION DENSITY (Y)
100
90
80
70
60
Y 50
40
30
20
10
0
0 10 20 30 40 50 60 70 80 90 100
X
Y=28·60+1·02X
IRRIGATION (X) AND PER CENT NSA (Y)

Fig. 8.3

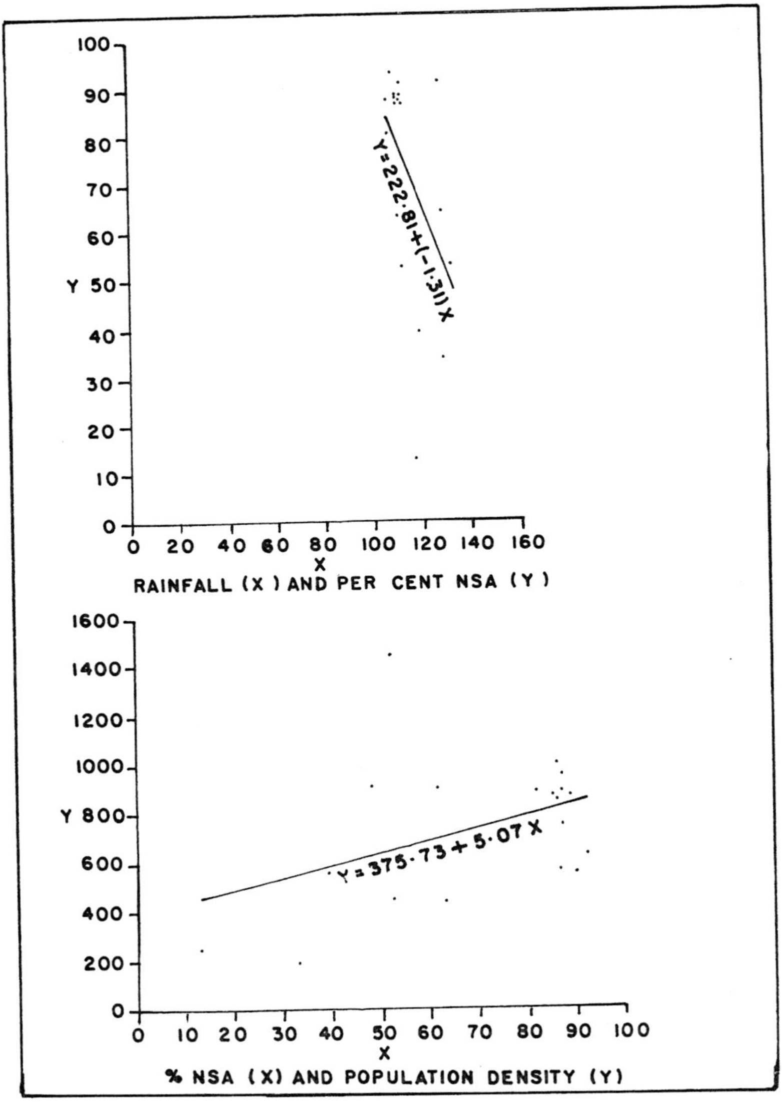
100
90
80
70
60
Y 50
40
30
20
10
0
Y=222.81+(-1.31)X
0 20 40 60 80 100 120 140 160
X
RAINFALL (X) AND PER CENT NSA (Y)
1600
1400
1200
1000
Y 800
600
400
200
0
Y=375.73+5.07X
0 10 20 30 40 50 60 70 80 90 100
X
% NSA (X) AND POPULATION DENSITY (Y)

Fig. 8.4

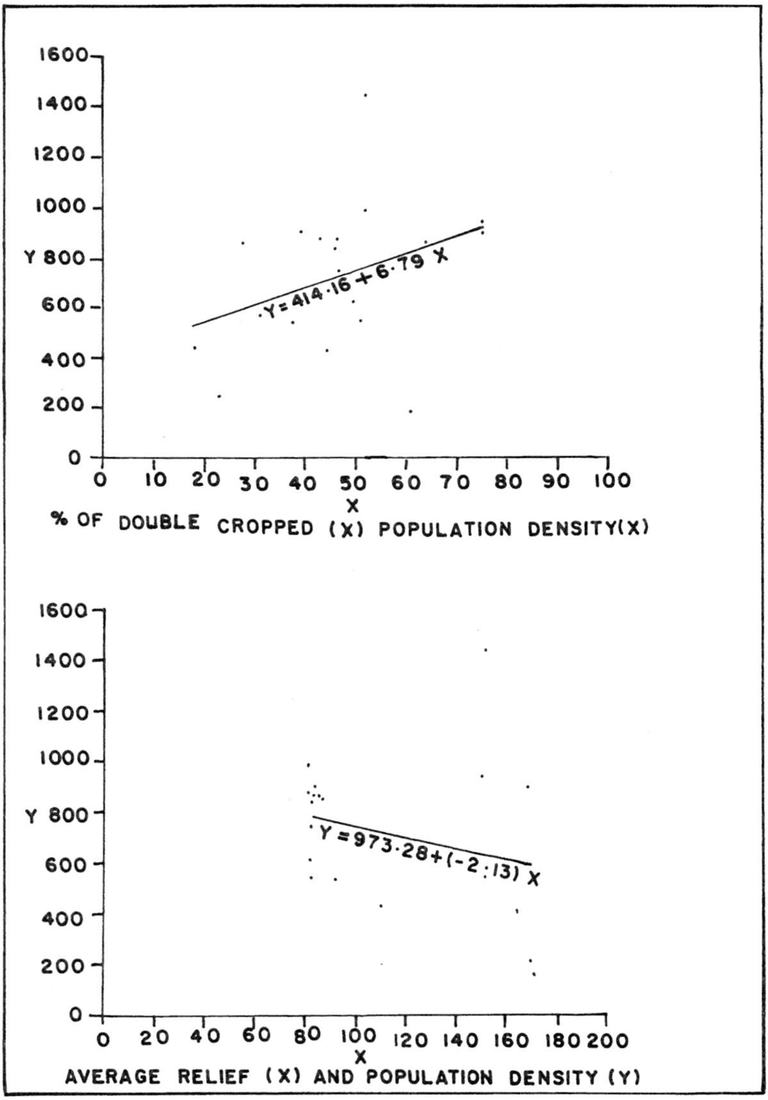
1600
1400
1200
1000
Y 800
600
400
200
0
0 10 20 30 40 50 60 70 80 90 100
X
Y = 414·16 + 6·79 X
% OF DOUBLE CROPPED (X) POPULATION DENSITY(X)
1600
1400
1200
1000
Y 800
600
400
200
0
0 20 40 60 80 100 120 140 160 180 200
X
Y = 973·28 + (-2·13) X
AVERAGE RELIEF (X) AND POPULATION DENSITY (Y)

Fig. 8.5

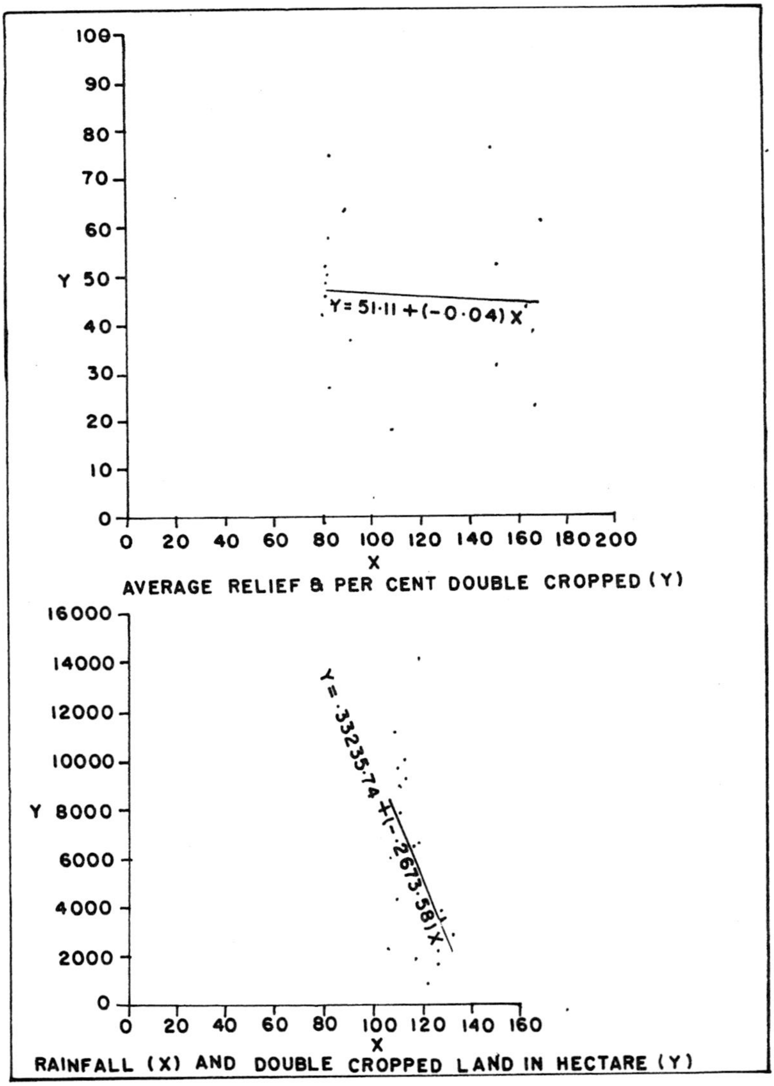
100
90
80
70
60
Y 50
40
30
20
10
0
Y= 51·11 +(−0·04) X
0 20 40 60 80 100 120 140 160 180 200
X
AVERAGE RELIEF & PER CENT DOUBLE CROPPED (Y)
16000
14000
12000
10000
Y 8000
6000
4000
2000
0
Y= ·33235·74 +(−·2673·58) X
0 20 40 60 80 100 120 140 160
X
RAINFALL (X) AND DOUBLE CROPPED LAND IN HECTARE (Y)

Fig. 8.6

population density (-0.59, 0.59) and % NSA (-0.45, 0.56). Thus, average relief, rainfall and irrigation taken together influence population distribution and density (fig. 8.6).

Generalising the results of analysis of variance it can be concluded that there exists a strong deterministic influence of physical environment (average relief and rainfall taken together) upon population distribution. This effect becomes more pronounced when we realise that the physical environment also influences land use and intensity of cropping and that the latter two combined together (relief and rainfall) influence population density. Thus the physical environment primarily controls land use and agriculture and secondarily population density. Of course there is an interaction between land use and population density, but this is only natural. There is always a close correspondence and an interaction between cultural elements in any area as land use, intensity of cultivation are manifestations of human occupance of land. The crucial question is whether man by his technological skill has been able to circumvent the influence of environment upon his activities and mode of habitat. In the region under study, the modification if any case has been observed negligible even of the deterministic influence of environment upon cultural elements is statistically proved to be significant.

As a result, the geographical patterns of distribution of various physical parameters seem to be in close correspondence with cultural elements in the Rohtas district. This justifies the carving out of geographical regions with homogeneous characteristics. These regions have already been discussed earlier in this chapter.

9

Chapter

Summary and Conclusion

SUMMARY :

This chapter brings together salient observations and major findings made in various chapters of the present study. The study area is a district of Bihar consisting of 3 sub-divisions and 19 development blocks. It comprises 2062 inhabited villages and 6 towns. The district embraces an area of 3839.32 km^2 with a total population of 2450748 (2001).

The study area has a long cultural history being part of the ancient Magadha Empire. Today it is intimately related to the cities of Patna and Gaya with which it has good transport links.

Geologically, the study area is characterized by Pre-vindhayan, Lower vindhayan, Upper vindhayan and Recent to sub-recent periods. Physiographically the district is divided into two divisions' viz. (i) Plateau Rohtas (ii) Plain Rohtas. The general slope is to the north-east along the drain line of river Son. However, the drainage system can be divided into Son, Durgawati and Kao systems. Climatically, it is very much a part of monsoonal type of climate, being characterized by heavy rainfall during the monsoon period and a long spell of lean period belonging to dry summer and winter. Winter rainfall occurs rarely as a result of westerly depression.

Texturally, soils of the Rohtas district can be divided into clayey, loamy clay and sandy loam. Alluvial soil is covered by more than 50% of geographical area. This soil is fertile soil but the red soil of the plateau region is not fertile. Forest is an important environmental asset for any geographical region. The study area covers 17% surface under the forest cover. Moreover this green cover is almost absent in the plain area.

Water resource of the study area depends upon physical attributes such as structure, topography, climate, forest cover, etc. Annual utilizable recharge of ground water is 1725.37 m. cum. whereas its annual net draft is 44.08 m. cum. Utilizable ground water is available in all 19 development blocks.

Limestone, Pyrite and sandstone are major minerals of the Rohtas district. Limestone is reserved over the vast area, Pyrite is found in Amjhore and Ghogha areas while sandstone is scattered in Karwandia - Tarachandi - Sasaram region.

Agriculture in the district is primitive and at subsistence level. In many parts it is almost entirely dependent upon the vagaries of rainfall. About 64 per cent of the total land is cropped annually. Other important categories of land use are forest and barren lands, land put to non- agricultural uses and current fallows. The northern fertile blocks of the district have more than 80 per cent of their land under net sown area. These blocks avail wet climatic conditions, a high ground water table, canal irrigation and better farm management. Nokha, Dinara, Bikramganj, Sanjhauli, Rajpur, Dawath blocks lie in the northern parts of the district. The southern hilly and forested blocks of Nauhatta and Rohtas have nearly 73 to 30 per cent of their total land under forest and barren lands categories.

The per capita cultivated land is low in the Rohtas district. It is extremely low in hilly areas. The capability status of land in this district has been determined on the basis of soil fertility, productivity and market price of land. Dih land containing loamy soil, though smallest in size, is the best type of agricultural land. It is attached with the dwelling and fetches the highest price in the market. Intermediate land occupies large areas of the village and has moderate value; the soil of this land is variable. During dry years a part of it is left fallow.

Low land is largely Ahar land and is waterlogged during the rainy months. The soil is clayey with high moisture retaining capacity. It is generally single cropped with paddy.

The pattern of land use varies in physical regions. The net sown area exceeds other categories of land in the North Plain. The northern plain has a high percentage (Dinara block 92.55% N.S.A.) of cultivated land. The net sown area in southern hilly region is poor and forest and barren lands are extensive (Rohtas 72.57% of the total land). The central high plain is fertile with more than 50 per cent of its total area under net sown area. The two hilly regions of Rohtas, Nauhatta and Sasaram have a high percentage of forest and barren lands on account of high slope, high rainfall and occurrence of alkaline or Reh patches.

The chief agricultural harvest is Aghani (July-November) covering 53.37 per cent of the total cropped land, although Rabi (winter) with 43.75 per cent. The cropped land can be divided into two categories (i) the uplands given to maize millet and coarse rice, and (ii) the plain lands given to paddy, wheat, sugarcane and dalhan. Paddy is cultivated on 53 per cent of the total agricultural land of the Rohtas district followed by wheat (42%), pulses (0.78%) and oilseed (3%).

The yield of rice is higher and requires less investment in hilly blocks. The same is smaller with higher investment in plain blocks. The former gets adequate rain while the latter compensates less rainfall with irrigation. The main sources of irrigation are canal and tubewells. Tubewells are impractical in hilly areas owing to a low water table.

Three agricultural regions have been identified on the basis of net sown area and land cropped more than once. The agricultural region I lie in the north and is noted for large area under agriculture. This region is plain and fertile. The water table is generally high and there is also better management of canal irrigation. This region covers 50.17 per cent of total area of the district. The agricultural region II contains both fertile plain and infertile hilly areas. Hence it is marked by a great variation in agriculture (Sheosagar 63% N.S.A., Tilauthu 39% N.S.A.). The agricultural region III contains both plain and hilly areas, but it is largely infertile. The water table is also low. The intensity of agriculture is, therefore, small.

The Rohtas district has variable growth and even negative growth of population up to 1921. The population increased rapidly after 1921 except during 1971-81. The rate also remained high during 1991-2001. The responsible factors are improved medical facilities and better agricultural conditions leading to economic prosperity. Population growth is comparatively higher in hilly blocks and lower in plain and fertile blocks. The probable causes are illiteracy and early marriage in hilly blocks. In plain areas people are relatively more literate and adopt family planning techniques.

The distribution of population is uneven. It is large in fertile agricultural areas and small in infertile hilly areas. The plain physical regions account for nearly 96 per cent of total population, the balance 4 per cent being located in hilly areas. 87 per cent of the total population is distributed in rural areas. The population concentration is highest in agricultural region I which is fertile and lowest in agricultural region III which is hilly and forested. Agricultural region II contains low to moderate population concentration. The population is, however, dense in some fertile pockets.

The highly populated zone embraces the plain and fertile blocks of the north. Here the population density in all blocks has been sharply increasing. The moderately populated zone comprises undulating areas throughout its span. The increase in population density in different decennial years is, therefore, medium. The thinly populated blocks are largely hilly and forested where the increase in density has been small.

The temporal population density and its variation are generally higher in plain and fertile physical regions. Hilly regions also exhibit striking density variation. The temporal density and its population are higher in agricultural region

I. This region is largely a fertile plain. The percentage of land under net sown area and double cropping is high. Other agricultural regions exhibit an increasing trend of population density but it is lower than in agricultural region I.

The male population exceeds female population in urban areas but is lower in some rural areas. For total population, the sex ratio shows a slight excess of females over males. The female population per thousand male has, however, come down both in rural and urban areas and in the Rohtas district. The high sex ratio in hilly and forested block is indicative of out-migration of male folk in search of jobs.

The Rohtas district is marked by a low level of literacy which is lower than that in Bihar State. Female literacy is only 17.36 per cent in 2001. The main reasons are poverty of the masses, inadequate transport facilities in hilly and forested areas and lack of educational institutions over large areas.

Literacy has increased in rural and urban areas in recent decades. The rate of literacy has always remained higher in urban areas, and in plain agricultural blocks as compared to rural or hilly and forested areas. The reasons are obvious. Further, male literacy has been higher than female literacy in almost areas during all decades.

Scheduled castes population is 18 per cent of total population of Rohtas district. They are distributed over the entire region. The percentage has remained between 15 to 22 out of total population in the majority of blocks in 1981 and 1991, but has slightly decreased in several blocks in 2001. The scheduled tribes population is negligible and is mainly concentrated in hilly and forested blocks of the Rohtas district.

The occupational structure is dominated by male workers. The proportion of workers is generally larger in blocks which have a bigger population size. The size of working force in rural areas is relatively larger than in urban areas. As the Rohtas district is largely rural and agricultural in character, the occupational structure is dominated by cultivators and agricultural labourers.

Three population regions can be distinguished on the basis of population density, literacy and sex ratio. The area of population region I is largely fertile agricultural land and it therefore, contains a high density of population (over 600 per sq. km.). As the economic condition is satisfactory, the percentage of literacy is also high. The sex ratio is low. The study of sample villages of this population region except minor exceptions attests to the aforesaid qualities.

The population region II contains a density of 400 to 550 persons per sq. km. The literacy percentage is medium. The sex ratio varies from 898 to 917 females per thousand males. The areas of this population region comprise land of low to medium fertility. The number of educational institutions and transport facility are also poor. This population region contains two sample villages of which Turky village reflects the characteristics of this region. The other two sample villages are more akin to population region III because these villages have infertile land and also represent poor educational facilities.

The population region III has a low density of population and low percentage of literacy. The sex ratio is also generally low. The areas of this population region are largely hilly and forested and the male members are compelled to out-migrate for livelihood. There are very few educational institutions. The sample villages also exhibit similar characteristics.

The sample villages of these population regions comprise a number of castes. This number is, however, relatively larger in sample villages of population regions I and II. The probable reason may be larger population size of these villages. In the sample villages of population region I and II, more than 45 per cent people belong to working age group but their share is much less in the sample villages of population region III.

A statistical analysis of six important block level parameters relating to the physical environment (average relief and rainfall), irrigation, land use, intensity of cropping and population density has been made. Values of Pearsonian Correlation Coefficients (r) and analysis of variance (r^2) lead us to the conclusion that there exists a strong deterministic influence of the physical environment directly upon land use and population density and indirectly upon population distribution and density in the region under study.

It has been found that relief has a very high correlation with the percentage of net sown area and low correlation with population density and intensity of cropping (% double cropped). Net sown area has a medium correlation with population density. Intensity of cropping has a medium correlation with population density. Rainfall and irrigation have high correlation with population density and medium correlation with net sown area. On the basis of above facts we come to the irresistible conclusion that relief, rainfall and irrigation control land use, agriculture and population distribution in Rohtas district. This has made it possible to establish economic the relationship between various physical, land use and population regions identified in different chapters.

A close distributional similarity between these regions and the close correspondence of the borders carved out for various parameters has led to the recognition of three geographical regions by applying sieve technique. Two of these fall in the plain parts and have varying degrees of soil fertility, intensity of agriculture and population density. The other one falls in hilly and forested parts of the study region and has a different character of land use and population distribution. These have been discussed in detail in chapter VIII.

CONCLUSION :

The above summary of findings explicitly portrays how Rohtas district has thoroughly been studied and analysed with regard to its physical features, population characteristics, nature of land use and many other geographical aspects of relevance. It has been found practical to divide the study area into physical, agricultural and population regions based upon various parameters taken for the present research work.

The physical regions have been identified on the basis of physical parameters of relief, slope, water table, climate and soils. There are three physical regions in the plain area where the land surface is reasonably level, ground water table is high and the soil is fertile. The hilly areas have similarly been divided into two region marked with high average slope, low ground water table, infertile soils, rocky surface and coverage of forests. These physical regions exhibit significant variations in land use and population characteristics.

The per capita cultivated land is usually low in the study area and extremely low in the hilly areas. The spatial pattern of land use varies in physical regions depending mainly upon slope, rainfall, ground water table and nature of soils. Plain regions contain relatively higher percentage of land under net sown area in comparison to hilly regions. On the other hand hilly regions have a high percentage of forest and barren lands on account of high slope and high rainfall. Irrigation facilities in various parts of the study area tend to modify the influence of relief rainfall and soils.

Three agricultural regions have been identified on the basis of net sown area and land cropped more than once. Agricultural region I lies in the north and is highly fertile and intensively cultivated. Agricultural region II is located in central part of the study area and includes both undulating plain and hilly areas. It is less fertile and marked by a great variation in spatial pattern of agriculture. Agricultural region III lies in the south. It is largely hilly and fertile. It also contains forest on some of its areas. As a result it represents poor cropping system.

The distribution of population in Rohtas district is

uneven. More than two third populations live in plain areas, the balance in hilly areas. However the population growth rate is lower in the former and higher in the later, mainly owning to poverty and illiteracy. Population density is the highest in fertile plain lands, moderate in undulating and the lowest in hilly and forested physical regions. The high sex ratio in hilly and forested blocks is an indicative of out migration of males in search of employment. The low level of literacy in these areas is also a result of poor economy. The occupational structure is dominated by cultivators and agricultural labourers in almost areas. There has been little urban development. Thus population characteristics exhibit a strong influence of natural environment and land use upon human activities.

Three population regions have been demarcated on the basis of population density, population distribution, literacy and sex ratio as these variables exhibit the largest spatial variation. Population region I generally covers the fertile agricultural areas in the north having a high density a relatively high literacy and a moderate sex ratio. The undulating population region II represents moderate condition in all these parameters. Population region III is hilly and forested and is marked by low density, low literacy and moderate to high sex ratio. The study of sample villages in these three regions clearly brings out these characteristics.

It has been observed that although the respective boundaries of physical, land use and population regions do not exactly coincide with each other, there is a sufficiently close correspondence and a distributional similarity to enable us to carve out geographical region with the help of sieve technique. Three geographical regions have been identified and discussed in the previous chapter. Two of these regions lie in the plain parts having varying degrees of soil fertility intensity of cultivation and population density. The hilly and forested areas have got poor soils, low level of agriculture and low density and distribution of population. Other characteristics of relief, soils land use, population also vary in these geographical regions which have been described in detail at appropriate places in various chapters.

A statistical analysis of correlation between six relevant parameters has been made and shown on six scatter diagrams fitted with regression lines. The study reveals that a high correlation exists between average relief and net sown area. Medium correlation exists between irrigation, rainfall, net sown area, density of population and more than once cropped land. This proves that environmental factors represented by slope / relief and rainfall directly control land use and population distribution. The deterministic influence of environment upon human activities i.e. cultural landscape thus stands proved. The similar result is found noticeable in the case of sample village studies made which attests to the fact that the statistical analysis is not an abstract but very much near to the truth or real.

To conclude it may be attempted to answer the questions posed in the first chapter while formulating, the hypothesis. The present research, thus, proves that Rohtas district can be divided into natural regions based on various physical parameters. These regions have a close relationship with regions carved out on the basis of land use and population characteristics. It has been witnessed that physical and land use attributes have deterministic influence upon population characteristics as the boundaries of these regions have a close correspondence even if they do not coincide. However, applying sieve technique it has become possible to identify geographical regions in study area based upon various parameters. The hypothesis that environment has a deterministic influence upon the cultural landscape in Rohtas district stands proved by the statistical and cartographic analysis carried out. The illustrations made by the sample village studies further support and authenticate the results achieved in the present study.

Bibliography

BOOKS :

Ackerman, E. A. (1954) : Population and Natural Resource, The Study of Population, ed. By Hauser, P.M. and Duncen, O.D.

Ambannavar, J.P. (1975) : Second Indian Studies, Population, The Macmillan Company of India Ltd. Delhi, Bombay, Madras, Calcutta.

Belshaw, H. (1956) : Population Growth and Levels of Consumption.

Bhattacharya, A. (1978) : Distribution of Population, Population Geography of India, Shree Publishing Company, New Delhi.

Bhende, Asha A. and Kanitkar, T. (1978) : Principles of Population Studies, Himalaya Publishing House.

Bogue, D.J. (1950) : Internal Migration in the Study of Population, ed. By Hauser, P.M. and Dunean, O.D., Chicago.

Caldwell, J.C. and Okonjo, C. (1969) : Population of Tropical Africa by T.E. Hilton, Longmans.

Chandra, R.C. & Sindhu, M.S. (1980) : Introduction to Population Geography, Kalyani Publishers, Ludhina, New Delhi.

Chaudhary, P.C. (1953) : Political History of Ancient India, Calcutta.

Clark, J.I. (1966) : Population Geography, Pergaman Press, London.

Clark, J.I. (1966) : What is Population Geography, Population Geography, Pergamon Press.

Clark, P.J. and Evans, F.C. (1954) : Distance to Nearest Neighbour as a Measure of spatial Relationship in Population, Ecology.

Clarke, B.D. (1972) : Iran : Changing Population Pattern, Population of the Middle East and North Africa, University of London Press Ltd.

Clarke, John I (1972) : Population Geography, Pergamon Press Oxford.

Clarke, John I. (1966) : What is Population Geography ? Pargamon Press, London.

Cole, J.P. and King, C. A.N. (1963) : Quantitative Geography, Wiley, New York.

Cox, P. R. (1961) : Demography.

Cunningham, (1929) : Ancient Geography of India, edited by S.N. Mazumdar, London.

Davis, Kingsley (1951) : The Population of India and Pakistan, Princeton University Press.

Dayal, P. (1953) : Bihar in Maps, Kusum Prakashan, Patna - 3.

Demko, G.J. (1970) : Spatial Pattern of Population Flows in Population Geography.

Demko, G.J. et. al. (1970) : Spatial Pattern of Population Geography, A Reader, McGraw Hill Book Company, New York.

Desai, P.B. (1967) : Patterns of Population Change in India, Bombay, Allied Publishers.

Dewdney, B.D. (1972) : Syria : Pattern of Population Distribution, Population of the Middle East and North Africa, University of London Press Ltd.

Enyedi, G. (1971) : The Land of Hungary and Its Agricultural Utilisation : Studies in Applied and Regional Geography, Edited by Md. Shafi and Mehdi Raza, Publication of Department of Geography Aligarh Muslim University, Aligarh.

Garnier, J.B. (1976) : Geography of Population, Longman, London.

Glass, D.V. and Grebenik, E. (1954) : The Trend and Pattern of Fertility in Great Britain : A Report of the Family Census of 1946.

Gosal, G.S. (1961) : Regionalism of Sex Composition of India's Population, Rural Sociology.

Gosal, G.S. (1964) : Literacy in India : An Interpretative Study, Rural Sociology.

Gould, W.T.S. and Prothero, R.M. (1976) : The Population Factor in African Studies, London.

Gyanchand (1972) : Population in Perspectives, Orient Longman.

Harrison, G.A. and Boyce, A.J. (1972) : The Structure of Human Population, Clarendon Press, Oxford.

Hassan, Mohammed Izhar (2005) : Population Geography Rawat Publications, Jawahar Nagar, Jaipur.

Howe, G.M. (1961) : The Geographical Variation in Disease Mortality in England and Wales in the Mid-Twentieth Century, Advancement of Science.

Isard, M. (1960) : An Introduction to Regional Analysis, New York, Chapter-2.

James, P.E. & Jones, E.F. (ed) (1954) : The Geographic Study of Population, American Inventory and Prospect, Syracuse University Press.

Kiser, Clyde, C. (1968) : The Aging of Human Populations, Population and Society, Boston Houghton Miffin Company.

Kosinski, L. (1970) : Distribution of Population, The Population of Europe, Longman.

Kuroda, T. (1972) : Migration, Distribution of Population and Development in Japan-Asian Population Study Series, No. 28, The second Asian Population Conference, Tokyo.

Law, B.C. (1954) : Historical Geography of Ancient India, Paris.

Lawless, R.I. (ed.) (1972) : Iraq : Changing Population Patterns, Population of the Middle East and North Africa, University of London Press Ltd.

Mahto, K. (1985) : Population Mobility and Economic Development in Eastern India, New Delhi : Inter India Publication.

Mehta, B.C. (1978) : Regional Population Growth :- A Case Study of Rajasthan, Research Books, Jaipur.

Mishra, R.P. (1989) : Population and Food Supply in M.P., New Delhi.

Mitra, A. (ed.) (1967) : Pattern of Population Change in India, Bombay, Allied Publishers.

Mitra, D.K. (1965) : India's Population and Food Supply, Observer, p. 11.

Mohammed, Ali (1978) : Situation of Agriculture, Food and Nutrition in Rural India, Concept publishing Company, Delhi.

Newton, M.P. (1957) : Internal Migration : Some Aspects of Population Movements Within England and Wales.

Pearl, Raymond (1939) : The Natural History of Population, Oxford University Press, Oxfords.

Punit, A.E. (1978) : Population, Social systems in Rural India, Sterling Publishers, Pvt. Ltd., New Delhi.

Qazi, S.A. & Qazi, Navaid Shabir (2006) : A.P.H. Publishing Corporation, New Delhi, 110002.

Roy Chaudhary, S.P. (1966) : Land & Soil, National Book Trust, New Delhi.

Sauvy, A. (1969) : General Theory of Population, Weidenfeld and Nicolson, London.

Saville, J. (1957) : Rural Depopulation in England and Wales.

Shah, S.L. (1969) : Growing Regional Disparities through Agricultural Development, Balanced Regional Development, Indian Economic Conference, Patna.

Singh, H.P. (1979) : Resource Appraisal and Planning in India, Rajesh Publication, New Delhi.

Singh, R.L., (ed.) (1971) : India : A Regional Geography, N.G.S.I., Varanasi.

Singh, R.P. & Kumar, A. (1970) : Monograph of Bihar, Bharti Bhawan, Patna.

Sinha, V.C. (1979) : Dynamics of India's Population Growth, National Publishing House New Delhi.

Sinha, V.N.P. (1976) : Socio-Economic Setting, Chotanagpur Plateau, K.B. publications, New Delhi.

Srivastava. O.S. (1983) : A Text Book of Demography, Vikash Publishing House, New Delhi.

Sulton, K. (ed.) (1972) : Algeria : Changes in Population Distribution, Population of the Middle East and North Africa, W.B. University of London Press Ltd.

Thakur, B. (1980) : Urban Settlements in Eastern India,

Entropy Changes and Pattern Analysis, Concept Publishing Co., New Delhi.

Thomas, B. (1968) ; Migration : Economic Aspects, International Encyclopaedia of Social Sciences.

Trewartha, G.T. (1972) : The Less Development Realm: A Geography of its Population, John Wiley & Sons, Inc., New York.

Verma, K.K. (1977) : Culture, Ecology and Population, National Publishing House, New Delhi.

Veyret-Verner, G. (1962) : Populations Movements, Structures, Repartition, Paris.

Vink, A.P.A. (1975) : Land Use in Advancing Agriculture, Springerveriok, Berlin, New York.

Woods, Robert (1982) : Theoretical Population Geography, Longman, London and New York.

Zelinsky, W. (1966) : A Prologue to Population Geography, Prentice-Hall Company Englewood Cliffs, N.J.

ARTICLES IN JOURNALS :

Ahmad, E. (1961) : Migrations in Bihar, Bombay Geographical Magazine, Vol. 8 and 9, No. 1.

Ahmad, K.S. (1941) : Environment and its Distribution of Population in India, Indian Geographical Journal, Vol. 16, No. 2.

Anantapadmanabhan, N. (1957) : Density of Rural Population and terrain Types in Madras State, Bombay Geographical Magazine, Vol. 5, No. 1.

Arunachalam, B. & Mathura, R.R. (1961) : Distribution of Population in the Ulhas Basin, Bombay Geographical Magazine, Vol. 8 and 9, No. 1.

Bhat, L.S. (1953) : A Population Map of the Upper Panchaganga Basin, Bombay Geographical Magazine,

Vol. 1, No. 1.

Bhat, L.S. (1961) : Population Density and Growth in India, 1951-61, Proceedings of the Indian Council of Geographers, Vol. 1.

Bhat, L.S. (1961) : Population Studies :The need for regional Approach, Bombay Geographical Magazine, Vol. 8 & 9, No. 1.

Bhatia, J.C. (1983) : Density of Population and Social Pathology in India, Indian Geographical Studies, R.B. No. 20, pp. 6-17.

Bidwai, B.K. (1951) : The variation of Population in Amravati District, Geographical Review of India, Vol. 13, No. 1.

Bohra, D.M. (1973) : Rates and Levels of Mortality and Fertility in Ajmer, Geographer, Vol. V, p. 25.

Bose, S.C. (1946) : Density and Pattern of Population in the Lower Damodar Basin, Calcutta Geographical Review, Vol. 8, No. 1 & 2.

Bose, S.C. (1952) : A Demographic Study of the Upper Damodar Basin, Indian Geographical Journal, Vol. 27, No. 3 & 4.

Brookfield, H.C. (1957) : Mauritius : Demographic upsurge and Prospect, Population Studies, Vol. 2, p. 102.

Chandana, R.C. (1967) : Female Working Force of Rural Punjab, Manpower Journal, Vol. 2, pp. 47-62.

Chang, Jen-her (1968) : The Agricultural Potential of the Humid Tropics, The Geographical Review, Vol. 58, No. 3, pp. 331-361.

Chatterjee, S.P. (1961) : Presidential Address : Physical Features and Population Distribution in West Bengal, Calcutta Geographical Review, Vol. 23, No. 1.

Chatterjee, S.P. (1962) : Regional Pattern of Density and

Distribution Population in India, Geographical Review of India, Vol. 24, No. 2.

Chatterjee, S.P. and Ganguli, A.T. (1943) : Population Distribution in two District of India, Calcutta Geographical Review, Vol. 5, No. 3.

Das, K.K.L. (1981) : Population Pressure in North Bihar Plain, west of Kosi : A Spatial Analysis, Indian Geographical Studies, R.B. No. 16, pp. 23-32.

Dayal, P. (1959) : Population Growth and Rural-Urban Migration in India, National Geographical Journal of India, Vol. 5, No. 4.

Duncan, O.D. (1957) : The Measurement of Population Distribution, Population Studies, Vol. 11, p. 27.

Franklin, S.H. (1956) : The Pattern of Sex Ratio in New Zealand, Economic Geography, Vol. 32, p. 162.

Geddes, A. & Learmonth, A.T.A. (1953) : Variability in Population Change in India and Regional Variations There in, (1921-40), Indian Geographical Journal, Vol. 28, No. 3 and 4.

Geddes, A. (1942) : The Population of India : Variability of Change as a Regional Demographic Index, geographical Review, Vol. 32, pp. 562-573.

Geddes, A. and Learmonth, A.T.A. (1953) : Variability in Population Change in India and Regional Variations Therein, Indian Geographical Review, Vol. 28.

Glass, D.V. (1960) : Population Growth, Fertility and Population Policy, Advancement of Science, Vol. 17, p. 353.

Gosal, G.S. (1958) : Occupational Structure of India's Rural Population, National Geographical Journal of India, Vol. 4, No. 3.

Gosal, G.S. (1961) : Internal Migration in India- a Regional

Analysis, Indian Geographical Journal, Vol. 36, No. 3.

Gosal, G.S. (1962) : Regional Aspects of Population Growth in India, Pacific View Point, Vol. 3, pp. 87-99.

Gosal, G.S. (1967) : Regional Aspects of Rural Literacy in India, Presidential Address, transactions of the Indian Council of Geographers, pp. 1-15.

Gosal, G.S. (1972) : Population Geography, A Survey of Research in Geography, Indian Council of Social Science Research, New Delhi, p. 173.

Gosal, G.S. and Krishan, G. (1965) : Occupational Structure of Punjab Rural Population, Indian Geographical Journal, p. 40.

Hoosan, D.J.M. (1960) : The Distribution of Population as the Essential Geographical Expression, Canadian Geographer, Vol. 17, p. 10.

Howe, G.H. (1964) : A National Atlas of Disease Mortality in the United Kingdom Geographical Journal, Vol. 130, p. 15.

Howe, G.M. (1960) : The Geographical Distribution of Cancer Mortality in Wales, 1947-53, Transactions and Papers of the Institute of British Geographers, Vol. 23, p. 189.

Kariel, H.G. (1963) : Selected Factors Areally Associated with Population Growth due to net Migration, Annals of the Association of American Geographers, Vol. 53, p. 210.

Kayastha, S.L. (1956) : Demographic Features of the Himalayan Beas Basin, National Geographical Journal of India, Varanasi, Vol. 2, No. 1.

Khan, M.N. (1956) ; Distribution of Population in Allahabad District, National Geographical Journal of India, Vol. 2, No. 4.

Kiser, C.V. and Whelpton, P.K. (1958) : Social and Psychological Factors affecting fertility, Milbank

Memorial Fund Quarterly, Vol. 36, p. 1323.

Krishan, G. (1968) : Distribution and Density of Population in Orissa, National Geographical Journal of India, Vol. 14, pp. 250-257.

Krishan, G. (1968) : Regionalism in Growth of Population in Punjab's Border Districts of Amritsar and Gurdaspur, Geographical Review of India, Vol. 30, pp. 1-17.

Krishan, G. and Shyam, M. (1973) : "Spatial Perspective on Progress of Female Literacy in India : 1901-71," Pacific View Point, Vol. 14, p. 204.

Krishnaswami, S.S. (1930) : Population of Coimbatore District, Journal of Madras Geographical Association, Vol. 5, No. 2 & 3.

Kumar, G. (1983) : Nagaland : A Study in Environmental Determinism of Population Distribution, Indian Geographical Studies, R.B. No. 20, pp. 38-41.

Kuriyan, G. (1936) : Population and its Distribution, Journal of Madras Geographical Association, Vol. 11, No. 1.

Kuriyan, G. (1938) : Population and its Distribution, Journal of Madras Geographical Association, Vol. 13, No. 2.

Lal, A. (1961) : Pattern of in-migration in Indian Cities, geographical Review of India, Vol. 23, No. 3.

Lokanathan, P.S. (1931) : Migration of Labour with Special Reference to South India, Journal of Madras Geographical Association, Vol. 6, No. 1.

Lowton, R. (1963) : Recent Trends in Population and Housing in England and Wales, Sociological Review, Vol. 11, p. 303.

Mahto, K. (1976) : Frontiers of Research in Population Mobility, Indian Geographical Studies, Patna, R.B. No. 6, pp. 61-66.

Mamoria, C.B. (1957) : Growth of Population in India,

Geographical Review of India, Calcutta, Vol. 19, No. 4.

Mandal, R.B. (1980) : Spatial Dynamics of the Centres of Population, Recent Trends and Concept in Geography, Concept Publishing Company, New Delhi, Vol. 3, pp. 275-283.

Mehta, S. (1967) : India's Rural Female Working Force and Occupational Structure, 1961-A Geographical Analysis, Indian Geographer, Vol. 12, No. 1 & 2, p. 50.

Mehta, S.K. (1969) : Aspects of Population of the Himalaya, west of Nepal, in Ram Rahul, ed. Social work in the Himalaya, Delhi School of Social work, University of Delhi.

Melezin, A. (1963) : Trends and Issues in the Soviet Geography of Population, Annals of the Association of American Geographers, Vol. 53, p. 144.

Murray, M. (1962) : The Geography of Death in England and Wales, Annals of the Association of American Geographers, Vol. 52, p. 130.

Nanad, N. (1966) : Distribution and Spatial Arrangement of Rural Population in East Rajashtan, Annals of Association of American Geographers, p. 6.

Padhye, S.S. (1961) : Melghat- a Study in Population, Bombay Geographical Magazine, Vol. 8 and 9, No. 1.

Pokshishevski, V.V. (1962) : Geography of Population and its Tasks, Soviet Geographical Review and Translation, Vol. 3, p. 9.

Prasad, A. (1956) : Population Distribution and the Dynamics of Supply of Labour in Bihar, Geographical Outlook, Vol. 1.

Raghavan, K.S. (1935) : Population of Anantapur District, Journal of Madras Geographical Association, Vol. 9, No. 4.

Raghavan, K.S. (1936) : Population of Salem District, Journal of Madras Geographical Association, Vol. 11, No. 2.

Raghavan, K.S. (1937) : Population of Tanjore District, Journal of Madras Geographical Association, Vol. 12, No. 3.

Raghavan, M.P. (1940) : Population of Tirunelvelley District, Journal of Madras Geographical Association, Vol. 15, No. 3.

Rajagopal, M.P. (1941) : Population of Chittor District, Indian Geographer, Vol. 16, No. 4.

Ramachandran, R. (1965) : Population Trend in Malnad, Deccan Geographer, p. 3.

Raza, M. (1950) : Is India Overpopulated ? geographer, Vol. 3, No. 1.

Rose, A.J. (1958) : The Geographical Pattern of European Immigration in Australia, Geographical Review, Vol. 48, p. 512.

Roy, S.R. (1977) : Growth of Population in Bhojpur and Rohtas, Indian Geographical Studies, R.B. No. 8, pp. 38-44.

Schwartzberg, J. (1965) : The Distribution of Selected Castes in North Indian Plain, Geographical Review, pp. 477-496.

Scott, P. (1957) : The Changing Population of Tasmania, Geographical Studies, Vol. 4, p. 13.

Sen, J.C. (1963) : The Sex Composition of the Population of India, The Deccan Geographer, pp. 43-62.

Sharma, T.R. (1960) : Historical and Cultural Geography of the Ganga Valley in Etah District, U.P., Agra University Research Journal, Vol. 8, No. 122.

Shastri, H.P. (1928) : Journal of the Bihar and Orissa Research Society, p. 330.

Singh, J.P. (1981) : Distributional Characteristics of Tribal

Population in India Geographical Studies, R.B. No. 17, pp. 1-10.

Singh, L.R. (1965) : Demographic Features of Nagaland, National Geographical Journal of India, p. 11.

Singh, R.L. (1947) : Trend in the Growth of Population in Uttar Pradesh, Bulletin of National Geographical Society of India (Varanasi), Vol. 3.

Singh, R.L. (1956) : Population and its Problem in the Umland of Banaras, proceedings of International Geography Seminar.

Singhal, G.D. (1981) : Some Features of Population Geography of New Gaya District, Indian Geographical Studies, Research Bulletin no. 16, March, geographical Research Centre, Patna- 5, p. 24.

Sinha, B.N. (1958) : Population Analysis of Orissa, National geographical Journal of India, Vol. 4, No. 4.

Sinha, B.N. (1962) : The Bearing of Population Growth on the Economy of Orissa, Deccan Geographer, Hyderabad, Vol. 1, No. 1.

Sinha, R.B. (March, 1981) : "Demographic Structure and Typology of Population Resource : A Case Study of Siwan District (Bihar), Indian Geographical Studies, research Bulletin no. 16, Geographical Research Centre, Patna-5, India, p. 35.

Sinha, V.N.P., Sinha, S. and Rashmi (1980) : Rural-urban Migration as a factor for Population Growth and Social Change, Indian Geographical Studies, R.B. No. 15, pp. 58-65.

Spate, O.H.K. (1956) : Population and Food in India, Proceedings of International geography Seminar.

Stamp, L.D. (1952) : Land For Tomorrow, The Underdeveloped World, Chapter Iv, Food for All, pp. 41-

45.

Stewart, J.G. and Warntz, W. (1950) : Some Parameters of the Distribution of Population, Geographical Review, Vol. 49, p. 270.

Sukhatma, P.V. (1972) : Population, Food Supply and Nutrition, Asian Population Study, Series No. 28, Population Strategy in Asia, The Second Asian Population Conference, Tokyo.

Tirath, Ranjit (1966) : Areal Patterns of Literacy in India, Manpower Journal, pp. 88-118.

Trewartha, G. T. (1953) : The Case for Population Geography, Annals of the Association of American Geographers, Vol. 43, p. 71.

Trewartha, G.T & Gosal, G.S. (1957) : The Regionalism of Population Change in India, Cold Spring Harbor Symposia in Quantitative Biology, Vol. 22, pp. 71-81.

Varma, S.D. (1956) : Density and Patterns of Population in Punjab, National geographical Journal of India, Varanasi, Vol. 2, No. 4.

Visaria, P.M. (1967) : The Sex Ratio of the Population of India and Pakistan and Regional Variations during 1901-61 in Ashish Allied Publishers.

Watson, J.W. (1955) : "Geography : A Discipline in Distance," Scottish Geographical Magazine, Vol. 71, pp 1-13.

Wolfenden, H.H. (1984) : Population Statistics and their Complication, Estimates of Population, J.A.S.A. Vol. XXXV, p. 390.

Yunus, M. (1941) : Trends of Population and Crop Production in Uttar Pradesh, Indian Geographical Journal, Vol. 16, No. 2.

Zelinsky, W. (1962) : Changes in the Geographic Pattern of Rural Population in the United States, 1790-1960,

Geographical Review, Vol. 52, p. 492.

OTHERS :

Chopra, P.N. (ed.) (1975) : The Gazetteer of India, Vol. III, Economic Structure and Activities, New Delhi, p. 140.

Determinants and Consequences of Population Trends, U.N. 1976, p. 64.

Gosal, G.S. (1956) : A Geographical Analysis of India's Population, Unpublished Ph.D. Thesis, Wisconsin University.

Jha, G.P. (1978) : Agricultural Land Use and Population in the Kamala Balan Plain, North Bihar, Unpublished Ph.D. Thesis, Patna University.

Jha, G.P. (1978) : Perspective in Land Utilisation Problems, Population and Agricultural Land Use in Kamla Balan Plain, Unpublished Ph.D. Thesis, p. 40.

Mahto, K. (1980) : Population Mobility and Economic Development in Eastern India, Unpublished Ph.D. Thesis, Patna University.

Mehta, S. (1970) : Some Aspects of Changes in the Demographic Character of Bist Doab : 1951-61, Unpublished Ph.D. Thesis, Punjab University.

Namboodiri, N.V. : Economic Times, September 23, 1976.

Prasad, S.N. (1980) : Land Use ; Land Use in Ranchi District, Unpublished Ph.D. Thesis, p. 75.

Prasad, S.N. (1980) : Land Use and Population in Ranchi District, Unpublished Ph.D. Thesis, Patna University.

Singh, L.K.P. (1984) : Spatial Pattern of Population and Settlement in Nawada Plain, Unpublished Ph.D. Thesis, Patna University.

Singh, M. (1969) : "Land Utilisation in North Eastern Uttar Pradesh," Unpublished Ph.D. Thesis, p. 106.

U.N. (1976) : Determinants and Consequences of Population Trends, p. 66.

GOVERNMENT PUBLICATIONS :

District Gazetteer of Shahabad (1966), p. 14.

Survey and Settlement Report, Hazaribagh, 1917, p.6.

Appendix - I
Land Use (in Acres), 2004-05

Sl. No.	Name of Blocks	Net Sown Area	Fallow Land	Cultivable Waste	Land Put to Non Agricultural uses	Forest and Barren	Land under Pasture and Plantation
1	Kochas	48808.77	202.55	15.70	6142.10	585.40	431.65
2	Dinara	71192.22	1788.45	145.75	3057.23	510.92	251.43
3	Dawath	21079.15	2895.00	70.60	570.93	1289.05	132.66
4	Suryapura	12226.24	285.33	-	24.20	1533.42	50.00
5	Bikramganj	988.62	-	32.14	4305.96	-	44.60
6	Karakat	45229.38	135.90	-	5791.79	32.93	266.10
7	Nasriganj	21224.37	-	-	9375.74	3118.10	-
8	Rajpur	14925.16	152.28	-	58.53	2256.51	16.46
9	Sanjhauli	14616.94	-	-	2173.65	-	-
10	Nokha	37517.31	-	-	4179.42	11.34	-
11	Kargahar	73817.4	266.50	-	6627.72	635.95	461.25
12	Chenari	32037.56	5865.19	139.20	5429.90	17169.81	43.19
13	Nauhatta	37442.38	8833.47	3740.49	25700.47	33826.93	986.09
14	Sheosagar	50710.22	62.25	-	234.41	2886.65	-
15	Sasaram	38826.01	3431.48	172.39	5628.18	32474.34	-
16	Akorhi Gola	21430.92	138.35	5.59	1707.09	1123.56	75.13
17	Dehri	20854.21	119.34	-	14733.75	2064.39	741.83
18	Tilouthu	15215.94	4262.60	301.82	9792.10	9127.85	172.60
19	Rohtas	10279.75	1702.60	52.27	9832.82	58150.89	107.59

Appendix - II
Cropping Pattern (in Acre), 2004-05

Sl. No.	Name of Blocks	Bhadai	Aghani	Rabi	Garma
1	Kochas	-	34641.50	39023.31	-
2	Dinara	-	61557.17	11680.78	-
3	Dawath	80.76	1711.80	13527.45	63.50
4	Suryapura	78.98	9620.53	8138.73	33.81
5	Bikramganj	2.93	24477.71	19822.38	-
6	Karakat	214.73	38466.63	25809.93	169.89
7	Nasriganj	164	19908.89	16960.2	230.62
8	Rajpur	100.34	12066.63	6661.57	202.86
9	Sanjhauli	3.19	13097.93	8436.30	-
10	Nokha	1.02	35333.15	26053.26	106.62
11	Kargahar	-	64871.57	36560.3	24.50
12	Chenari	108.84	21801.58	15832.98	-
13	Nauhatta	2038.75	6172.13	6448.07	-
14	Sheosagar	-	37245.07	36082.83	3.21
15	Sasaram	76.49	29236.36	24612.65	15.82
16	Akorhi Gola	159.91	18852.84	18193.61	401.88
17	Dehri	431.79	16429.71	14315.84	486.59
18	Tilouthu	674.07	9624.94	9018.47	702.25
19	Rohtas	685.05	5645.58	5986.27	386.59

Appendix - III
Total Population (Male and Female , 2001)

Sl. No.	Name of the Blocks	Total Male	Total Female
1	Kochas	62998	56578
2	Dinara	100527	91764
3	Dawath	48292	44695
	Rural	40086	37086
	Urban	8206	7609
4	Suryapura	24924	23298
5	Bikramganj	71666	65037
	Rural	51325	46970
	Urban	20341	18067
6	Karakat	92951	86244
7	Nasriganj	62042	57514
8	Rajpur	31498	29112
9	Sanjhauli	26934	24531
10	Nokha	76061	69701
	Rural	64428	58980
	Urban	11633	10721
11	Kargahar	94570	84986
12	Chenari	56293	50980
13	Nauhatta	39525	36339
14	Sheosagar	75203	68973
15	Sasaram	156446	139783
	Rural	86764	78293
	Urban	69682	61490
16	Akorhi Gola	51665	46948
17	Dehri	123593	110242
	Rural	60053	54725
	Urban	63540	55517
18	Tilouthu	47089	43121
19	Rohtas	41208	37417

Source : Census of India, Patna.

Appendix - IV
Literacy, 2001

Sl. No.	Name of Blocks	Literate persons	% of literate persons out of total population of block
1	Kochas	56730	47.44
2	Dinara	89909	46.75
3	Dawath	44552	47.91
4	Suryapura	21927	45.47
5	Bikramganj	71269	52.13
6	Karakat	88212	49.22
7	Nasriganj	58141	48.63
8	Rajpur	28785	47.49
9	Sanjhauli	26707	51.89
10	Nokha	68784	47.18
11	Kargahar	88025	49.02
12	Chenari	46999	43.81
13	Nauhatta	27518	36.27
14	Sheosagar	67809	47.03
15	Sasaram	159876	53.97
16	Akorhi Gola	48543	49.22
17	Dehri	133583	57.12
18	Tilouthu	42034	46.59
19	Rohtas	35884	45.63

Source : Self Calculated from census data.

Appendix - V
No. of Households (2001)

Sl. No.	Name of Blocks	No. of Household
1	Kochas	16046
2	Dinara	26538
3	Dawath	12880
	Rural	10602
	Urban	2278
4	Suryapura	6587
5	Bikramganj	19638
	Rural	13826
	Urban	5812
6	Karakat	25283
7	Nasriganj	17044
8	Rajpur	8667
9	Sanjhauli	7064
10	Nokha	20059
	Rural	17015
	Urban	3044
11	Kargahar	23399
12	Chenari	14854
13	Nauhatta	12085
14	Sheosagar	20973
15	Sasaram	41905
	Rural	23680
	Urban	18225
16	Akorhi Gola	14050
17	Dehri	33566
	Rural	16086
	Urban	17480
18	Tilouthu	13161
19	Rohtas	12243

Source : Census of India, Patna.

Appendix - VI
Occupational Structure

Sl. No.	Name of Blocks	Cultivators	Agricultural Labourers	Household Industry Workers	Other Workers	Marginal Workers
1	Kochas	15973	9547	530	3910	7213
2	Dinara	23504	16751	1271	5896	17868
3	Dawath	10752	6376	445	3125	5459
4	Suryapura	6133	3195	126	1888	1425
5	Bikramganj	11672	8240	712	8658	7592
6	Karakat	17130	11330	1321	6641	18648
7	Nasriganj	8817	6459	1042	6995	12840
8	Rajpur	6734	5421	656	269	6216
9	Sanjhauli	6381	3019	280	1825	4271
10	Nokha	14327	13320	1144	6071	12003
11	Kargahar	23188	15252	1056	4797	14231
12	Chenari	12007	8071	851	4302	9193
13	Nauhatta	5346	5997	622	2691	12598
14	Sheosagar	15007	12778	854	4956	12416
15	Sasaram	13755	12948	3146	33991	18352
16	Akorhi Gola	8710	7645	1235	3804	10318
17	Dehri	10585	6728	2713	26859	15507
18	Tilouthu	8591	5367	574	5496	6961
19	Rohtas	3925	4161	641	6396	6341

Source : Census of India, Patna.

Questionnaires

SAMPLE VILLAGES

Date of Survey :

1. (a) Name of Village : ....

(b) Thana No. : ....

(c) Area : ....

(d) Location : North.......... South......... East........ West......

(e) Distance from Block Headquarter : ....

(f) Distance from School : ....

(g) Distance from P.S. : ....

(h) Distance from R.S. : ....

(i) Distance from P.O. : ....

(j) Distance from Road : ....

(k) Distance from Market / Hat : ....

2. (a) Population : Total .... Male......... Female ....

(b) Population by age structure :

Below 5 yrs ... 5-15yrs ...... 15-60yrs ...... Over 60yrs ......

Male : ....

Female : ....

(c) Literacy : Total .... Male .... Female ....

(d) Caste Division :

S.N.	Name of Hamlets	Caste	Total Population	Male	Female
1........					
2........					
3........					

(e) Religion :

S.N.	Name of Hamlets	Caste	Total Population	Male	Female
1					
2					
3					

(f) Occupational Structure :

Occupational Structure	Total	Male	Female
....			
....			
....			
....			

3. Services :

(a) (i) P.O. : ....

(ii) T.T.O. : ....

(iii) Dispensary : ....

(iv) Hospital : ....

(v) Doctor (Type) : ....

(vi) Electricity : ....

(vii) Piped Water Supply : ....

(viii) Panchayati House : ....

(ix) Literacy : ....

(b) (i) No. of Tank : ....

(ii) Nature of Link Road : ....

(a) Metalled : ....

(b) Unmetalled : ....

(c) Cart-track : ....

(iii) No. of Retail Shops and Type :

Type	No.
1..	
2..	
3..	
4..	

4. Physical Character of Landscape :

(a) Nature of scope -Regular gentle, regular steep, irregular gentle, irregular steep.

(b) Direction of slope

(c) Upland area

(d) Nature of Crops

(i)	Single Cropped Area		Double Cropped Area
	Triple Cropped Area		Horticulture Area
(ii)	Aghani	Rabi	Bhadai Garma

(e) Irrigation Facilities :-

Hand Pump Well Tubewell Canal Tank
Electricity Pump

(f) Forest Area :

(g) Waste Land :

(h) Water-table :

(i) in Summer

(ii) in Winter

(iii) in Rainy Season

(iv) Hot Season

(i) Drainage character :- Nala River Tank.

5. Village Problems : Discuss and note down.

....

....

....

....

Note :

1. Draw sketch of physical character
2. Take photo of
3. Collect land use data.

Glossary

GLOSSARY OF LOCAL TERMS

Aghani Crops	-	Crops grown during monsoon months.
Ahar	-	Water body.
Bhadai Crops	-	Crops which are harvested in the month of Bhado or August-September.
Chamar	-	A caste associated with leather work.
Dhankhet	-	Land put to paddy crops.
Dihland	-	Fertile upland near village.
Garma Harvest	-	Crops grown during summer months.
Koeri	-	A caste known for intensive agriculture.
Kumhar	-	Potter caste.
Oraon	-	Scheduled Tribe.
Paswan	-	A Scheduled caste associated as agricultural Labourers.
Pyne	-	Narrow irrigation channels.
Rabi Crops	-	Winter harvest.
Yadav	-	Milkman.